PSYCHOTIC ENTELECHY

The Dangers of Spiritual Gifts Theology

Stan A. Lindsay

University Press of America,® Inc.
Lanham · Boulder · New York · Toronto · Oxford

Copyright © 2006 by
University Press of America,® Inc.
4501 Forbes Boulevard
Suite 200
Lanham, Maryland 20706
UPA Acquisitions Department (301) 459-3366

PO Box 317
Oxford
OX2 9RU, UK

All rights reserved
Printed in the United States of America
British Library Cataloging in Publication Information Available

Library of Congress Control Number: 2006923755
ISBN-13: 978-0-7618-3493-9 (paperback : alk. paper)
ISBN-10: 0-7618-3493-1 (paperback : alk. paper)

∞™ The paper used in this publication meets the minimum
requirements of American National Standard for Information
Sciences—Permanence of Paper for Printed Library Materials,
ANSI Z39.48—1984

To the elders: Rod, Tim, and Dennis

Contents

Acknowledgements		vii
Chapter 1	Spiritual Gifts and Psychotic Entelechy	1
Chapter 2	The Waco Disaster	17
Chapter 3	The Rhetoric of bin Laden's Battle	37
Chapter 4	The Cure for bin Laden's Rhetoric	55
Chapter 5	Muslims, Christians, & Jews *versus* Secular Psychotic Entelechies	69
Chapter 6	A Brief History of Jewish, Christian, and Islamic Spiritual Gift Theology	95
Chapter 7	An Examination of New Testament Spiritual Gifts Theology	105
Chapter 8	Motivation: Why Gifts Theology	127
Chapter 9	Perspectivism: The Eldership Approach	147
Conclusion		159
Bibliography		191
Index		199

Acknowledgements

This book is a further development of a chapter ("Waco and Psychotic Entelechy") from my book, *Implicit Rhetoric: Kenneth Burke's Extension of Aristotle's Concept of Entelechy* (University Press of America, 1998). That chapter was reworked into a journal article, "Waco and Andover: An Application of Kenneth Burke's Concept of Psychotic Entelechy" published in *Quarterly Journal of Speech* (1999). Following the terrorist attacks of September 11, 2001, I presented a paper entitled "Burke and bin Laden: Psychotic Entelechy and the Comic Frame" at the Triennial Conference of the Kenneth Burke Society in May, 2002, at New Orleans. Those materials have been reworked, developed, and incorporated here.

I quote throughout this work from *Implicit Rhetoric*, plus three of my other books, *Revelation: The Human Drama* (Lehigh University Press, 2001), *The Seven Cs of Stress: A Burkean Approach* (Say Press, 2004), and *Persuasion, Proposals, and Public Speaking* (Say Press, 2004). Chapter 9, "Perspectivism: The Eldership Approach" is a Burkean reworking of an article, "Restore Eldership," first published in *The Christian Standard* (August 22, 1976).

Chapter 1

Spiritual Gifts and Psychotic Entelechy

What do Osama bin Laden, Adolph Hitler, David Koresh, Jim Jones, Gene Applewhite, and the slayers of abortion doctors all have in common? They all base their dangerous and destructive actions to a large extent on some particular message they believe they have received from God. The receipt of messages from God is called, in many religious circles, spiritual gifts theology.

On October 10, 2005, the BBC offered a press release with the headline: "God told me to invade Iraq, Bush tells Palestinian ministers." The press release quotes Palestinian Foreign Minister (now Palestinian Information Minister) Nabil Shaath, referring to his first meeting with President George W. Bush in June 2003:

> President Bush said to all of us: "I'm driven with a mission from God. God would tell me, 'George, go and fight those terrorists in Afghanistan.' And I did, and then God would tell me, 'George, go and end the tyranny in Iraq . . .' And I did. And now, again, I feel God's words coming to me, 'Go get the Palestinians their state and get the Israelis their security, and get peace in the Middle East.' And by God I'm gonna do it."[1]

Scott McClellan, White House spokesman, immediately denied the charge: "That's absurd. He's never made such comments."[2]

True. That story is absurd and extremely doubtful in light of the evidence that Bush has never claimed such inspiration even among Evangelical Christian groups in all of his political campaigns. Such rhetoric might have swayed some Evangelical Christians, but it would be ridiculous to assume that it could sway Palestinian Muslims. The Palestinian Prime Minister, the other Palestinian leader in attendance at the meeting in June 2003, identified by *breitbart.com* as Mahmud Abbas and by *bbc.co.uk* as Abu Mazen, recounts Bush's comments as follows: "I have a moral and religious obligation. So I will get you a Palestinian state."[3] This second account, by the Palestinian Prime Minister, is much more credible and much less indicative of psychotic entelechy based on a spiritual gifts theology. It is one thing to say that one's religious beliefs lead one to a moral obligation. It is quite another to assert that God sent a personal message to fight specific wars. Perhaps, Mr. Shaath elaborated on the message he heard from the President in accordance with his own preconceived notions of the President's religious views, or perhaps he intentionally distorted the President's words to cause Bush to appear to be a Christian fanatic to Moslem or Western audiences. Regardless of the circumstances of this incident, it is quite characteristic of many American Christians to claim the type of divine inspiration President Bush denied claiming.

In the last quarter of the twentieth century, spiritual gifts theology swept the churches in America. Congregation after congregation, denomination after denomination began to teach and practice various spiritual gifts—both those listed in the New Testament and other newly discovered gifts that appear to have developed over the years.

Clearly, the Charismatic Movement is largely responsible for this trend. The defining doctrine of this movement is that the spiritual gifts mentioned by the Apostle Paul—including such obviously supernatural abilities as the ability to prophecy, heal, perform miracles, speak in tongues, and interpret tongues—have continued to exist in the church from the first century to the twenty-first century. Moreover, according to many Charismatics, the trend should even be expected to increase "in the last days."

The Church of Jesus Christ Latter Day Saints (also known as Mormonism) capitalizes on the biblical prophecy that in the last days God will pour out His Spirit on all flesh. Staking its claim to comprise these saints of the latter days, this relatively young (as compared to Islam, Christianity, and Judaism) yet rapidly growing religion asserts that its leaders (and members) possess these supernatural gifts. So sure is the Mormon Church that prophecy and other gifts continue that the Book of Mormon is afforded equal status with the New and Old Testaments as supernaturally inspired messages from God. The Book of Mormon was purportedly discovered in North America by Joseph Smith. The book asserts that Native Americans are actually the ten lost Israelite tribes who disappeared after the northern tribes were defeated by Syria in the sixth or seventh century B.C. The angel Moroni helped Smith translate the original tablets on which the book was written. After the book was translated, the original tablets disappeared. Other recognized prophecies of the church have also been considered divinely inspired. These prophecies range from a prohibition of drinking alcoholic beverages, coffee, and tea to the (now abandoned) acceptance of polygamy as a family style.

One of the world's three largest religions, Islam, is founded on the premise that the gift of prophecy continued to exist at least as late as the seventh century A.D. Mohammed, living in that century, claimed to be a prophet of God and wrote the Koran. Most of his prophetic hortatory messages are entirely in line with Judeo-Christian values. Like Judaism and Christianity, Mohammed proclaimed the God of Abraham the true God and opposed sins such as murder and adultery. Like Christianity, Mohammed proclaimed Jesus the Messiah, the son of the virgin Mary. Like the church of Jesus Christ Latter Day Saints, Islam prohibits the drinking of alcoholic beverages. Like the Catholic Church and many conservative Protestant churches, Islam opposes the practice of abortion. Unlike the Catholic Church, Mohammed resisted the elevation of Mary to divine status and denied the doctrine of the Trinity. To Mohammed, Jesus was not the Son of God. On the more dangerous side, the world currently faces a serious problem with Mohammed's controversial hortatory messages to slay infidels.

Fortunately, the vast majority of hortatory messages that have resulted from the acceptance of spiritual gifts over the years have had positive results. Since the church has solidly established a biblical code of ethics over the past two millennia, most hortatory messages delivered in the context of Bible-believing churches are very much in line with that biblical code of ethics. When the occasional "messenger from God" exclaims that God wants us to kill someone, to steal, to commit adultery, or to lie, the church quickly condemns this person as a "false prophet." The biblical warnings about "false prophets" are simultaneously an admission of and a cure for the dangers of spiritual gifts theology. As an example of a hortatory spiritual gifts message that has had a positive result, I cite a note given to me recently by one who believes in modern-day spiritual gifts:

> Several weeks ago, the Holy Spirit told me that I needed to sow a financial blessing into this single mother. I kept seeking who this person would be. All day, I sought after a single mother and nightfall was approaching and I needed to do this before I call it a night. So, the Holy Spirit told me who to go to and I said no. Since I tarried all day, I thought he would [allow?] me to sow into this potential single mother. Roughly, around 9 pm that night I got up and went to the single mother that I wanted to sow into. While driving over to the girl's home, the Holy Spirit told me that this was not the girl He wanted me to sow into. So, I kept on driving until I got to her house. In the meantime, I became extremely hot and neither the air condition[ing] nor the windows in the car did anything for me. When I arrived, she was not home. I said ok[ay], maybe she's at her mother's house. Again, the Holy Spirit told me that this was not the person. So, I drove over to her mother's house and nobody was there. The Holy Spirit told me that, "You're going to listen to me yet—now go and sow into the person I told you earlier. So, I called the person that the Holy Spirit told me and guess where she was—at the grocery store trying to buy groceries. I felt really bad because the Holy Spirit had told me early to go and find her. So I went to the grocery store where she was at and sowed into her family. It was just what she lacked at the register.

Regardless of what other reactions readers may have to this account, most can agree that the result of the hortatory message was not negative. One individual assisted another individual financially. Benevolence is considered a positive result in most cases.

I am, however, aware of another circumstance in which the result of a benevolence-related hortatory message was somewhat damaging. In the 1970s, a woman I knew was watching the PTL Club. She heard Jim Bakker state that the Spirit had told him someone in the television audience needed to send a gift of $5000.00 to the ministry. She perceived that this message from the Holy Spirit was intended for her. She dutifully wrote a check for $5000.00 and sent it to the PTL Club. A few nights later, the Spirit told Bakker that the person who had sent $5000.00 before needed to send another $5000.00. The woman complied again. Unfortunately, she did not have the money in her checking account to cover either check. Both checks bounced, resulting in NSF fees. I do not consider it negative that the PTL Club was unable to cash either check, but the bounced checks and NSF fees damaged the woman's relationship with her bank and with her husband.

Many hortatory messages offered in spiritual gifts contexts are far more damaging than the preceding example. Jim Jones' People's Temple, Gene Applewhite's Heaven's Gate, David Koresh's Branch Davidians, and Osama bin Laden's al-Qaida all based their hortatory messages on the validity of spiritual gifts. To ignore them is to continue to see cult followers and their enemies incur possible death. In his Preface to *Modern Rhetorical Criticism*, Roderick P. Hart lists some reasons for a current "renewed interest in the study of rhetoric":

> Hitler's rise to power, the Iran-Contra hearings, the resurgence of David Duke, televised evangelism, the politicized novel, advocacy journalism, apartheid protest rallies, AIDS awareness campaigns, Weight Watchers International, soap operas, and the Ayatollah Khomeini. All of these characters and events collect in the rhetorical arena. All of them change people's lives. To ignore them is to incur possible political, moral, health, and financial risks.[4]

Surely, we could legitimately add to Hart's list of rhetorical situations that produce risks the religious cults and movements mentioned earlier. The fact that such cults and movements continue to arise indicates that rhetorical critics need to find methods not only of understanding such rhetorical processes but also of curing the underlying rhetorical excesses. Using Kenneth Burke's concept of psychotic entelechy, we are able to find such methods.

Recently, an expert on "diversity training" remarked in an interview that no religion is superior and none are inferior. If that is true, then Jim Jones' People's Temple, Gene Applewhite's Heaven's Gate, Osama bin Laden's terrorist version of Islam, and David Koresh's Branch Davidians are all equal in validity to mainstream Christianity. Here is the difference between a dangerous religion and a scholarly approach to the Bible, for example: In a dangerous religion, the interpreter (typically claiming some *spiritual gift* such as "prophecy") provides his followers with *the correct* interpretation of his scriptures. Then, since this "gifted prophet" is considered *infallible*, his followers do whatever he says (even if it means staying inside burning buildings or drinking cyanide or committing suicide in other ways). A scholar will submit his/her views to his peers for review, feedback, recalcitrance, etc.

I do not place religion in general in the category of psychotic entelechy. I do not place Kenneth Burke in the category of those overly affected by psychotic entelechy, either. Burke was opposed to technologism as was Theodore Kaczynski (the Unabomber). Nevertheless, only one of those two was motivated by psychotic entelechy as it relates to anti-technologism. Kaczynski killed people in his anti-technologistic entelechy. Likewise, not all members of a given religion are motivated by psychotic entelechy. We all need the courage to doubt our own opinions from time to time. The biggest danger associated with "end time" prophecies in the Bible is when someone KNOWS (not just believes) that his/her *interpretation* of the Bible is *the correct interpretation*. (As I will demonstrate later, it is not necessary or even advisable to try to persuade the dangerous person that the *scripture* is not to be believed. Recalcitrance usually just needs to cause the person to question the inerrancy of his/her *interpretation*.) Absolute conviction that he was right caused Jim Jones to make his followers drink cyanide-laced Kool-Aid. Absolute conviction that bin Laden was right caused nineteen men to commit suicide in the 9/11 terrorist attack. If they were not convinced they would definitely go to paradise upon completing this deed, they probably would not have willingly killed themselves (and others). This is psychotic. It is also entelechial. They were operating on the conviction (not just assumption) that this attack on America would get them into paradise (their *telos*). If the terrorists are wrong, the world needs to be informed about how to diagnose their dangerous malady and seek solutions.

To eliminate all spiritual gifts theology from society would virtually eliminate religion as we know it, something neither feasible nor wise. Conversely, to embrace all religions—and, by extension, all spiritual gifts theology—currently present in society invites disaster. Nevertheless, advocates of each of these extreme positions exist at the present time. Some might infer, based on the title of this book, that I prefer the first option. That inference would be incorrect; I do not. I do not favor the second extreme, either. While the doctrine of equality among all religions sounds noble, it exposes society to dangers from certain religious sectors. Our choice is not an either-or choice.

Another option is to choose a single religious position and to systematically eliminate other religious positions. Such a position is held by some militant Moslems today as it was held by various Jewish, Roman Catholic, and Protestant sectarians in various parts of the world in years past. Not only is this option contrary to America's historic freedom-of-religion principle, it supports a position that has served as the underpinning for religious wars throughout human history.

The option I advocate accommodates Postmodernist arguments, religious scriptures and claims, and American principles of religious tolerance. Twentieth century philosopher of human communication Kenneth Burke made no claims that his observations were inspired by God. Despite the arguments of some Burkeans that Burke was a theologian,[5] and the arguments of other Burkeans that Burke was a thoroughgoing secularist who studied theological language only to understand how language works, I take Burke at his word. He indicates that he is an agnostic.[6] Unlike Burke, I am not an agnostic; I am a Christian. Yet, I hold a master's degree in Hebrew from the Department of Near Eastern Languages and Cultures at Indiana University. I had a Christian, a Moslem, and a Jew on my thesis committee. I have great appreciation for Judaism. I learned a great deal about my own religion by studying Rabbinic Judaism. I also have considerable respect for Islam. I find some Islamic values closer to my own than those of some Christian communities. I also find in the writings of Kenneth Burke, the agnostic, much wisdom.

Throughout the history of religion, practices that harm individuals and society in general have existed. Jewish and Babylonian worshippers of the god Molech sacrificed their children by burning them to death. The Greek king Agamemnon, following the dictates of the Delphic oracle, sacrificed his daughter, Iphigenia, to Greek gods. The ancient Mayans sacrificed their noblest children to their gods. Modern-day Christians who believe in faith healing have denied their children access to medicines and medical procedures that might have prolonged their lives. They did this in order to demonstrate their faith in the spiritual gifts of their "healers."

Of course, religions are not the only sources of dangerous practices. Darwinist theories of evolution contributed strongly to racial supremacy views. Darwinist views devalued the lives of members of some races and the victims of some illnesses. Amoral pragmatic philosophies have paved the way for abortion and the infanticide of baby girls in Communist China. All of these practices I classify as psychotic entelechy, a phrase that is not specifically used by Kenneth Burke but that is certainly implicit in his works.

More than two millennia ago, Aristotle coined the term entelechy [*entelecheia*] to indicate a process. The process to which entelechy refers in Aristotle's writings is not an extreme process. The process is not an uncommon process; rather, it is the *most* common process. Entelechy, according to Aristotle, refers to *natural* processes. Aristotle thinks of seeds, for example, as possessing within themselves the "final cause" or *telos*--the goal of what the mature plant will be. He believes that there exists within a grain of wheat the formula that makes the seed first produce roots and a sprout, then grow a blade, which grows into a stalk, until finally an ear of new grain develops. The plan for the fully-grown stalk with its ear of grain is implicit in the seed. To use a computer metaphor, the seed is in a sense "programmed" to produce a fully developed wheat plant. The *telos* (or goal) of the fully developed plant is held in the seed and in the plant throughout the growth process. Hence, Aristotle calls the process "entelechy." "En" means "within." "Tel" is short for *telos*, the goal. "Ech" means "to have." "Y" indicates "process." Thus, "En-tel-ech-y" means: the process of development (*cf. Attitudes Toward History*, hereafter ATH, 107) while having one's *telos* within oneself. Entelechy, like many of Burke's terms, can be best understood in terms of a "philosophical vocabulary" that Aristotle bequeathed to subsequent generations. Burke's friend, Classicist Richard McKeon, comments:

> [Aristotle's] influence on the vocabulary of philosophy may be taken as typical of his influence in general . . . for the technical terminology of later philosophical discussion is taken largely from his distinctions, but the terms to which he gave prominence were for the most part used in other senses than he gave them and in other contexts of arguments and suppositions than his.[7]

When Burke extends Aristotelian entelechy from the biological realm to the symbolic realm, he leaves intact most of Aristotle's definition. Burke employs the term entelechy in his theorizing in 1945, where his comment on the matter is little more than a brief summary of Aristotle's use of the "concept of the 'entelechy,' which [Burke, then] might call the individual's potentialities for becoming a fully representative member of its class" (*A Grammar of Motives*, hereafter GM, 27). Although Burke there presents the notion that Aristotle's concept of entelechy was derived in a sense from a "Platonic theory of forms," he also distinguishes the "Aristotelian" view from that of the "realist" or the "nominalist." Later, in GM, Burke defines the Aristotelian entelechy as "the striving of each thing to be perfectly the kind of thing it was" (GM 249). This sometimes biological, sometimes physical, "striving" is, of course, a "temporizing of essence." The essence, for example, is already completely located, dormant in the seed. The temporizing is the time-bound process of sprouting, growing, maturing, and producing new seeds. Again, Burke distinguishes "Aristotle's more 'scientific' brand" from Platonism since "the Aristotelian 'entelechy' resided in the things of sensory experience" as opposed to "the heavenly family identity" (GM 253). Still commenting on the Aristotelian entelechy, Burke offers one more definition of entelechy in GM: "having its end [or purpose] within itself" (GM 261).

Burke finds it necessary, however, to replace the implicit determinism of Aristotelian biological entelechy with the implicit freedom of human action in his concept of entelechy. Certainly, by 1961, Burke has put in place the logological framework that characterizes the Burkean entelechy in its extension of the Aristotelian entelechy. Burke here speaks of "terminologies that can be developed in connection with the 'logic of perfection.' (A bright Greek will treat it in terms of . . . the 'entelechy')" (*The Rhetoric of Religion*, hereafter RR, 300). And while Burke acknowledges that "[t]he Aristotelian concept of the 'entelechy' is essentially a biological analogy," that locates the "entelechy . . . as residing not just in the . . . seed, but in the . . . *process as a whole*" (RR 246-247), Burke is moving to "extend" Aristotle's biologically-contextualized entelechy to his own logologically-related entelechy.

Burke later states: "By entelechy, I refer to such use of symbolic resources that potentialities can be said to attain their perfect fulfillment" (*Dramatism and Development*, hereafter DD, 39). Since Burke's concept of entelechy is described in the final clause in his definition of [hu]man--which definition, at its outset, distinguishes between the human's biological nature (animality) and his/her logological nature (symbolicity)--Burke is concerned with tracking down the logic of perfection implicit in symbols, terminologies, nomenclatures. This concern is Burkean, not Aristotelian.

Implicit in the action of Burkean entelechy is what Burke calls the "temporizing of essence." Burke declares that the "temporizing of essence" is "a major Dramatistic property":

I refer to Dramatism's investment in what (in my *Grammar of Motives*) I called the "temporizing of essence," and which I have later developed further. I might approach the issue thus: Recall, in Chapter VII of the *Poetics*, where Aristotle propounds the proposition that "A whole is what has a beginning, middle, and end." There are few statements that are more platitudinous, and even fewer that are more fertile. In particular, owing to my study of dramatic and narrative forms, I became involved in somewhat paradoxical considerations whereby, if a work is integrally formed, then whereas a beginning, middle, or end must be *explicitly* exactly as it is, each such stage must *implicitly* contain the other two, in anticipation (as regards a beginning), in retrospect (as regards an end), while the middle would somehow contain the "substance" of both.[8]

If beginning, middle, and end all contain each other "*implicitly*," the temporizing of essence is a thoroughly entelechial concept. Burke elaborates on his concept of the temporizing of essence on pages 430-440 of GM. In simplest terms, the temporizing of essence is a way of "translat[ing] back and forth between logical and temporal vocabularies" (GM 430). As Burke puts it, "There is no *temporal* sequence in the premises and conclusion of a syllogism though the *stating* of the propositions involves the passing of time."[9] Yet narrative includes temporal sequence.

The term entelechy, as Burke and Aristotle use it, may be defined as: *the process of changing from what something is into what something should become, which process is directed by an internal principle of change that allows the thing to possess internally the final form toward which the thing is changing.*[10] The Aristotelian basis for Burke's concept of entelechy is hardly "extremist." Burke is extending a thoroughly natural concept, and Burke frequently uses the terms entelechy and entelechial in contexts that do not suggest extremism. For instance, in Burke's first published use of the term he states: "[A] philosophy is an 'entelechy'" (ATH 107n). Philosophies are usually not regarded as extremist, yet they are usually very systematic and thorough. On certain occasions, however, Burke definitely discusses entelechy in extremist contexts.

Rhetorical scholars are familiar with Burke's final clause or "wry codicil" in his definition of (hu)man: "*and rotten with perfection*" (*Language as Symbolic Action*, hereafter LSA, 16). In Burke's discussion of this clause, he explicitly ties the clause to the term entelechy. He makes some non-extreme connections, such as: "The

Spiritual Gifts and Psychotic Entelechy 11

mere desire to name something by its 'proper' name, or to speak a language in its distinctive ways is intrinsically 'perfectionist'" (LSA 16). In the same discussion, he mentions extremist applications for the term entelechy. Burke offers Freud's "repetition compulsion" as an application of the principle (LSA 17). He suggests that a "'perfect fool' or a 'perfect villain'" is "precisely" what he has "in mind when in [his] wry codicil [he] refer[s] to [the hu]man as being 'rotten' with perfection" (LSA 18). Burke then moves to Hitler's identification of the Jew as a "'perfect' enemy" (LSA 18). Burke offers as an example of "'terministic compulsion' to carry out the implications of one's terminology . . . [the example of] an astronomer [who] discovered by his observations and computations that a certain wandering body was likely to hit the earth and destroy us." Burke opines that the astronomer "would nonetheless feel compelled to *argue for the correctness of his computations*, despite the ominousness of the outcome" (LSA 19).

Although Burke does not discuss his concept of entelechy in great detail until GM, he implicitly recognizes the possibility of this extremist type of entelechy--what might be called psychotic entelechy--as early as his first book of criticism, *Counter-Statement* (hereafter CS). Burke's pertinent line is: "'Madness' is but meaning carried to the extreme" (CS 180).

In his second book of criticism, *Permanence and Change: An Anatomy of Purpose* (hereafter, PC), Burke uses the terms "psychosis" and "psychotic" as John Dewey used them--not in a psychiatric sense, but referring simply to "a *pronounced character* of the mind" (PC 40). Burke views Dewey's concept of "occupational psychosis" as being interchangeable with Veblen's concept of trained incapacity. Burke's own way of putting the point is: "A way of seeing is also a way of not seeing" (PC 49).

Burke's use of the terminology "seeing" and "not seeing" brings to mind the concepts of selective perception, selective organization, and selective interpretation, as taught by interpersonal communication specialists Berko, Rosenfeld, and Samovar.[11] They cite H. M. Tomlinson: "We see things not as they are, but as we are." The point that all of these thinkers make is that humans perceive the world partially, selectively. However, it did not take Burke, Dewey, Veblen, or Berko, *et. al.*, to notice that humans are capable of "not seeing" quite a bit. A proverb that runs throughout the gospels and Acts in the New Testament reflects the same observation: "Though seeing they do not see; though hearing, they do not hear or understand" (Matthew 13:13 NIV; *Cf.,* also Mark 4:12 and 8:18, Luke 8:10, John 9:39, and Acts 8:26). Matthew attributes the proverb to the Old Testament book of Isaiah (6:9-10):

" . . . In them is fulfilled the prophecy of Isaiah: 'You will be ever hearing but never understanding; you will be ever seeing but never perceiving. For this people's heart has become calloused; they hardly hear with their ears, and they have closed their eyes. Otherwise they might see with their eyes, hear with their ears, understand with their hearts and turn, and I would heal them' . . . ." (Matthew 13:14-15 NIV)

Given the prominence of the biblical proverb concerning seeing and not seeing, it is ironic that religious leaders so frequently fall prey to the proverb. In November of 1978, members of the People's Temple, led by Jim Jones and transplanted from San Francisco to South America, killed Congressman Leo Ryan and four others before committing mass suicide in their compound. In October of 1994, in Cheiry and Les Granges, Switzerland, forty-eight members of a Swiss cult called the Order of the Solar Tradition became victims of a mass murder-suicide. According to Alexander G. Higgins of the Associated Press, "the Swiss cult . . . draws on Roman Catholicism and predicts the end of the world."[12] In March of 1997, thirty-nine members of the Heaven's Gate cult in southern California shed their "vehicles" (earth-bound bodies) by committing mass suicide in order to hitch a ride on the chariot that was coming in the tail of the Hale-Bopp comet. Applewhite, the leader of the Heaven's Gate cult, identified somewhat with the Branch Davidians of Waco, Texas.

One of the most tragic of the death-related cult events is the case of David Koresh and the Branch Davidians. In April of 1993, eighty-six persons died in a fire at the Branch Davidian compound after a fifty-one-day standoff with federal agents. What should the deaths at Waco be called? Suicides? Murders? Accidents? Should these deaths be categorized with the deaths at Jonestown, Switzerland, and California-- even if they are termed accidents? I think so. Regardless of the term used to describe the deaths, the deaths appear to have resulted from psychotic entelechy, just as did the other cult deaths mentioned.

While Burke following Dewey uses the term psychotic to refer only to a pronounced character of the mind, I have in mind a somewhat stronger connotation for the term when I speak of psychotic entelechy. Though not yet using the term in a psychiatric sense, I use the term psychotic entelechy to refer to *the tendency of some individuals to be so desirous of fulfilling or bringing to perfection the implications of their terminologies that they engage in very hazardous or damaging actions.* This definition of psychotic entelechy is in line with Burke's example of the astronomer who, upon calculating the coming of a human-life-ending cosmic event "would nonetheless feel compelled to *argue for the correctness of his computations,* despite the ominousness of the outcome" (LSA 19). It would aptly encompass Freud's "repetition compulsion" and Hitler's attitude toward the Jew as the "perfect enemy."

As a religious example, it is not uncommon among religious groups for individuals to believe in the necessity of controlling their sexual appetites. Yet, some in the Heaven's Gate cult found that their sexual temptation was too difficult to control in light of the fact that permitting sensual arousal in thought or action was considered a major offense in the cult. According to Mark Miller, before DiAngelo joined the cult:

> [T]wo members had quietly gone to Mexico to be castrated. The others increasingly talked about getting "neutered." Finally, . . . Do [Applewhite] himself decided to lead the way. "He did it to his own vehicle just to make sure. He protected us in every way," says DiAngelo. Do had trouble finding a doctor willing to perform the operation, however; most wanted him to see a psychiatrist. The one [castration surgery] Do got "goofed," as DiAngelo put it. Do healed very slowly. Still five others eagerly followed. "They couldn't stop smiling and giggling," says DiAngelo. "They were excited about it."[13]

This example fits Burke's definition of madness as "meaning carried to the extreme." The specific "meaning" here could be defined as a principle of religious purity--the implicit desire to conquer or control the sexual appetite. This is not an unethical *telos*. Castration, however, takes this principle too far. In an effort to bring to perfection the implications of religious purity terminology, the Heaven's Gate cult engaged in very hazardous or damaging actions.

The search for a method of understanding and curing the underlying rhetorical excesses of religious cults and movements begins with a search for a theory that explains the rhetoric. Kenneth Burke offers such a theory in his extension of Aristotle's highly Naturalistic concept of entelechy. Burke utilizes the deterministic framework of biological entelechy, but eliminates the determinism. In the place of determinism or motion, Burke inserts human choice, or free will, or action. Despite the implications of free will in Burke's theory, he finds that frequently humans (however free) subject themselves to near-deterministic compulsions supplied by their own terminologies. These logical (or logological) compulsions are easily carried to the extreme or to psychotic levels. I use the term psychotic entelechy. I refer to *the tendency of some individuals to be so desirous of fulfilling or bringing to perfection the implications of their terminologies that they engage in very hazardous or damaging actions.*

Notes

[1] "God Told Me to Invade Iraq, Bush Tells Palestinian Ministers," *BBC.co.uk* 10/16/05. Available: http://www.bbc.co.uk/print/pressoffice/pressreleases/stories/2005/10_october/06/bush.shtml (10/6/05).
[2] "White House Denies Bush Claimed Divine Inspiration," *Breitbart.com* 10/17/05. Available: http://www.breitbart.com/news/2005/10/07/051007131357.nstalu7a.html (10/7/05).
[3] "God Told Me" and "White House Denies."
[4] Roderick P. Hart, *Modern Rhetorical Criticism* (Glenview, Illinois and London: Scott, Foresman/Little, Brown Higher Education, 1990), i.
[5] Edward C. Appel, "Kenneth Burke: Coy Theologian," *Journal of Communication and Religion* 16 (1993): 99-110, and Wayne C. Booth, "The Many Voices of Kenneth Burke, Theologian and Prophet, as Revealed in His Letters to Me," in *Unending Conversations: New Writings by and about Kenneth Burke* eds. Greig R. Henderson and David Cratis Williams (Carbondale: Southern Illinois University Press, 2001), 179-201.
[6] Stan A. Lindsay, *Implicit Rhetoric: Kenneth Burke's Extension of Aristotle's Concept of Entelechy* (Lanham, MD: University Press of America, 1998), 91 & 134.
[7] Richard McKeon, *Introduction to Aristotle* 2nd ed. rev. (Chicago and London: University of Chicago Press, 1973), xlii.
[8] Kenneth Burke, "Poetics and Communication," in *Perspectives in Education, Religion, and the Arts* eds. Howard E. Kiefer and Milton K. Munitz (Albany: State University of New York Press, 1970), 415 (emphases, Burke's).
[9] Burke, "Poetics and Communication," 416.
[10] Lindsay, *Implicit*, 5.
[11] Roy M. Berko, Lawrence B. Rosenfeld, and Larry A. Samovar, *Connecting: A Culture-Sensitive Approach to Interpersonal Communication Competency* 2nd ed. (Fort Worth, TX: Harcourt Brace College Publishers, 1997), 67-77.
[12] Alexander G. Higgins, "48 in Swiss Religious Sect Die," *Journal and Courier*, 6 October 1994, sec. A.
[13] Miller, 32.

Chapter 2

The Waco Disaster

Biblical scholar James D. Tabor, professor of religion at the University of North Carolina, Charlotte, claims that the Branch Davidian disaster could have been avoided. With his co-author, Eugene Gallagher, Tabor provides an analytical overview of the Waco siege.[1] According to Tabor's testimony at the U. S. House hearings on July 25, 1995, Tabor and his colleague Philip Arnold "elicited a promise that Koresh and his followers would leave the compound once he [Koresh] had written down his own interpretation of the Book of Revelations [sic]."[2]

In the Waco incident, specific meanings were carried to extremes. A definite source of meanings is indicated in Koresh's conditional promise to leave the compound. No doubt, Koresh believed that his cult was playing a role in the fulfillment of the prophecies of Revelation. For the several days preceding the Waco conflagration, Koresh worked on a manuscript that would contain, according to Koresh, the "decoded message of the Seven Seals" of Revelation.[3] Ruth Riddle, a survivor of the conflagration, had typed the manuscript as Koresh dictated it. She carried out a computer disk with Koresh's unfinished manuscript and this manuscript was published as an appendix to Tabor and Gallagher's book on the Waco incident.[4] With the publication of the text of Koresh's unfinished manuscript, Burkean scholars may proceed to analyze Koresh's entelechial framework.

The Poem

The manuscript begins with a poem entitled "Eden to Eden." The poem, apparently composed by Koresh, speaks of two lovebirds. Halfway through the poem, the two lovebirds are identified as Adam and Eve. Eve is identified as Adam's "spirit." Finally, "the Christ" is mentioned along with "a bride." Since Adam's "spirit" is Eve, one can interpret the language Koresh uses regarding the bride of the Christ: "The wife with cloven tongues of fire, / Of whom the Christ has loved." Cloven tongues of fire were the sign that the Holy Spirit had descended upon the Christians on the day of Pentecost, according to the book of Acts. Hence, Koresh appears to be saying that the Holy Spirit is the bride of the Christ as the spirit Eve was the bride of Adam. Two matters are unclear--the identity of the Christ and in what sense the Holy Spirit somehow may be identified with a human bride for the Christ.

By virtue of the title of the poem, "Eden to Eden," Koresh appears to be thinking entelechially. He seems to indicate that "the marriage of the King" in the *final* line of the poem would provide a symmetrical mirror-image conclusion to the first couple, "Adam and . . . Eve" who were *originally* designed "[t]o share the kingdom fair." As I demonstrate elsewhere,[5] the biblical book of Revelation contains a thorough entelechy that is in some respects similar to that which Koresh explicates. There is a clear contest/agon between a metaphorical woman and a metaphorical dragon. The text of Revelation implicitly equates the woman in a sense with Eve in Genesis and with the bride of the Lamb, New Jerusalem, at the end of time. The first Adam and Eve lost the contest with the dragon. As Koresh puts it, "when they sinned they lost their crown." Near the end of Revelation, the Lamb and his bride both overcome the dragon. There is a marriage of the Lamb (the second Adam?) and his bride. Koresh correctly identifies at least this one *telos* of Revelation. What is important to watch in Koresh's interpretation, however, is the identity of "the Christ" and his "bride."

Most Revelation scholars place the drama of Revelation in the context of the first century. They interpret all of the terms of Revelation as being historically understandable to the book's original audience. The Beast, for example, is the Roman Empire. The seven heads of the Beast are individual emperors. The number six hundred sixty-six can easily be identified with emperor Nero Caesar. In the positive cluster, the

Lamb is Jesus. The conquerors are the witnesses/martyrs who died or who were to die for their faith in the first century.

However, most apocalyptic cults, such as the Branch Davidians, reinterpret Revelation's symbols in order to apply them to their own generation, and (more specifically) to themselves. Tabor testified to congress that:

> David Koresh, whether understood as con man, "cult" leader, psychotic or messiah, operated within his own elaborate system of biblical symbols and codes. Indeed this was his claim to fame and the key to his hold upon his followers. They all uniformly report that they had become unalterably convinced of Koresh's prophetic role as a final "Christ Figure" because he alone could unravel the complexities of the entire Scriptures, particularly the obscurities of the biblical prophets and the mysterious Seven Seals Book of Revelation.[6]

Specifically, according to Tabor, the group believed "that those outside were indeed the prophesied enemy and that the 'time of the end' had arrived." Koresh's followers identified themselves as "the people of God [who] were to finally confront an evil governmental system." Tabor suggests that to Koresh the FBI was "Babylon."[7]

The term Babylon was important to Koresh because of his interpretation of Isaiah 40-66. Tabor and Gallagher write:

> The . . . figure [of a messiah riding his horse triumphantly in Psalm 45 and other texts] is mentioned in Isaiah 45:1 and called by name: "Thus says the LORD to his anointed (Christ), to Cyrus ("Koresh" in Hebrew), whose right hand I have held, to subdue nations before him." This Cyrus, or Koresh, is called "Christ" and his mission is to destroy Babylon. Historians have understood the reference to be to the ancient Persian king Cyrus, who destroyed ancient Babylon. But there is a deeper spiritual and prophetic meaning according to Koresh and, for that matter, to the author of the biblical book of Revelation. The whole religious-political system is called "mystery Babylon the Great." As the text says, "Babylon is fallen, is fallen" (Rev. 18.2). Koresh took the repetition of the verb to indicate a *double* meaning and fulfillment, that is, not only the fall of ancient Babylon but also the fall of her counterpart at the end of history. This last Babylon, Western society, is to be defeated by the last Christ/King/Koresh, who is also the Branch of David, according to Koresh.[8]

The Introduction

Following his opening poem, Koresh provides an introduction to the seven seals. The first paragraph of the introduction is a verbatim quotation of John 18:33-38. Although Koresh does not state which Bible version he uses, all of his quotations are from the King James Version. In the passage cited, Pilate had asked Jesus if he was the *King* of the Jews. Instead of answering directly, Jesus asked whether Pilate says this himself or someone said this to Pilate. Jesus never explicitly answers the question. Koresh's first comment following the quotation is a cryptic one: "Strange indeed for the judgment of man, for who knows within himself that his judgment be true?" Of whose judgment was Koresh speaking? Jesus' or Pilate's?

Koresh's poem ends with the marriage of the "King." The issue in Koresh's introductory quotation is whether or not Jesus is the "King." Koresh follows with the cryptic question cited above, then asks questions: "Who was this Jesus? Who was this Saviour that nearly a whole religious nation rejected? . . . .'Who is this Christ and what remains to be the mystery of Him?'"[9] Koresh does not yet answer these questions, but he points to several New Testament books for those who are interested in the answer. The "most awe inspiring . . . [and] the most misunderstood"[10] record of who Christ is may be found, according to Koresh, in the book of Revelation.

Koresh next turns to "unfold[ing] this mystery . . . not us[ing] great techniques of scholarly display nor in-depth reasonings of philosophy, no sophisticated, congenial language, . . . just simple talk and reason."[11] Koresh claims that Revelation contains "past, present, and future events"[12] and dispenses quickly with the past (i.e., Revelation 2-3). Koresh is more interested in what he sees as "the events that are to be after John's time," found in "chapters 4-22."

Koresh quotes the entire fourth chapter of Revelation and makes only three sentences of commentary on it. Sometime after John's time, a God will sit on His throne, surrounded by a jury of twenty-four elders. Koresh quotes the entire fifth chapter and makes six sentences of commentary. Essentially, Koresh believes that chapter five presents the Christ's role as High Priest. He then quotes 19 verses from the book of Hebrews. These verses, as Koresh explains, demonstrate that "Christ is the mediator of the New Covenant . . . which is contained in the seven seals."[13] "[T]he opening of these seven seals by Christ," Koresh argues, amounts to the "salvation ready to be revealed in the last times," referred to in I Peter 1:3-5. Koresh next asks the rhetorical question, "[A]re we in the last days?"[14] The question needs no answer. Koresh proceeds on the assumption that we are.

After quoting three passages from the Psalms, Koresh is ready to expound upon the meaning of the seven seals. Unfortunately, Koresh had only enough time to explain the first seal before his demise. That Koresh is thinking entelechially is indicated in the final paragraph of his introduction: "[E]very book of the Bible meets and ends in the book of Revelation. . . . [W]hen has grace ever been needed more than now in the time of which we live?"[15]

The First Seal

The text of the first seal in Revelation (6:1-2) is brief and worth quoting here:

> And I saw when the Lamb opened one of the seals, and I heard, as it were the noise of thunder, one of the four beasts saying, Come and see. And I saw, and behold a white horse; and he that sat on him had a bow; and a crown was given unto him: and he went forth conquering, and to conquer.

Koresh ties this reference to a white horse to another reference to a white horse in Revelation 19. Although scholars might disagree that the rider in the first seal is the Lamb, it is much clearer that the rider on the white horse in Revelation 19 is the Lamb. Furthermore, chapter 19 makes reference to "the marriage supper of the Lamb" (19:9), thus tying in the poem with which Koresh begins his manuscript.

As Koresh observes earlier, "[E]very book of the Bible meets and ends in the book of Revelation."[16] This marriage supper appears to be the point at which all books meet. Throughout his commentary on the first seal, Koresh interprets Psalm 44, what appears to be the paradigmatic wedding supper of a King. Koresh brings in Matthew 22:1-14, Jesus' parable that compares the kingdom of heaven to a king who made a marriage feast for his son. Koresh cites Isaiah 33:17: "Thine eyes shall see the king in his beauty." We must assume that the king would be dressed for this affair. Koresh points us to Isaiah 61:8-10 where God "hath clothed me with the garments of salvation, . . . the robe of righteousness; as a bridegroom decketh himself with ornaments; and as a bride adorneth herself with her jewels."[17]

In Jeremiah 23 and 33, Koresh sees that God "will raise up unto *David* a righteous *Branch*" and that this "*Branch* of righteousness [will] grow up unto *David* [emphasis mine]." In Ezekiel 37:24-25, God's "servant *David* shall be their prince for ever [emphasis mine]." Daniel 12:1 then says, "And at that time shall Michael stand up, the great prince . . . and there shall be a time of trouble, such as never was since there was a nation . . . and at that time thy people shall be delivered." Surely, we are meant to infer that the "David" of the "Branch" Davidians will be our prince.

Hosea 2:14-23 is next invoked to present the picture of God preparing for Marriage. Hosea 3:5 indicates the one whom the bride should be seeking--"*David*, their king [emphasis mine]." Joel 2:15-16 instructs "the bridegroom [to] go forth from his chamber, and the bride out of her closet." Who is the bride? David Koresh says, "Should we not eagerly ourselves be ready to accept this truth and come out of our closet."[18] Earlier, he comments, "If we, the church of God, stand in the counsel of Christ, especially in the light of the seven seals, shall we not be a part of that beautiful bride spoken of in Jeremiah 33?"[19] Although Koresh uses the first person pronoun "we" in this quotation to refer to both the church of God and the beautiful bride of Jeremiah 33, I do not believe he intends to include himself as part of the bride; rather, he is the "Christ" to whom he refers in the third person in the same quotation. Jeremiah 33 mentions the term "bride," but not the term "Christ." Koresh's own system of equations has inserted this term into Jeremiah 33. God promises that in the streets of Jerusalem will once again be heard "the voices of bride and bridegroom (Jer. 33:11)." The promise of a return of good times to Israel are made clear: "In those days and at that time I will make a righteous Branch sprout from David's line; he will do what is just and right in the land (Jer. 33:15)."

If the church (understand: the Branch Davidians), then, is the bride of the new Christ (understand: Koresh), what may be said about the reference to the "Spirit" as the bride of Christ? Koresh had implied in his beginning poem that Holy Spirit is the bride of the Christ as the spirit Eve was the (spirit and) bride of Adam. Koresh had already "married" in a physical sense several of the women and girls in the Branch Davidians. Perhaps, the spirit language suggests that he also considered the males (as well as the females) in the Branch Davidians to be his spiritual bride. If the entire group of followers is understood to be his bride, his sexual relationships with whomever he chose implicitly follows a marriage entelechy, however misguided. The marriage entelechy implicitly contains presumed sexual acts between the husband and the bride.

In closing the chapter on the first seal, Koresh quotes Amos 9:11,14,15, and Obadiah 21, promising that God will "raise up the tabernacle of *David* that is fallen [emphasis mine]" and that "the kingdom shall be the LORD's." As Tabor and Arnold observe, David Koresh claimed to be neither God nor Jesus, but he did claim to be "the Lamb, or the 'Root [Branch] of David,' who alone is able to open this mysterious book sealed with Seven Seals (Rev. 5:5)."[20] Koresh believed that he was a "second 'Christ' figure, who is called a 'ravenous bird from the east' in Isaiah 46:11." The references to lovebirds in Koresh's poem may relate to this bird terminology.

The Letter

The unfinished manuscript is not the only text generated by David Koresh that emerged from the compound. Five days before the conflagration, Koresh wrote a letter to federal negotiator Richard DeGuerin. In that letter, Koresh presents his plans for the conclusion of the standoff:

> I am presently being permitted to document . . . the decoded messages of the Seven Seals. Upon the completion of this task, I will be freed of my "waiting period." I hope to finish this as soon as is possible and to stand before man to answer any and all questions regarding my actions.
> . . .
> I was shown that as soon as I am given over into the hands of man, I will be made a spectacle of, and people will not be concerned about the truth of God, but just the bizarrity [*sic*] of me--the flesh (person).
> . . .
> I will demand the first manuscript of the Seals be given to you. . . . I will keep a copy with me. As soon as I can see that people, like Jim Tabor and Phil Arnold have a copy I will come out and then you can do your thing with this Beast.[21]

Regarding Koresh's plan to write his message and then surrender, Tabor comments:

> We know through the negotiation tapes of those last three days and the computer disk containing Koresh's first chapter of his treatise, that

survived the fire, that he went to work immediately. It is obvious in the tapes that he felt the situation was resolved, that an agreement had been reached, and that the negotiators were going along with the plan, though urging him to move quickly.[22]

Why then did the twenty-one children and fifty-three adults of the Branch Davidians die in a fiery blaze on April 19, 1993? If Koresh and his followers were willing to give themselves up, eventually, what prohibited that from happening? Perhaps we can find some answers by employing Burkean analysis.

Burkean Analysis

In 1974, Jeanne Y. Fisher conducted "A Burkean Analysis of the Rhetorical Dimensions of a Multiple Murder and Suicide."[23] Fisher utilized Burkean pentadic analysis in an attempt to determine the implications of the non-verbal message of Joseph William White who committed suicide after murdering four female co laborers. White left no clear verbal statement indicating the reason for his actions. The pentad is useful in "assigning" motives, but most of the conclusions Fisher drew from her analysis, while fascinating, were quite speculative. No text could be found to corroborate her conclusions. Even so, the closest Fisher came to identifying some entelechy that was driving White to extreme behavior was White's apparent dissatisfaction with his birth name, Joseph William Blank. Children teased him in high school, saying "Blank is a blank."[24] He later changed his name to White.[25] This terminological entelechy might lead Blank to become a social blank, so to speak. Conversely, the terminological entelechy might lead Blank to become an adept socialite. This is the reactionary response to an entelechy.[26] The entelechy of his new name might lead White to become pure. But, there is nothing in either of these entelechies that suggests that White possessed an entelechy that, if carried to the extreme, would result in his suicide and the murder of four women.

Burke comes closer to an entelechy similar to Koresh's in his analysis of Milton's *Samson Agonistes* in RM. Burke demonstrates that Milton identified himself with the blind, fallen, Old Testament hero. The suicidal motive was implicit in Samson's pulling the temple down upon himself and his enemies. If Jeanne Fisher had been able to show that Joseph White was as deeply interested in the life of Samson as was Milton, she would have gone a long way toward demonstrating an entelechy behind his murder-suicide. Burke's own analysis of Milton's

Samson entelechy stops short of demonstrating *psychotic* entelechy, as well. Burke writes:

> [Y]et Milton's religion strongly forbade suicide. Compelled by his misfortunes to live with his rage, gnawed by resentments that he could no longer release fully in outward contest, Milton found in Samson a figure ambivalently fit to symbolize both aggressive and inturning trends. Here . . . would be "literature for use" (RM 5).

Unlike Joseph William White, David Koresh left texts that might be analyzed in order to account for his motives. Certainly, Koresh's non-verbal actions might be pentadically analyzed, as White's were. The conclusions, however, should still depend for corroboration upon the textual evidence. Unlike White, Koresh had a clear sense of entelechy. He thought he was a Christ figure who would usher in the predictions of Revelation. His entelechy, however, depended to a large part upon his interpretation of Revelation. His interpretation continued to show signs that it was still being molded.

Like Milton, Koresh found an authoritative entelechy in the Bible. Unlike Milton's, Koresh's entelechy was a prophecy. Milton could "use" the "literature" of Samson to poetically reenact Samson's role. Koresh, meanwhile, found in his interpretation of prophecy a compulsion to literally live out the entelechy. Unlike the symbolic action in the writings of Milton, the writings of Koresh laid down his own *telos*. He was persuaded that he must live it out.

Burke's cluster-agon method may be employed to find ways in which Koresh may have linked the terms of Revelation to one another. Revelation scholars agree that the Beast of Revelation is an evil governmental system. There is some dispute concerning the identity of Babylon, the harlot, however. Nevertheless, the terms that represent the enemies of the people of God in Revelation have a tendency to cluster together, as Burke suggests. Clearly, Tabor claims that to Koresh the FBI was "Babylon."[27] There is even the element of synecdoche operative in the clusters. There is the sense that one term in a cluster represents the other terms in the cluster. For that matter, many biblical students and some scholars refer to the Antichrist of Revelation despite the fact that the term Antichrist is not even found in the book. In Christian literature, the terms that refer to the enemies of the church operate synecdochically--they tend to stand for each other.[28]

In this respect, it is not difficult to understand the view that the FBI is Babylon, even though a clearer reference to an evil government system in Revelation is the term Beast. Koresh refers to himself as a "Beast" in his letter to DeGuerin five days before the Waco fire, although it is not clear whether he was using the term ironically. If Koresh saw himself as the Beast of Revelation, it is interesting to note that it is the Beast who, in Revelation, destroys Babylon. Koresh may have distinguished between the Beast, whom he may have seen as another Cyrus/Koresh messiah and Babylon as the evil entity to be destroyed by Cyrus/Koresh. Perhaps, if we had Koresh's writings on the final six seals, we would understand his take on the Beast better. The view of Koresh as Beast would be particularly hard to accept, though, if Koresh believed in the entire Book of Revelation. Later, God casts the Beast into the Lake of Fire, which is the Second Death (or Hell).

One part of the Book of Revelation that may have been operative on the specific day of the conflagration, however, mentions neither Babylon nor Beast. Gog and Magog are evil political entities similar to Babylon and the Beast. Revelation 20:9 (NIV) records the drama: "They [Gog and Magog] marched across the breadth of the earth and surrounded the camp of God's people, the city he loves. But fire came down from heaven and devoured them."

The Branch Davidians considered themselves to be God's people. Whoever Gog and Magog are, they are clearly an evil governmental system. It is possible that Koresh and his followers identified them with the Bureau of Alcohol, Tobacco, and Firearms (BATF). It is not much of a stretch to identify them with the FBI, the Justice Department, or the entire United States Government. Clearly, to the Branch Davidians, these governmental representatives were "surround[ing] the camp of God's people," the Branch Davidian compound known as Mount Carmel. On Monday, April 19, when the "fire" began, the *telos*/end of the psychotic entelechy might have become easy for Koresh and his followers to accept. Nevertheless, we have no record of an explicit teaching by the Branch Davidians that incorporates the fiery Gog and Magog ending.

Indeed, the textual evidence suggests much more strongly that Koresh and the Davidians thoroughly intended to come out peacefully within a brief period of time. Koresh had clearly begun to work on his manuscript. He had notified Richard DeGuerin by letter that he expected to "stand before man," to be "given over into the hands of man," since he would "come out." There is absolutely no credible evidence that Koresh was planning to start the fires himself.

Even the psychotic entelechy that caused the cult members to fire upon the BATF agents at the outset of the siege seems to have abated before the conflagration. Nevertheless, clearly the cult's action of firing upon the BATF agents initially qualifies as psychotic entelechy. The action certainly demonstrates *the tendency of some individuals to be so desirous of fulfilling or bringing to perfection the implications of their terminologies that they engage in very hazardous or damaging actions.* What were these individuals trying to bring to perfection? Koresh's unfinished manuscript informs us: the marriage supper of the Lamb. This marriage supper occurs in Revelation 19, immediately following the destruction of Babylon. Since Babylon is the FBI and BATF, the sooner they are destroyed, the sooner the marriage supper will come. Only after Tabor and others persuaded Koresh that the timing of these events did not easily fit within Koresh's interpretive schema did Koresh consider writing his manuscript and exiting the compound.

Perhaps the fiery conclusion to the standoff was purely accidental; yet somehow the compound caught fire. High winds exacerbated the problem. The Branch Davidians may have thought it was the end of the world. It was--for them.

The Solution

Unlike Jeanne Y. Fisher's application of Burkean method to the analysis of tragic deaths, the value I find in applying Burkean insights is the curative value. I believe that the Waco incident is actually an important example of how Burkean methods might work to solve psychotic entelechy. Burke offers several tools for dealing with psychotic entelechy. His cluster-agon method may be used to diagnose the problem, to delineate protagonist and antagonist terms. His concept of recalcitrance suggests the attitude that must be taken when counseling/treating those who incline toward psychotic entelechy. His concepts of discounting and the four master tropes supply the prescription for treating or curing psychotic entelechy.

Diagnosis

The first step in treating any malady is diagnosis. The healer must thoroughly understand the malady and its causes. For the Branch

Davidians, a contest existed between good and evil, between the Branch and Babylon. This was the primary agon. Koresh's followers considered themselves to be the bride of the Lamb (or Branch). They awaited the marriage supper of the Lamb. The BATF and the FBI were in the Babylon cluster with such terms as (Beast,) Gog and Magog, and serpent.

The very fact that the "woman *versus* serpent" agon of Revelation is reminiscent of Eve's encounter with the serpent in Genesis introduces a powerful entelechy. There is a sense in which the Branch Davidians are Eve and the government agents are the serpent. Dialogue takes place between the two, but Eve must always be suspicious of the motives of the serpent. Eve should not be so naïve as to trust the word of the serpent. Hence, the Branch Davidians must guard themselves against trusting the (evil) government agents. Koresh states this point poetically: "Love birds . . . / Shot down for gambled play, / . . . For the hunter felt it best that way."[29] The negotiators who seemed to be most successful in gaining the trust of Koresh were biblical scholars--James Tabor and Philip Arnold. According to Tabor, these two scholars were genuinely concerned for the physical well being of cult members:

> [Our] intentions, . . . in offering our expertise to the FBI, were singular and resolute: to see the tragic situation that developed on February 28 resolved peaceably with no further loss of life. Our essential aim was to enter into the complex and technical biblical world-view that Koresh and his followers inhabited, to try to listen and make sense of his stream of biblical rhetoric, and to identify all possible variables in what appeared to be a "set" apocalyptic scenario that would inevitably lead to disaster and further death.[30]

The scenario Tabor describes is a clear example of a psychotic entelechy, and the approach Tabor and Arnold took was the correct diagnostic approach. It was necessary first to understand Koresh's meaning--his entelechy. In the attempt to enter into the biblical world-view of Koresh and to identify all possible variables, Burke's cluster-agon method might have been quite useful to Tabor and Arnold, had they been familiar with it. Clearly, however, the insertion of two biblical scholars into the Eve *versus* serpent entelechy offered Eve someone other than the serpent with whom to negotiate. The genuine concern of the scholars and their willingness to listen to the views of Koresh apparently made an impact. When Koresh wrote to federal negotiator (and Koresh's lawyer) DeGuerin, he commented, "As soon as I can see that people, like Jim Tabor and Phil Arnold have a copy [of my book] I will come out . . . ."[31] The language Koresh uses seems to imply trust and appreciation for the two scholars. By using negotiators who were detached from Babylon, the evil government entity, a trusting negotiation was made possible.

The type of malady toward which Koresh and his followers tend is what Freud calls "repetition compulsion" or "destiny compulsion" or a "psychopathic tendency." Burke considers the tendency "in the light of an 'entelechial' principle having wider functions than the manifestations with which Freud is . . . concerned" (DD 39-40). The problem is not that Koresh is merely irrational, but that he is super-rational. He carries his meaning to the extreme. Burke's discussion of carrying matters to the extreme recurs in the footnotes to the second edition of PC: "[A] cult of perspective carried to extremes which far outstrip the possibilities of communication . . . can have its roots in irrational emotional conflicts" (PC 114). Burke and Freud mean that certain traumatic experiences earlier in the life of a psychopath can cause the psychopath to reinterpret all new and unrelated experiences in accordance with the patterns of the earlier experience. Burke argues, "Is not the sufferer exerting almost superhuman efforts in the attempt to give his life a certain form . . . ?" (DD 40).

While the form Koresh applies to his life does not necessarily result from earlier traumatic experiences, the result is very similar. The form Koresh applies comes from his interpretation of the Lamb *versus* Babylon conflict in Revelation. The cult thoroughly infuses the federal government with all of the attributes of the serpent, (the Beast,) Babylon, and possibly Gog and Magog. The cult also thoroughly infuses itself with all of the attributes of the Lamb and his bride. What may seem irrational to onlookers is just meaning carried to the extreme.

Recalcitrance

Burke uses the terms "recalcitrant" and "recalcitrance" in discussions of persuasion. He views the "recalcitrant reader" of a piece of literature as someone whom "the author can reduce . . . to acquiescence" (CS 176) by means of "corrosion obtained by thoroughness, thoroughness manifest either as accuracy, or as profusion, or as both" (CS 178).

But, Burke sees recalcitrance as not only something to be overcome but also as a method of overcoming, of correcting. Burke notes that recalcitrance "refers to the factors that *substantiate* a statement, the factors that *incite* a statement, and the factors that *correct* a statement" (ATH 47). He suggests that "communicative problems and procedures" may be "corrected by the principle of *recalcitrance*" (PC lix). Burke teaches: "In classical eras, eras of pronounced social conformity, . . . anarchistic tendencies of the individual artist or thinker are corrected by the recalcitrance of the social body. In the very act of attempting to socialize his position, the artist is forced to revise his statements to such an extent that he himself is reclaimed in the process" (PC 115). This influence toward "social conformity" is very similar to the influence of the church through the centuries in opposition to "false prophets" or even heretics.

Burke stresses *"the term 'recalcitrance,' as an* essential corrective *of the 'poetic metaphor'"* (PC 168). According to Burke, "the poet meet[s] with considerable recalcitrance in arranging the materials of his poem" (PC 255). Even one's view of the universe is corrected by recalcitrance. Says Burke: "Such a position . . . does not imply that the universe is merely the product of our interpretations. For the interpretations themselves must be altered as the universe displays various orders of recalcitrance to them" (PC 256). Burke comments further: "[A]n *interpretation* . . . [is] a reading of the recalcitrant factors favorable and unfavorable to the point of view. But an interpretation can be wrong. . . . But where there is the possibility of a wrong interpretation, there is also the possibility of a right one. The *freedom to err* argues a *freedom to be right*" (PC 257). In order to fulfill its corrective function, Burke holds that "recalcitrance requires specific points of view before it can be disclosed" (PC 263). Burke is a perspectivist. He recommends the consideration of multiple points of view.

This recommendation is at odds with someone who is following a psychotic entelechy. The single common denominator of the Branch Davidians, the People's Temple, Heaven's Gate, and the Order of the Solar Tradition is that *all of these groups believed in the modern-day gift of prophecy*. Furthermore, they all believed that their leader(s) possessed this gift. Implicit in the term "prophet" is the notion of infallibility. If an infallible prophet supplies an interpretation of the Hale-Bopp comet, no other point of view is needed. If an infallible prophet claims that the FBI and the BATF are Babylon, no further perspective is allowed. Tabor describes the view of the Branch Davidians: "[I]f the Bible is true, then Koresh is who he claims to be. Those who had become schooled in Koresh's teachings, through hundreds of hours of meticulous, verse-by-verse, Bible study, had come to equate leaving the group with leaving God, rejecting the Bible and abandoning the truth."[32] Some Burkean recalcitrance would be useful in dealing with such a singular perspective. Burke says his "concept of recalcitrance could lessen sectarian divisions by prompting a man to remember that his assertions are necessarily *socialized by revision* . . ." (PC 265). Burke surely would have advised Koresh "to recommend his position by considering such orders of recalcitrance and revising his statements accordingly" (PC 272).

Discounting

Discounting is the Burkean prescription for curing the malady of psychotic entelechy. According to Burke: "The naïve take philosophic symbols at their face value--and the logical positivists are simply the naïve turned upside down. Neither extreme knows how to 'discount.' The naïve rate the symbol at 100; the logistically sophisiticate rate it at zero. Zero is not a discount--it is a massacre" (ATH 246). Too frequently in current vernacular the term discount is used by students synonymously and interchangeably with the term disregard.[33] Take the following sentence, for example: I always discount what salespersons say about their product and research it myself. If I mean by this sentence that I totally disregard anything a salesperson says about his/her product, I am carrying a meaning to an extreme. If my response becomes extremely hazardous or damaging, I have developed my own case of psychotic entelechy. For example, if every salesperson says that I need to have the brakes repaired on my car, but I totally disregard what every salesperson says, preferring to wait until I have the time to check out the brakes myself, I may be engaging in psychotic entelechy. I may be exercising my tendency to perfect the implications of my terminology to the extent that I have engaged in extremely hazardous or damaging actions. To reiterate, zero is not a discount--it is a massacre.

For Tabor and Arnold to have attempted to persuade Koresh to totally disregard his entire system would not have worked. Instead, the scholars realized:

> Koresh . . . was operating first and foremost within [his own] closed world of biblical exposition. Accordingly, any effective communication with him or his followers would have to be from within that framework. . . . As things appeared to us . . . a peaceful resolution of the Mt. Carmel standoff, if one were even possible, would rest on a

combination of three factors: a trustful relationship between those inside Mt. Carmel and the FBI negotiators; a resolution of the legal issues involved in effecting an exit; and an alternative biblical apocalyptic scenario that would allow for interpretive flexibility--or, to put it in Davidian terms--a postponement of the "Fifth Seal."[34]

It would have been a gross error for negotiators to have suggested to the cult that the truth claims of the Bible (and, hence, the book of Revelation) be disregarded. To have suggested such a thing would have immediately permitted the cult to place the negotiators in the dragon cluster with the Beast and Babylon. Instead, the negotiators were *biblical scholars* who "tried to gain [Koresh's] trust, offer a respectful hearing of his prophetic view, and offer in the most subtle way alternative interpretive possibilities."[35] Certainly, biblical scholars could agree with Koresh that the enemy in Revelation is an evil governmental system. Points of agreement between Koresh and the negotiators would and did allow Koresh to "identify" with the negotiators (*Cf.*, RM 55-59).

Such points of agreement can be related to Burke's understanding of the curative nature of psychoanalysis: "The patient, with pious devotion, ha[s] erected a consistent network of appropriatenesses about the altar of his wretchedness, the thoroughness of the outlying structure thus tending to maintain the integrity of the basic psychosis" (PC 126). Following McDougall's amended form of psychoanalysis, Burke would not recommend the obliteration of the psychotic's entire network. Instead a partial "conversion" should be attempted, which should not be "a revaluation of *all* values, but should appeal to any normal standards which the patient still held intact" (PC 131). While Burke does not buy into psychoanalysis in a wholesale fashion, he does disclose: "[T]hese theories might be expected to have genuine curative effects" (PC 132). Burke elaborates: "For one can cure a psychosis only by appealing to some aspect of the psychosis. The cure must bear notable affinities with the disease: all effective medicines are potential poisons" (PC 126). Burke is not being cynical here. He is honestly looking for those "normal standards" that even psychotics still possess. Once normal standards are located within the system of the psychotic, the process of discounting may begin.

According to Burke, the four master tropes--metaphor, metonymy, synecdoche, and irony--are examples of discounting at work. Burke, for example, claims that "all metaphor involves a . . . feeling for the discount" (*The Rhetoric of Religion: Studies in Logology*, hereafter, RR, 19). Burke writes that even language, "to be used properly, must be 'discounted.' We must remind ourselves that . . . the *word* 'tree' is *NOT* a tree" (RR 18).

This appears to be precisely what Tabor and Arnold attempted to do at Waco. They supplied recalcitrance. They attempted to persuade Koresh to discount some of his interpretations of his own prophecies:

> "[W]e tried to gain his trust, offer a respectful hearing of his prophetic view, and offer in the most subtle way alternative interpretive possibilities. We particularly argued that his confrontation did not have the marks of the "end," based on his own biblical prophetic scheme. We maintained that the very texts he focused on allow more time and that if the people of God were to finally confront an evil governmental system this was not the place nor the time."[36]

Far from serving as proof that psychotic entelechy cannot be dealt with, the Waco incident actually demonstrated the utility of many of Burke's concepts in dealing with psychotic entelechy. Unlike Jeanne Y. Fisher's dramatistic analysis of a multiple murder and suicide, this book approaches psychotic entelechy as a malady that may be diagnosed and cured. It is a shame that an accident or the lack of patience disrupted a process that now appears to have been working, a Burkean-style cure for a type of psychotic entelechy.

Conclusion

The psychotic entelechial rhetoric of David Koresh is a suitable subject for rhetorical study. Koresh left us not only the texts of a poem, an introduction, and one chapter of his *Seven Seals*, but also of a letter to Richard DeGuerin, in addition to his conversations with James Tabor and Phillip Arnold (as they have recalled them). These various texts help us to understand David Koresh's entelechy. Koresh's followers assume that he possesses an infallible prophetic gift when interpreting the book of Revelation (and the rest of the Bible). Koresh's interpretation claims that he is the Lamb of the book of Revelation and that various U.S. Government agencies are Babylon. Hence, Koresh views his *telos:* to conquer/destroy these agencies.

Biblical scholars Tabor and Arnold, while not contesting Koresh's view that he is the Lamb, use a Burkean-style recalcitrance in suggesting that Koresh's own interpretation seems to suggest a different timetable for the events that he is expecting. Using tools quite similar to Burkean identification, discounting, cluster-agon analysis, tropes, and recalcitrance, Tabor and Arnold nearly succeeded in persuading a cult compelled by psychotic entelechy to step back from the brink of disaster. Indeed, according to Tabor and Arnold, they *did* succeed. The intrusion of government tanks and the resulting conflagration was a tragedy that could have been averted.

Given the plausibility that Burkean methods may be able to defuse such psychotic time bombs, rhetorical scholars capable of applying Burkean psychotic entelechial insight might be quite valuable allies in handling future Waco's when they arise.

Notes

[1] James D Tabor and Eugene V. Gallagher, *Why Waco?: Cults and the Battle for Religious Freedom in America* (Berkeley, CA: Univ. of California Press, 1995).

[2] Editor, "Bible Scholar Claims Branch Davidian Disaster Could Have Been Avoided," *Religious Studies News* 10, no. 3 (1995): 3.

[3] Tabor and Gallagher, 189.

[4] Tabor and Gallagher, 189.

[5] Stan A. Lindsay, *Revelation: The Human Drama* (Bethlehem, PA: Lehigh University Press, 2001).

[6] James D. Tabor, "Introductory Remarks," *Religious Studies News* 10, no. 3 (1995): 3

[7] Tabor, "Introductory," 3.

[8] Tabor and Gallagher, 206.

[9] Tabor and Gallagher, 193.

[10] Tabor and Gallagher, 193.

[11] Tabor and Gallagher, 193.

[12] Tabor and Gallagher, 193.

[13] Tabor and Gallagher, 196.

[14] Tabor and Gallagher, 196.

[15] Tabor and Gallagher, 197.

[16] Tabor and Gallagher, 197.

[17] Tabor and Gallagher, 197-200.

[18] Tabor and Gallagher, 203.

[19] Tabor and Gallagher, 201.

[20] Tabor and Gallagher, 205.

[21] David Koresh, "Letter from David Koresh to Richard DeGuerin [14 April 1993]," *Religious Studies News* 10, no. 3 (1995): 3.

[22] Tabor, "Introductory," 3.

[23] Jeanne Y. Fisher, "A Burkean Analysis of the Rhetorical Dimensions of a Multiple Murder and Suicide," *Quarterly Journal of Speech* 60 (1974):175-189.

[24] Fisher, 178.

[25] Fisher, 179.

[26] Stan A. Lindsay, *Implicit Rhetoric: Kenneth Burke's Extension of Aristotle's Concept of Entelechy* (Lanham, MD: University Press of America, 1998), 8-10.

[27] Tabor, "Introductory," 3.

[28] Lindsay, *Revelation*, 69-94

[29] Tabor and Gallagher, 191.
[30] Tabor, "Introductory," 3.
[31] Koresh, "Letter," 3.
[32] Tabor, "Introductory," 3.
[33] I owe this observation to Don M. Burks who teaches this to his classes on Burke at Purdue University.
[34] Tabor, "Introductory," 3.
[35] Tabor, "Introductory," 3.
[36] Tabor, "Introductory," 3.

Chapter 3

The Rhetoric of bin Laden's Battle

Roderick P. Hart, as cited earlier, indicates that rhetorical critics should pay attention to the Islamic leader Ayatollah Khomeini. Now, an even more dangerous Islamic leader, Osama bin Laden, has emerged. To ignore such religious leaders is to continue to see cult followers and their "religious" enemies incur death. In the instance of the Islamic terrorist attack on the Pentagon and the World Trade Center on September 11, 2001, specific interpretations of Islamic scripture were carried to extremes. By his use of the Koran, Osama bin Laden sought to persuade his fellow Muslims that America should be attacked.

Bin Laden was not totally successful. Most governments of Islamic countries chose either to wait on the sidelines or to assist (however slightly) the United States at least in its prosecution of the war against the Taliban and bin Laden. Fewer Islamic governments supported the war to depose Saddam Hussein in Iraq. Despite the support of any of the official governments, however, many citizens in these Islamic countries have indeed been swayed by bin Laden. What seems clear is that the rhetoric of Osama bin Laden has many receptive ears. Whether or not bin Laden is personally motivated by psychotic entelechy, many in the Islamic world appear to be open to the psychotic entelechy expressed in bin Laden's rhetoric.

My procedure in addressing the specific psychotic entelechy I find present in bin Laden's rhetoric is first to review the text of the Koran to see what sources of entelechy may be found there. Then, I examine the texts in which bin Laden interprets the Koran. The specific psychotic entelechy on which bin Laden's rhetoric rests is elucidated.

September 11, 2001 served as a wake-up call to the world. Just as Burke's essay, "The Rhetoric of Hitler's Battle," analyzed the universal dangers of Hitler's rhetoric, rhetoricians should be analyzing the universal dangers of bin Laden's rhetoric.

In the Waco incident, specific interpretations of scripture were carried to extremes, but the danger was restricted to a small band of followers. A definite source of meanings is indicated in the "promise that Koresh and his followers would leave the compound once he had written down his own interpretation of the Book of Revelations [sic]."[1] Koresh believed that his cult was playing a role in the fulfillment of the prophecies of Revelation. In the instance of the Islamic terrorist attack on the Pentagon and the World Trade Center on September 11, 2001, specific interpretations of Islamic scripture were carried to extremes. By his use of the Koran, Osama bin Laden sought to persuade his fellow Muslims that America should be attacked.

Bin Laden's rhetoric has persuaded some in the Moslem world. A Reuters news story reports:

> Abdel-Rahman Saleem, spokesman for Islamic group al-Muhajiroun (the immigrants), . . . [which] describes itself as "the voice, the eyes, the ears of Muslims" [stated] . . . "Now, and after the British and American allies . . . have embarked on bombarding in Afghanistan, . . . [British Prime Minister Tony Blair] has also become a legitimate target . . . This means that if any Muslim wanted to kill him or to get rid of him, I would not shed any tears."
> . . . "From an Islamic legal point of view, if Blair entered a Muslim country, then he would become one of the legitimate targets because he had committed aggression against the land of the Muslims."[2]

Another Reuters story reported online support for bin Laden:

> "I swear he made me shiver when he appealed to the Muslim world for help . . . ."
>
> "How strong this man is! He has a solid faith and power of will. With those he can accomplish the impossible . . . ."
>
> "I hope to see America's end soon, God willing . . . I am very optimistic. What bin Laden said carries a lot of indications."[3]

Although Yasser Arafat used police force to put down a rally supporting bin Laden, Hamas claimed that the majority of Palestinians were not accepting the Palestinian Authority's policies.[4] Even though Pakistan was helpful in prosecuting the war against the Taliban, as many as 100,000 Pakistanis may have joined the Taliban in their Jihad against the U.S.[5] Syria's President Assad invited Tony Blair to his country, then proceeded to blast the U.S. led bombing in Afghanistan. The hostility was echoed later in Riyadh. The Saudi government, while helping in other ways, refused to allow use of its air bases for attacks on Afghanistan.[6] Dateline NBC aired a focus group interview in Egypt on October 21, 2001. Comments from the Egyptian interviewees ranged from wondering why the U.S. would bomb Afghanistan to calling American support of Israel "terrorist" to labeling the U.S. "a big bully" to expressing a general agreement that the Masad (the Israeli CIA) is behind the September 11th attacks. All interviewees believed the assertion that four thousand Jewish workers in the World Trade Center did not show up for work on September 11th. On the weekend following the terrorist attack, in mosques throughout the Middle East, worshipers were sympathetic toward America, but *USA Today* reported:

> [T]he day's sermons--traditionally an important indicator of national sentiments--also offered a passionate reminder of the hatreds and hardships that fuel the region's conflicts. In mosques from Baghdad to Beirut, from Tehran to Gaza City, the airborne attacks against America were portrayed as an inevitable consequence of U.S. support for Israel, and as retribution for an array of American policies seen as bullying and unfair toward Arabs and Muslims.[7]

What seems clear is that the rhetoric of Osama bin Laden has many receptive ears. Whether or not bin Laden is personally motivated by psychotic entelechy, many in the Islamic world appear to be open to the psychotic entelechy expressed in bin Laden's rhetoric.

To unite Muslims everywhere, bin Laden's appeal is to the one source of authority that transcends all of the factionalism in Islam--the Koran. My procedure in addressing the specific psychotic entelechy I find present in bin Laden's rhetoric is first to review the text of the Koran to see what sources of entelechy may be found there. Next, I examine the texts in which bin Laden interprets the Koran. Finally, in a future chapter, I apply Burkean principles to seek a cure.

The Koran

Perhaps the biggest conflict in values American culture has with the Koran is in the area of religious pluralism. American culture was built on a foundation of religious toleration. In America, Moslems, Jews, Buddhists, and Christians of all varieties may practice their various religions without governmental interference. Even though many Christians believe Heaven is reserved for Christians, American Christians do not routinely engage in hate crimes against members of other religious parties (although, admittedly, it does happen from time to time). There are passages in the Christian New Testament that have been used by some Christians as a basis for anti-Jewish attitudes and actions. There are also passages in Jewish rabbinic literature that have been interpreted by Jews as anti-Christian. There is nothing in either Jewish or Christian authoritative scripture that is anti-Moslem because, of course, Mohammed was not born until long after the Jewish and Christian bibles were codified.

Yet (probably because the Koran was competing-for-acceptance with Judaism and Christianity), there are several anti-Jewish and anti-Christian comments in the Koran:

- "Never will the Jews be satisfied with thee, neither the Christians, not till thou followest their religion." (I:43)

- "No; Abraham in truth was not a Jew, neither a Christian; but he was a Muslim and one of pure faith." (I:83)

- "Some of the Jews pervert words from their meanings . . . but God has cursed them for their unbelief, so they believe not except a few." (I:107)

- "So, for their breaking the compact, and disbelieving in the signs of God, and slaying the Prophets . . . and for their saying, 'We slew the Messiah, Jesus son of Mary . . . And for the evildoing of those of Jewry, we have forbidden them certain good things that were permitted to them . . . ." (I:123)

- "And with those who say 'We are Christians' . . . We have stirred up among them enmity and hatred, till the Day of Resurrection . . . ." (I:130)

- "They are unbelievers who say, 'God is the Messiah, Mary's son.'" (I:130, 139)

- "O believers, take not Jews and Christians as friends; they are friends of each other. Whoso of you makes them his friends is one of them. God guides not the people of the evildoers." (I:136)

- "Let not the believers take the unbelievers for friends" (I:76)

- "O believers, take not the unbelievers as friends instead of the believers." (I:121)

- "They are unbelievers who say 'God is the Third of Three.' No god is there but One God." (I:140)[8]

Furthermore, the Koran makes the previously demonstrated conflict even more difficult to resolve. While identifying Jews and Christians as "unbelievers" and "evildoers," the Koran recommends conducting holy war against unbelievers and evildoers:

- "And fight in the way of God with those who fight with you, but *aggress not*: God loves *not the aggressors*. And *slay* them wherever you come upon them and expel them from where they expelled you; persecution is more grievous than slaying. But fight them not by the Holy Mosque until they should fight you there; then, if they fight you, slay them--such is the recompense of *unbelievers*." (I:53, italics mine)

- "Fight them, till there is no persecution and the religion is God's; then if they give over, there shall be no enmity save for *evildoers*. . . . Whoso commits *aggression* against you, do you commit aggression against him like as he has committed against you." (I:54, italics mine)

- "Prescribed for you is fighting though it be hateful to you. . . . Say: 'Fighting in [the holy month] is a heinous thing, but to bar from God's way and disbelief in Him and the Holy Mosque, and to expel its people from it--that is more heinous in God's sight; and persecution is more heinous than slaying.' They will not cease to fight with you, till they turn you from your religion, if they are able; and whosoever of you turns from his religion, and dies disbelieving-- . . . those are the inhabitants of the Fire; therein they shall dwell forever." (I:57-58)

- "Hast thou not regarded the Council of the Children of Israel, after Moses, when they said . . . 'we will fight in God's way.' . . . Yet when fighting was prescribed for them, they turned their backs except a few of them; and God has knowledge of the *evildoers*." (I:63, italics mine)

- "They wish that you should *disbelieve* as they *disbelieve*, and then you would be equal; therefore take not to yourselves friends of them, until they emigrate in the way of God; then, if they turn their backs, take them, and slay them wherever you find them; take not to yourselves any one of them as a friend or helper . . . ." (I:113, italics mine)

- "It belongs not to a *believer* to slay a *believer*, except it be by error." (I:114, italics mine)

- "I shall cast into the *unbelievers'* hearts *terror*; so smite above the necks and smite every finger of them!" (I:198, italics mine)

- "O believers, when you encounter the *unbelievers* marching to battle, turn not your backs to them. Whoso turns his back that day to them, unless withdrawing to fight again or removing to join another host, he is laden with the burden of God's anger, and his refuge is Gehenna." (I:198-199, italics mine)

- "O Prophet, urge on the believers to fight. If there be twenty of you, patient men, they will overcome two hundred; if there be a hundred of you, they will overcome a thousand *unbelievers* . . . . *It is not for any Prophet to have prisoners until he makes wide slaughter in the land.*" (I:204-205, italics mine)

- "Assuredly God will defend those who believe . . . who were expelled from their habitations without right . . . . How many a city We have destroyed in its *evildoing*, and now it is fallen down upon its *turrets*! How many a ruined well, a *tall palace*!" (ii:32, italics mine)

- "When you meet the *unbelievers*, smite their necks, then, when you have made wide slaughter among them, tie fast the bonds . . . . And those who are slain in the way of God [i.e., believing martyrs] . . . He will admit them to Paradise." (ii:220, italics mine)

- "If you are slain or die in God's way, forgiveness and mercy from God are a better thing than that you amass; surely if you die or are slain, it is unto God you shall be mustered." (I:93)

Discussion of "evildoers" is suggestive of a tragic frame. If Christians, Jews, or Muslims are viewed as "evil" rather than "mistaken," the tragic frame demands victimage. On the other hand, if Islamic extremists are being motivated by psychotic entelechy, they may be understood as "mistaken"--a comic frame. Burke prefers the comic frame. Nevertheless, the Koran speaks of evildoers. Americans who believe the Islamic extremists may be appeased are naïve indeed. The *telos* of a tragedy is victimage. If Americans are perceived as "evildoers," they will be victimized by those who perceive them in that manner. Therefore, it is encouraging that President Bush makes a nuanced distinction between the regimes he terms "axis of evil" and the citizenry those regimes govern:

> North Korea is a regime arming with missiles and weapons of mass destruction, while starving its citizens. Iran aggressively pursues these weapons and exports terror, while an unelected few repress the Iranian people's hope for freedom. . . . The Iraqi regime has plotted to develop anthrax and nerve gas and nuclear weapons for over a decade. This is a regime that has already used poison gas to murder thousands of its own citizens, leaving the bodies of mothers huddled over their dead children. This is a regime that agreed to international inspections, and then kicked out the inspectors. This is a regime that has something to hide from the civilized world.[9]

Bush's language allows for both the comic and the tragic frames. The regimes may be evildoers, but the citizenry may be considered victimized or mistaken.

Bin Laden's Rhetoric

Meanwhile, bin Laden's language generally does not make such a nuanced distinction between the American government and its people. In a post to h-rhetor@h-net.msu.edu, Byron Keith Hawk offered a quotation from bin Laden that comes close to making a nuanced distinction: "The Western regimes and the government of the United States . . . bear the blame for what might happen." Bin Laden recommends that, if citizens want to be safe, "they should seek to elect governments . . . truly representative of them . . . that can protect their interests."[10] Spaniards took bin Laden's threat to heart and elected a new government following the terrorist bombings in Spain. Bin laden used a similar tactic to attempt to sway the 2004 U.S. presidential elections:

> People of America this talk of mine is for you and concerns the ideal way to prevent another Manhattan . . . your security is not in the hands of Kerry, nor Bush, nor al-Qaida. No.
> Your security is in your own hands. And every state that doesn't play with our security has automatically guaranteed its own security.[11]

Many inferred from bin Laden's remarks that he was willing to make a nuanced distinction between the Red states and the Blue states. If a particular state votes against Bush, it automatically guarantees its own security. One might guess that Kerry states will be free from al-Qaida attacks for four years. Yet, New York and Washington, D.C. are two of the strongest Democrat voting blocs; that characteristic did not protect them from 9/11. Nevertheless, the goal of bin Laden's November 2004 rhetoric was to intimidate American voters, not to make distinctions between government and citizenry. This is a terrorist tactic. Before his May 1998 interview with John Miller of ABC, bin Laden said his followers "differentiate between the western government and the people of the West." He suggested the people were duped by their government. Yet, he states:

> It is not enough for their people to show pain when they see our children being killed in Israeli raids launched by American planes, nor does this serve the purpose. What they ought to do is change their governments which attack our countries.[12]

Despite assertions that al-Qaida differentiates between governments and people, all Americans who worked in the World Trade Center, flight attendants, pilots, and innocent passengers aboard the hijacked planes were considered by bin Laden to be legitimate targets. Despite the fact that not all Americans are Christians or Jews, that many in the world are neutral toward religion, bin Laden sees no such nuanced distinctions: "The crusader war against Islam has intensified . . . The world is split into two. Part of it is under the head of infidels Bush, and the other half under the banner of Islam. . . . Standing against wrong will strengthen us."[13] Whoever, then, is not under the banner of Islam, we would assume, is for bin Laden an infidel, an evildoer. Two and one-half years before 9/11, bin Laden and his associates issued a statement that purported "to be a religious ruling (fatwa) requiring the killing of Americans, both civilian and military":

> On that basis [among other things, America's "eagerness to destroy Iraq"], and in compliance with God's order [understand: the Koran], we issue the following fatwa to all Muslims:
>
> The ruling to kill the Americans and their allies—civilians and military—is an individual duty for every Muslim who can do it an any country in which it is possible to do it, in order to liberate the al-Aqsa Mosque and the holy mosque [Mecca].[14]

By contrast, Bush generally welcomes all willing Moslems to his cause. He was careful, for example, to include Moslem cleric Imam Muzammil H. Siddiqi in the National Day of Prayer and Remembrance, following the 9/11 disaster.[15] Siddiqi read two passages from the Koran condemning "those that lay the plots of evil" and teaching: "Goodness and evil are not equal."[16] The choice of Koranic texts condemning "evil" is probably not accidental. Bush's choice of the term "evildoers" to refer to bin Laden and his followers is strategic.

On October 7, 2001, bin Laden made his first verified comments regarding the 9/11 attack. He referred to George W. Bush as "head of the infidels," said that the world was now divided into "the camp of the faithful and the camp of the infidels," and made no distinctions between the American government and its citizens: "As to America, I say to it and its people a few words: I swear to God that America will not live in peace before peace reigns in Palestine, and before all the army of infidels depart the land of Mohammad."[17]

Analyzing the bin Laden statement, Rawhi Abeidoh observed that both Saddam Hussein and bin Laden have "invoked terminology from Islam's holy book, the Koran, to win the hearts and minds of their co-religionists." Abeidoh noted: "Bush and other Western leaders have sought to dispel fears among the world's 1.2 billion Muslims that they are waging war on Islam or the Afghan people, rather than on terrorism."[18]

Arab world specialist at the Library of Congress Mary-Jane Deeb provided a brief textual analysis of the bin Laden statement. Specifically, the Deeb piece claims that the imagery of bin Laden's

October 7th statement "is drawn from the Koran; its form . . . is scripturally framed; and its setting . . . was chosen to appeal to the masses."[19] Deeb observes that bin Laden alludes to one of the passages from the Koran mentioned earlier, concerning the buildings that were destroyed: "How many a city We have destroyed in its *evildoing*, and now it is fallen down upon its *turrets*!" (ii:32, emphasis mine). Deeb also claims bin Laden's Koranic imagery is taken from Sura 33: "O believers, remember God's blessing upon you when hosts came against you, and we loosed against them a wind." (It is worth noting that, based on this Koranic text [to a psychotic Islamic extremist], hurricane damage to Florida, Alabama, Mississippi, Louisiana, and Texas in the years following 9/11 are easily appropriated as further evidence that God wants to destroy America.)

David Spiech mentioned Deeb's analysis in a post to the kb@purdue.edu list serve on November 8, 2001. Spiech observes:

> She makes it clear that bin Laden understands which elements of Islam are necessary to justify his point of view; therefore he applies appropriate rhetorical pressure on questionable points, such as who has the right to speak for Islam as a whole. . . . In particular, the 11/7 statement goes further to tease out political justifications based on a common religious worldview. He is quite aware that he has no qualification to be an imam in a purely religious sense, and so he lays claim to it as a political position, like the former caliph. To the degree that Islam relies on a politically active expression of faith, this argument could be justified as using representations inherent to religion, which could be said of any politician's rhetoric. Furthermore, all politicians could be said to labor under the delusion that they represent the will of the people, divine establishment, a perfect fulfillment of their constituency's hopes and dreams, acting always in their best interest.

Two significant terms not discussed in the Deeb analysis are the terms "believers" and "evildoing." As demonstrated in the Koranic texts cited earlier, the "unbelievers" and "evildoers" are easily associated in the Koran with Christians and Jews. According to the AP text of his statement, bin Laden states: "These events have divided the whole world into two sides. The side of *believers* and the side of *infidels*" (emphasis mine). America is explicitly identified as being "hit by God" in a reference to its "greatest buildings [which] were destroyed." If

Deeb is correct, "evildoing" is implicitly connected Koranically with the cities "destroyed."

Some have questioned whether bin Laden really believes his own rhetoric or whether, like Saddam Hussein, he is simply using the Koran as a means of motivating fellow Muslims. An official of the United Arab Emirates commented: "Instead of fighting Israel, Saddam invaded a fellow Arab country. Tell me of any military operation bin Laden launched against Israel? None." Abdel Moneim Said, director of the Cairo-based al-Ahram Centre for Strategic Studies observed: "These fanatics are hungry for power . . . . I haven't seen them doing anything for the poor, for the unemployed, or talking about freedom."[20]

According to Caroline Drees of Reuters:

> Some analysts said bin Laden . . . proved what a sinister manipulator he is. But to many in the Islamic world, he just spoke from the heart, saying what they feel but are afraid to express.
>
> "If there had been a referendum [October 7, 2000] in the Arab world (on bin Laden's performance), he would have got 99 percent," said Walid Kazziha, a political science professor at the American University in Cairo (AUC).
>
> "It gave me goosebumps," said an Arab photographer in Kuwait . . . . "I have never in my life heard somebody pledge such conviction and determination."
>
> Mustafa Alani, a Middle East consultant . . . in London . . . said . . . "He is a deep believer. He left millions of dollars to live in a cave. That tells you about the depth of his belief in what he is doing."[21]

In his essay, "The Rhetoric of Hitler's Battle," Burke wrestles with the question of whether Hitler's anti-Semitism was genuine or contrived. In the instance of the current war on terror, the issue of whether bin Laden's motivation is genuine or contrived is largely irrelevant. Regardless of whether bin Laden is personally motivated by psychotic entelechy or is simply a power-hungry manipulator like Saddam Hussein, many in the Islamic world are motivated by the type of psychotic entelechy articulated by bin Laden. Before an interview with ABC's John Miller in May 1998, bin Laden seems to allude to the Koranic texts which warn against making friends with Christians or Jews because they are friends of each other: "The call to wage war against America was made because . . . [t]heir presence . . . is to offer support to the Jews in Palestine who are in need of their Christian brothers."[22] He is also well aware of the Koranic prohibition against being the aggressor, unless aggressed against: "The terrorism we practice is of the commendable kind for it is directed at the tyrants and the aggressors . . . . America heads the list of aggressors against Muslims." He claims America has aggressed against the people of Iraq and by occupying (having troops in) the Moslem holy land of Saudi Arabia.[23]

In a statement from bin Laden and his associates dated February 23, 1998, Jihad against Jews and the United States is called for, citing the Koran: "But when the forbidden months are past, then fight and slay the pagans wherever ye find them, seize them, beleaguer them, and lie in wait for them in every stratagem (of war)."[24] Here, the fatwa cites a passage that does not specifically refer to the United States (understand: Christians) or Jews, but it is clear that bin Laden interprets it as applying to these two entities.

Burke is cautious whenever assigning motives for any action, and any assignment of motives in the war on terrorism must also be cautiously handled. In an October 2001 post to kb@purdue.edu, Kumar Ramanathan objected to my statement that the Koran is the text by which the terrorists justify their actions to their fellow Muslims. Ramanathan states: "Terrorism (speaking within the context of September 11) is not only religiously motivated violence. It is also politically motivated violence." He goes on to cite America's "sanctions against Iraq" and "the Jewish occupation in Palestine," two political issues that constantly arise in the terrorist debate context. Ramanathan argues: "Dr. Lindsay, . . . you do not delve enough into the political and imply that religion is the sole motivation behind the motives of 'terrorists.'" I responded to Mr. Ramanathan:

> [T]here was no discussion of "motives" in my email. Burkeans know why that is true. I only commented that the Koran was being used to justify murder. I'm not even claiming that the Koran is the only thing being used to justify murder. I only suggest that it is being used to justify the murder for other Muslims. The other issues Kumar

mentions are certainly being used to justify the murder for other audiences.

When I refer to justifications to other audiences, I have in mind something like the bin Laden speech to America on the eve of the 2004 presidential election. Here, bin Laden understood that his audience did not comprise fellow Muslims. His justifications sound quite different:

> [I]t never occurred to us to strike the towers. But after . . . we witnessed the oppression and tyranny of the American/Israeli coalition against our people in Palestine and Lebanon, it came to my mind. . . . [I]n 1982 . . . America permitted the Israelis to invade Lebanon and the American Sixth Fleet helped them in that.
> . . . [T]he intentional killing of innocent women and children is a deliberate American policy. . . . This means the oppressing and embargoing to death of millions as Bush Sr. did in Iraq in the greatest mass slaughter of children mankind has ever known, and it means the throwing of millions of pounds of bombs and explosives at millions of children—also in Iraq—as Bush Jr. did.
> . . . [Bush Sr.] took dictatorship and suppression of freedoms to his son and they named it the Patriot Act, under the pretence of fighting terrorism. In addition, Bush sanctioned the installing of sons as state governors, and didn't forget to import expertise in election fraud . . . to Florida.
> . . . [T]he Bush administration has also gained . . . [by] the shady Bush administration-linked mega-corporations, like Halliburton . . . .[25]

The Koran is not mentioned here, because it is not powerful rhetoric in American society. Besides, it is questionable that bin Laden actually cared that much for Palestine and Iraq. As the official of the United Arab Emirates commented: "Instead of fighting Israel, Saddam invaded a fellow Arab country. Tell me of any military operation bin Laden launched against Israel? None." The comments about the Patriot Act, the Florida election of 2000, and Halliburton were gratuitous. How could these have provoked the 9/11 attack?

Even if one stipulates that Muslims worldwide are unhappy with the Israeli-Palestinian situation, political issues are not the concern of this book. Psychotic entelechy is the concern here. A Koranic allusion crept into bin Laden's November 2004 speech to America: "[A]l-Qaida spent $500,000 on the event, while America, in the incident and its aftermath, lost . . . more than $500 billion. Meaning that every dollar of al-Qaida defeated a million dollars."[26] This sounds very much like the Koranic promise: "O Prophet, urge on the believers to fight. If there be twenty of you, patient men, they will overcome two hundred; if there be a hundred of you, they will overcome a thousand *unbelievers* . . . ." (I:204-205, italics mine). What amounts to the psychotic entelechy is the concluding hortatory message of this same Koranic passage: "It is not for any Prophet to have prisoners until he makes wide slaughter in the land."

The *Telos* of bin Laden's Entelechy

Is the passage just cited the *telos* of bin Laden's Jihad entelechy—to make wide slaughter in the land? How much slaughter is "wide slaughter"? If all non-Moslems are evildoers, how can bin Laden's followers stop with a minimal view of wide slaughter? The Koran says: "Fight them, till there is no persecution and the religion is God's; then if they give over, there shall be no enmity save for *evildoers*" (I:54, italics mine). Does this mean to bin Laden's followers that they should allow only two options to non-Moslems—convert or die? Prior to the May 1998 interview with John Miller of ABC, bin Laden was asked by some of his followers at his mountaintop camp in southern Afghanistan to "address the people" of America and Europe. This was his response:

> [O]ur call is the call of Islam that was revealed to Mohammed. It is a call to all mankind. We have been entrusted with good cause to follow in the footsteps of the Messenger and to communicate his message to all nations. It is an invitation that we extend to all the nations to embrace Islam . . . . We, nonetheless, fight against their governments and all those who approve of the injustice they practice against us . . . we fight them, and those who are part of their rule are judged in the same manner.[27]

When the ancient Israelites left their captivity in Egypt and were led to the Promised Land, God told them:

> When the Lord your God brings you into the land you are entering to possess and drives out before you many nations . . . and you have defeated them, then you must destroy them totally. Make no treaty with them, and show them no mercy. . . . Break down their altars,

smash their sacred stones, cut down their Asherah poles and burn their idols in the fire (Exodus 7:1-5 NIV).

Is this the fighting-in-God's-way entelechy bin Laden's followers have in mind when they read in the Koran:

Hast thou not regarded the Council of the Children of Israel, after Moses, when they said . . . "we will fight in God's way." . . . Yet when fighting was prescribed for them, they turned their backs except a few of them; and God has knowledge of the *evildoers* (I:63, italics mine).

Do the Islamic terrorists believe that the later, merciful treatment the ancient Israelites were reported to have given to the nations in the Promised Land was their downfall—the reason Mohammed labeled them evildoers? If this is the fighting-in-God's-way entelechy bin Laden's followers have in mind, perhaps their greatest *telos* is found in the following Koranic passage: "If you are slain or die in God's way, forgiveness and mercy from God are a better thing than that you amass; surely if you die or are slain, it is unto God you shall be mustered" (I:93). The ultimate entelechy might be to make wide slaughter among the unbelievers, so that you might become an Islamic martyr. If you become an Islamic martyr, you shall be mustered unto God. Or as the Koran states it in another passage:

When you meet the *unbelievers*, smite their necks, then, when you have made wide slaughter among them, tie fast the bonds . . . . And those who are slain in the way of God [i.e., believing martyrs] . . . He will admit them to Paradise. (ii:220, italics mine)

With this reference to making "wide slaughter among" the unbelievers, we have come full circle to the passage cited on page 50. Mohammad was a student of Jewish and Christian teachings. No doubt, he was aware that after the walls of Jericho fell, the ancient Israelites "destroyed with the sword every living thing in [Jericho]—men and women, young and old, cattle, sheep and donkeys" (Joshua 6:21). Similarly, they destroyed Ai, except that they kept the cattle alive. They annihilated Jerusalem, Hebron, Jarmuth, Lachish and Eglon. They destroyed Makkedah, Libnah, Gezer, and Debir. The Bible says:

> Joshua subdued the whole region, including the hill country, the Negev, the western foothills and the mountain slopes, together with all their kings. He left no survivors. He totally destroyed all who breathed (Joshua 10:40).

This total destruction is reported to have continued throughout Joshua's lifetime, but after he died, the Israelites' resolve to rid the land of all its inhabitants began to weaken. The original inhabitants were allowed to remain; their local gods became a part of Israelite culture, and the Bible condemned that idolatry. This may be the basis for the fighting-in-God's-way references in the Koran. Perhaps, Mohammed was calling for his followers to totally annihilate their enemies. Perhaps, bin Laden's followers are accurately interpreting the Koran on at least this point. So, where does that leave us?

If bin Laden is successful in labeling all Jews and Christians the unbelievers and evildoers referred to in the Koran, and if the Koran prescribes slaying as the treatment intended for all unbelievers and evildoers, and if all Muslims who die a martyr's death in this battle are guaranteed admission to God's presence, bin Laden's rhetoric is infused with a most dangerous psychotic entelechy. It is highly unlikely that his followers will be satisfied with what bin Laden originally cited as his *telos*, to get U.S. troops out of the land of Saudi Arabia:

> The call to wage war against America was made because America has spear-headed the crusade against the Islamic nation, sending tens of thousands of its troops to the land of the two Holy Mosques over and above its meddling in its affairs and its politics, and its support of the oppressive, corrupt and tyrannical regime that is in control. These are the reasons behind the singling out of America as a target.[28]

Notes

[1] Editor, "Bible Scholar Claims Branch Davidian Disaster Could Have Been Avoided," *Religious Studies News* 10, no. 3 (1995): 3.

[2] Reuters, "Islamic Group Says Blair 'Legitimate Target,'" *Yahoo! News* 10/10/01. Available: http://uk.news.yahoo.com/011010/80/c8h17.html (10/10/01).

[3] Reuters, "Bin Laden Fans Voice Online Admiration," *Yahoo! News* 10/10/01. Available: http://uk.news.yahoo.com/011008/80/c71f8.html (10/10/01).

[4] Uri Dan and Andy Geller, "Arafat on Hot Seat for Putting Down Protests," *NYPOST.COM* 10/11/01. Available: http://www.nypost.com/news/world news/33750.html (10/11/01).

[5] Riaz Khan, "Pakistanis Leave for Holy War" *Yahoo! News* 10/27/01. Available: http://dailynews.yahoo.com/h/ap/20011027/ts/attacks_holy_war riors_4.html (10/27/01).

[6] Philip Webster, Christopher Walker, and David Charter, "Assad Ambushes Blair" *The Times* 11/1/01. Available: http://www.thetimes.co.uk/article/0,,200 1370005-2001380490,00.html (10/31/01).

[7] "Sympathy for U.S. in Mosque Pulpits,'" *USA Today* 11/7/01. Available: http://www.usatoday.com/news/nation/2001/09/14/mosque-pulpits.htm (11/7/01).

[8] All quotations from the Koran are from A. J. Arberry, *The Koran Interpreted* 2 vols. (New York: MacMillan, 1955). The passage locations parenthetically following each quotation are the respective volume and page numbers.

[9] George W. Bush, "State of the Union Address," 1/29/02, Available: http://www.washingtonpost.com/ac2/wp-dyn/A58285-2002Jan29?language=pri nter (1/30/02).

[10] Byron Keith Hawk's post was dated September 14, 2001 and offered as a source the following link: http://www.pbs.org/wgbh/pages/frontline/shows/ binladen/who/.

[11] "Full Transcript of bin Ladin's Speech," *Aljazeera.net* 11/1/04. Available: http://english.aljazeera.net/NR/exeres/79C6AF22-98FB-4A1C-B21F-2BC36E 87F61F.htm (1/24/05).

[12] "Frontline: Interview with Osama bin Laden" 5/98. Available: http://www.pbs.org/wgbh/pages/frontline/shows/binladen/who/interview.html (10/1/01).

[13] "Bin Laden Urges Pakistanis to Defend Islam-Jazeera," *Yahoo! News* 11/1/01. Available: http://dailynews.yahoo.com/htx/nm/20011101/ts /attack_binladen_letter_dc_4.html (11/1/01).

[14] "Jihad Against Jews and Crusaders: World Islamic Front Statement" 2/23/98. Available: http://www.fas.org/irp/world/para/docs/980223-fatwa.htm (10/1/01).

[15] "Prayer Service Speakers List," *Yahoo News* 9/14/01. Available: http://dailynews.yahoo.com/h/ap/20010914/us/prayer_service_list_2.html (9/19/01).

[16] "National Day of Prayer and Remembrance." Available: http://www.holyfamilyhmb.org/US_Tragedy/Litany_and_Prayer/Islamic_Prayer/islamic_prayer.html (2/20/02).

[17] Sami Aboudi, "Defiant bin Laden Vows No Peace for U.S.," *Yahoo News* 10/8/01. Available: http://uk.news.yahoo.com/011008/80/c713y.html (10/10/01).

[18] Rawhi Abeidoh, "Focus-Bin Laden Adopts Saddam's Line in Fight Against U.S." *Yahoo News* 10/8/01. Available: http://uk.news.yahoo.com/011008/80/c7kw4.html (10/10/01).

[19] Mary-Jane Deeb, "A Closer Look at the Words of an Image Maker," *Washington Post* 10/28/01. Available: http://www.washingtonpost.com/ac2/wp-dyn/A60014-2001Oct26?language=printer (11/13/01)

[20] Rawhi Abeidoh, "Focus-Bin Laden Adopts Saddam's Line in Fight Against US" *Yahoo! News* 10/8/01. Available: http://uk.news.yahoo.com/011008/80/c7kw4.html (10/10/01).

[21] Caroline Drees, "Bin Laden Speech Hits Right Chord" *Yahoo! News* 10/8/01. Available: http://uk.news.yahoo.com/011008/80/c7nf1.html (10/10/01).

[22] John Miller, "Interview: Osama bin Laden," *Frontline*. Available: http://www.pbs.org/wgbh/pages/frontline/shows/binladen/who/interview.html (10/1/01).

[23] "Frontline" 5/98.

[24] "Jihad Against Jews and Crusaders: World Islamic Front Statement," Available: http://www.fas.org/irp/world/para/docs/980223-fatwa.htm (10/1/01)

[25] "Transcript" 11/01/04.

[26] "Transcript" 11/01/04.

[27] "Frontline" 5/98.

[28] "Frontline" 5/98.

Chapter 4

The Cure for bin Laden's Rhetoric

Is bin Laden's *telos* the removal of U.S. troops from Saudi Arabia? Would a simple withdrawal of U.S. troops from Saudi Arabia cure the world's problems? No. Yet, such a withdrawal will probably occur before too long. *The Washington Post* reported in 2002 that the Saudis might ask the United States to remove its forces from that country:

> [S]enior Saudi rulers believe the United States has "overstayed its welcome" and its forces have become a political liability. ... If asked to leave, the United States would no longer have regular use of the Prince Sultan Air Base, where American forces have maintained a presence since the 1991 Gulf War. ... The presence of U.S. military forces in Saudi Arabia—currently numbering about 5,000—has been repeatedly cited by bin Laden as a key reason for his violent opposition to Saudi Rulers. ... Pentagon spokeswoman Victoria Clarke declined to answer when asked whether Saudi Arabia has told the United States it will ask for an American withdrawal. ... [N]othing would be done precipitously. ... Crown Prince Abdulla ... did not want to create the impression that he was responding to pressure from bin Laden.[1]

If the U.S. withdraws from Saudi Arabia, militant Islamists will use another justification for continuing the anti-American Jihad. The presence of American troops in Iraq fits the bill. But America has stated its intention to leave Iraq once the democratically elected government is capable of defending the country. Would, then, a withdrawal of U.S. troops from both Saudi Arabia and Iraq satisfy the terrorists? No. The militants will use another justification for continuing the anti-American Jihad. Bin Laden has stated:

> The enmity between us and the Jews goes far back in time and is deep rooted. There is no question that war between the two of us is inevitable. For this reason it is not in the interest of Western governments to expose the interests of their people to all kinds of retaliation for almost nothing. It is hoped that people of those countries will initiate a positive move and force their governments not to act on behalf of other states and other sects.[2]

In other words, so long as any nation remains an ally of the State of Israel, bin Laden's followers will continue to terrorize that nation. Bin Laden comments:

> Your position against Muslims in Palestine is despicable and disgraceful. America has no shame. . . . We do not have to differentiate between military or civilian. As far as we are concerned, they are all targets, and this is what the fatwah says . . . . The fatwah is general (comprehensive) and it includes all those who participate in, or help the Jewish occupiers in killing Muslims.[3]

If bin Laden were out of the picture, powerful militant Muslims would continue to wage campaigns against Israel. Gareth Smyth reports:

> Mahmoud Ahmadi-Nejad, Iran's fundamentalist president, . . . declared that Israel should be "wiped off the map" and warned Arab countries against developing economic ties with Israel in response to its withdrawal from Gaza.
> . . . U. S. analysts noted that the president's remarks were not a departure from hard line Iranian rhetoric and did not represent a new policy.
> . . . "As the Imam said, Israel must be wiped off the map," Mr. Ahmadi-Nejad said, citing Ayatolla Ruhollah Khomeini, the founder of Iran's Islamic revolution.
> . . . "Anybody who recognizes Israel will burn in the fire of the Islamic nation's fury," he said, in remarks aimed at Arab states.[4]

If the U.S. were to completely abandon Israel (an extremely unlikely event), would the anti-American Jihad end? No. It would be seen as a sign of weakness, and the Jihad would be pressed even harder. CNN aired a February 2002 television interview with bin Laden in which he exulted over the fact that U.S. forces pulled out of Somalia "after 18 U.S. special operations personnel were killed during a raid against a warlord faction in the capital Mogadishu."[5] Bin Laden's anti-Americanism was not assuaged by America's hasty withdrawal from Somalia; it was emboldened. In the earlier ABC interview he bragged:

> After our victory [over Russia] in Afghanistan ... our boys ... went to Somalia and prepared themselves carefully for a long war. ... They were stunned when they discovered how low was the morale of the American soldier. America had entered with 30,000 soldiers in addition to thousands of soldiers from different countries in the world. ... [O]ur boys ... realized that the American soldier was just a paper tiger. He was unable to endure the strikes that were dealt to his army, so he fled, and America had to stop all its bragging. ... After a few blows, it ... rushed out of Somalia in shame and disgrace, dragging the bodies of its soldiers.[6]

What, then, will satisfy bin Laden and his followers? He answers in the ABC interview:

> We are certain that we shall—with the grace of Allah—prevail over the Americans and over the Jews, as the Messenger of Allah promised us in an authentic prophetic tradition when He said the Hour of Resurrection shall not come before Muslims fight Jews and before Jews hide behind trees and behind rocks.
> We are certain—with the grace of Allah—that we shall prevail over the Jews and over those fighting with them. Today however, our battle against the Americans is far greater than our battle was against the Russians. Americans have committed unprecedented stupidity. They have attacked Islam and its most significant sacrosanct symbols ....
> We anticipate a black future for America. Instead of remaining United States, it shall end up separated states and shall have to carry the bodies of its sons back to America.[7]

In the CNN-aired interview, he states: "We will work to continue this battle, God permitting, until victory or until we meet God."[8] Did it matter to terrorists that the U.S. helped broker a peace agreement between Israel and Egypt, returning to Egypt territory that Israel had captured in the 1967 war? Anwar Saddat was assassinated for having negotiated with Israel. Did it matter to terrorists that the U.S. took the side of Kosovars over (Christian?) Serbs? The animosity remained.

ABC's John Miller offered an incredibly gratuitous piece of flattery to bin Laden:

> In America, we have a figure from history from 1897 named Teddy Roosevelt. He was a wealthy man, who grew up in a privileged situation and who fought on the front lines. He put together his own men—hand chose them—and went to battle. You are like the Middle East version of Teddy Roosevelt.[9]

Did that matter? Bin Laden responded with his ultimate *telos*:

> I am one of the servants of Allah. We do our duty of fighting for the sake of the religion of Allah. It is also our duty to send a call to all the people of the world to enjoy this great light and to embrace Islam and experience the happiness in Islam. Our primary mission is nothing but the furthering of this religion. . . . Let not the West be taken in by those who say that Muslims choose nothing but slaughtering. Their brothers in East Europe, in Turkey and in Albania have been guided by Allah to submit to Islam and to experience the bliss of Islam.[10]

So, is this the West's ultimate either-or choice—submit to Islam or be slaughtered? There are at least two other options. One option would be for the West to utterly destroy the militant Muslims. This option would surely involve a massive bloodbath similar to what bin Laden may envision for America and Israel. Neither bloodbath option is acceptable. The coerced submission to Islam is not acceptable, either. Another option involves the Burkean cure for psychotic entelechy.

The Burkean Cure

As was the case with the entelechy of David Koresh, Burke's analysis of Milton's *Samson Agonistes* in RM comes close to an entelechy similar to bin Laden's. Burke demonstrates that Milton identified with the blind, fallen, Old Testament hero. The suicidal motive was implicit in Samson's pulling the temple down upon himself and his enemies. Milton's religion forbade suicide (RM 5); bin Laden's clearly does not. But does Islam actually forbid suicide? One Islamic website claims that suicide is forbidden based on the following text: "O ye who believe! . . . [do not] kill yourselves, for truly Allah has been to you Most Merciful. If any do that in rancour and injustice, soon shall We cast him into the Fire. . . . " (Qur'an 4:29-30).[11] Precisely this type of difference in interpretive possibilities, according to Burke, can supply the basis for a cure for psychotic entelechy. What if bin Laden's interpretation is wrong and the website's interpretation is right? Instead of being mustered to Allah for dying a martyr's death, the suicide bomber or suicidal plane hijacker may experience eternal punishment, according to the Koran!

Like Milton, bin Laden found an authoritative entelechy in scripture. Like Samson, bin Laden's entelechy was a command to slay unbelievers and evildoers. Like Samson, the notion of committing suicide as a side effect of destroying one's enemies appealed to bin Laden and his followers. Milton could "use" the "literature" of Samson to *poetically* reenact Samson's role. Bin Laden, meanwhile, found in his interpretation of the Koran a compulsion to *literally* live out the entelechy. Unlike the symbolic action in the writings of Milton, the writings of bin Laden laid down the Islamic *telos*. He was persuaded that Muslims must live (or, more precisely, die) it out.

As I demonstrated in the previous chapter, Burke's cluster-agon method could (using equations) be employed to demonstrate that the Koran commands Muslims to slay Christians and Jews. Even the imagery of tall towers being destroyed in great cities is present in the Koran. The psychotic entelechy is reinforced. If dying a martyr's death while fighting a holy war takes one directly to paradise, the entelechy is complete.

For the Islamic terrorists, a contest/agon exists between good and evildoers, between the believers and unbelievers. To the terrorists, the unbelievers or evildoers comprise Christians (most prominently, Americans) and Jews (most prominently, Israelis). This is the primary agon. Is there any element of this psychosis we may safely accept? I think so. Even George W. Bush agrees that a contest exists between good and evildoers. He has so stated on several occasions. His use of the term "evildoers" to designate the enemies of America has been roundly condemned by many American and foreign political leaders. Yet, President Bush uses the term "evildoers" advisedly. Perhaps, the Islamic world can be persuaded that America and Islam have a common enemy, "evildoers." The issue is: Who are the evildoers? In his first State of the Union Address following 9/11, President Bush referred to "states like" Iraq, Iran, and North Korea as "an axis of evil, arming to threaten the peace of the world":

> By seeking weapons of mass destruction, these regimes pose a grave and growing danger. They could provide these arms to terrorists, giving them the means to match their hatred. They could attack our allies or attempt to blackmail the United States.[12]

The years subsequent to the president's January 2002 address have shown that all three regimes were actually "*seeking* weapons of mass destruction," even if they have thus far been largely unsuccessful. If the president is able to persuade the Moslem world that this behavior should be classified as evildoing, he might even have the Koran on his side.

Never once does the Koran explicitly command Muslims to fight and kill "Christians and Jews," although it is easy to see how some Muslims may interpret these passages as such a command. Clearly, the primary unbelievers and evildoers who aggressed against Mohammed and his followers in Mohammed's lifetime were not Christians and Jews; they were pagan Arabs. The Islamic website mentioned earlier explains:

> In pre-Islamic Arabia, retaliation and mass murder was commonplace. If someone were killed, the victim's tribe would retaliate against the murderer's entire tribe. This practice was forbidden in the Qur'an (2:178-179). Following this statement of law, the Qur'an says, "*After this, whoever exceeds the limits shall be in grave chastisement*" (2:178). No matter what wrong we perceive as being done against us, we may not lash out against an entire population of people.[13]

What if the "unbelievers" and "evildoers" the Koran commands Muslims to fight and kill are NOT Christians or Jews—two groups the Koran also identifies as people of the Book? What if Mohammed meant only to fight against pagan unbelievers and evildoers, which is what Mohammed did? Even if "unbelievers" and "evildoers" were to be correctly interpreted as referring to Christians and Jews in Mohammed's mind, are the Christians and Jews of the third millennium the same Christians and Jews as the Christians and Jews of the first millennium (at the time the Koran was written)?

For a few years, I taught communication courses for Loyola University Chicago. My classes contained many Muslims, Jews, Protestants, Buddhists, Hindus, and Roman Catholics. No religious hatred or treachery was clearly visible from any of these groups. It is possible for individuals to adhere to different religions yet get along with each other. America has defended persecuted Muslims in Kosovo and Bosnia. America has brokered peace agreements between Egypt and Israel. America has defended Arab countries from their aggressive neighbor, Saddam Hussein. America has handed over the governance of Iraq to Iraqis after deposing Saddam Hussein. Although the United States of America is predominantly Christian in religion, America protects the rights of members of other religions to freely worship God in their own ways. This is not the same Christianity associated with the Crusades in ages past. Although an issue remains concerning the proper disposition of various parts of the Holy Land, Israel has shown good faith in its willingness to relinquish land to Egypt in exchange for secure peace agreements. Israel has shown it is willing to discuss similar matters with other Arab countries. This is not the same Judaism encountered by Muslims in the first millennium. Is it not possible for Christians, Jews, and Muslims to share in some way the ownership of the Holy Land? The land is holy to all three religions. What if bin Laden's interpretation is simply wrong?

The Samson entelechy is interesting because Christians and Jews understand it. A great Jewish hero was captured and blinded by his enemies. Then he was made a slave. Upon regaining his tremendous strength, he pulled a building down on himself and his captors. Is this justifiable suicide? Even assuming it is, is it the same type of suicide as that practiced by suicide bombers and the 9/11 hijackers? The Islamic website mentioned earlier counters:

> The Qur'an admonishes those who oppress others and transgress beyond the bounds of what is right and just. *"The blame is only against those who oppress men with wrongdoing and insolently transgress beyond bounds through the land, defying right and justice. For such there will be a chastisement grievous (in the Hereafter)"* (42:42)
>
> Harming innocent bystanders, even in times of war, was forbidden by the Prophet Muhammad (peace be upon him). This includes women, children, noncombatant bystanders, and even trees and crops. **Nothing** is to be harmed unless the person or thing is actively engaged in an assault against Muslims.
>
> . . . Muslims around the world condemn attacks against innocent civilians, while recognizing the Palestinians' right to struggle against occupation.[14]

What if bin Laden's tactic of suicide bombing innocent bystanders is not martyrdom, but insolently transgressing beyond bounds? Sheik Mohammed Sayed Tantawi at Cairo's Al-Azhar mosque told worshippers after the 9/11 incident:

> He who kills a person without necessity . . . will never go to heaven . . . . It's not courage in any way to kill an innocent person or to kill thousands of people, including men and women and children.[15]

The type of malady toward which bin Laden and his followers tend is what Freud calls "repetition compulsion" or "destiny compulsion." The problem is not that bin Laden is merely irrational, but that he is super-rational. He carries his meaning to the extreme. The views of bin Laden would not be so dangerous if they were not backed up by an appeal to the Koran. The Moslem world agrees that the Koran was given through (the spiritual gift of) prophecy. Their Prophet Mohammed spoke for God. Anything he wrote is powerful rhetoric to a Muslim.

Any compulsions in orthodox Islam should be easier to deal with than compulsions in Minister Louis Farrakhan's group, for example:

> Orthodox Islam has always abhorred the Nation [Farrakhan's group], believing it distorts the Muslim central profession that "there is no god but God and Mohammed is his Prophet."
> The Nation has taught that "Allah appeared in the Person of Master W. Fard Muhammad" and that this mysterious Detroit teacher was also the messiah of Muslims and Christians. After Fard Muhammad disappeared in 1934 his successor, Elijah Muhammad, came to be revered as the final prophet instead of Mohammed of Arabia.[16]

By limiting the messages from God to those uttered and written by Mohammed of Arabia, the possibility arises that the psychotic entelechy of bin Laden's followers may be cured. We are dealing with "interpretations."

It is extremely unlikely that Christians and/or Jews will be able to persuade Muslims motivated by psychotic entelechy that they are somewhat mistaken, but other Muslims might be able to do so. Just as Christian scholars Tabor and Arnold were able to persuade David Koresh that his own interpretations might be flawed, Islamic scholars may be able to persuade many Muslims that there are significant questions pertaining to the interpretations of the Koran supplied by bin Laden. By questioning whether the specific passages referring to holy war are correctly interpreted as referring to modern-day Christians and Jews, recalcitrance may wear down the psychosis.

It would be a gross error for any negotiators to suggest to the Moslem world that the commands of the Koran be disregarded. To suggest such a thing would immediately permit the extremists to categorize the recalcitrant as evildoers. Instead, like the *biblical scholars* who "tried to gain [Koresh's] trust, offer a respectful hearing of his prophetic view, and offer in the most subtle way alternative interpretive possibilities,"[17] points of agreement with the Koranic interpreters should be sought.

Such points of agreement can be related to Burke's understanding of the curative nature of psychoanalysis. Following McDougall's form of psychoanalysis, we would not recommend the obliteration of the psychotic's entire network. Instead a partial "conversion" should be attempted. In this chapter, I have offered several possibilities, most of them borrowed from Muslim interpreters of the Koran. I will offer one more.

Even if the Koran should be interpreted as commanding war against Christians and Jews of any variety in all ages, there is one final caveat stressed by the Koran: War is only permitted if the evildoers and unbelievers (not the believers) are the aggressors:

- "And fight in the way of God with those who fight with you, but *aggress not*: God loves not the *aggressors*." (I:53, italics mine)

- "Whoso commits *aggression* against you, do you commit *aggression* against him like as he has committed against you." (I:54, italics mine)

- "Let not detestation for a people who barred you from the Holy Mosque move you to commit *aggression*." (I:127, italics mine)

Despite Saddam Hussein's protestations to the contrary, the United States needs to persuade the Moslem world that it was not the aggressor in the Gulf War. Rather, Hussein and his armies aggressed by invading Kuwait. America and several Islamic Arab countries together repulsed the aggressor from Kuwait. A ceasefire in that War was achieved by Hussein's agreement to follow the stipulations laid down by the United Nations. The UN found Hussein in violation of the agreement on several occasions. The coalition that removed Hussein from power was completing the earlier Gulf War, not beginning a new war. While Americans enjoy the right to freedom of speech, those who insist upon calling the Iraq War a U.S. "invasion" are playing into the hands of Moslem extremists who seek to justify Jihad. Invasion implies that the U.S. is clearly the aggressor. Even a neutral terminology such as "war" or "conflict" is preferable to the terminology that implies aggression on the part of the U.S.

America should find it easier to persuade the Moslem world that it did not aggress against Bin Laden. He and his terrorists attacked the United States. Until the September 11, 2001 attack, the United States had only retaliated when attacked. The devastating terrorist attack on New York and Washington was unprovoked. Claiming the spirit of justice and self-defense advocated by Mohammed in the Koran, America has the right to defend itself from an aggressor. Even in this instance, however, there is an attempt among Muslims and Americans to make the U.S. appear to be the aggressor.

Terrorists—whether Islamic, Christian (such as the Irish Republican Army), or Jewish (such as the Zealot party, discussed below)—are difficult to reason with. The Jewish Zealot party of the 1st century is an example of this point. Louis Finkelstein summarizes some of the events that led to the overtly rebellious activities of the Zealot party:

> After the death of Agrippa the country was once again reduced to the status of a province to be governed by procurators; for the next twenty-two years they did everything to make confusion worse confounded. Fadus demanding that the High Priest's vestments be deposited, as once before, with the Romans; Tiberius Alexander symbolizing apostasy triumphant; Cumanus unable to maintain discipline among his own soldiers and aggravating Samaritan-Jewish relations; Felix outraging everyone and encouraging local banditti, and on trifling charges ordering the imprisonment of excellent persons--these men destroyed every possibility for peace and established a precedent for pillage and anarchy.
>
> Such a state of affairs strengthened the Zealot group, and a number of extremists in their midst now abandoned restraint altogether. At every public gathering, wherever huge crowds assembled and order was at a minimum, these extremists created panic by stabbing their enemies with hidden daggers. They formed an underground movement and spread terror throughout the country. Everyone trembled at the mention of the Sicarii (they were so called because of their murders with the sica, dagger), for their weapons were raised not only against Romans but against any Jews suspected of counseling "collaboration."[18]

The problem with negotiating with terrorists is that even members of their own religion whom they suspect of counseling collaboration with the enemy are themselves targets for terrorist activity. Anwar Saddat discovered this. Iraqis who are cooperating with the new democratically elected government are discovering this.

Nevertheless, to stop the march of tragedy on a worldwide scale, rational Muslims must have the courage to take the initiative. One such Muslim group did. The remarks of this group follow:

> After September 11, many in the Muslim world chose denial and hallucination rather than face up to the sad fact that Muslims perpetrated the 9-11 terrorist acts and that we have an enormous problem with extremism and support for terrorism. Many Muslims, including religious leaders, and "intellectuals" blamed 9-11 on a Jewish conspiracy and went as far as fabricating a tale that 4000 Jews did not show up for work in the World Trade Center on 9-11. Yet others blamed 9-11 on an American right wing conspiracy or the U.S. Government which allegedly wanted an excuse to invade Iraq and "steal" Iraqi oil.
>
> After numerous admissions of guilt by Bin Laden and numerous corroborating admissions by captured top-level Al-Qaida operatives, we wonder, does the Muslim leadership have the dignity and courage to apologize for 9-11?
>
> If not 9-11, will we apologize for the murder of school children in Russia?
>
> If not Russia, will we apologize for the train bombings in Madrid, Spain?
>
> If not Spain, will we apologize for suicide bombings in buses, restaurants and other public places?
>
> If not suicide bombings, will we apologize for the barbaric beheadings of human beings?
>
> If not beheadings, will we apologize for the rape and murder of thousands of innocent people in Darfour?
>
> If not Darfour, will we apologize for the blowing up of two Russian planes by Muslim women?
>
> What will we apologize for?
>
> What will it take for Muslims to realize that those who commit mass murder in the name of Islam are not just a few fringe elements?
>
> What will it take for Muslims to realize that we are facing a crisis that is more deadly than the Aids epidemic?
>
> What will it take for Muslims to realize that there is a large evil movement that is turning what was a peaceful religion into a cult?

> Will Muslims wake up before it is too late? Or will we continue blaming the Jews and an imaginary Jewish conspiracy? The blaming of all Muslim problems on Jews is a cancer that is destroying Muslim society from within and it must stop.
> . . . Only moderate Muslims can challenge and defeat extremist Muslims. We can no longer afford to be silent. If we remain silent to the extremism within our community then we should not expect anyone to listen to us when we complain of stereotyping and discrimination by non-Muslims; we should not be surprised when the world treats all of us as terrorists; we should not be surprised when we are profiled at airports.
> Simply put, not only do Muslims need to join the war against terror, we need to take the lead in this war.
> . . . For more information visit our website at: www.freemuslims.org.[19]

Agreed. This psychotic entelechy can only be cured by Muslims like these.

The search for a method of understanding and curing the underlying rhetorical excesses of Islamic terrorists begins with a search for a theory that explains the rhetoric. Kenneth Burke offers such a theory in his extension of Aristotle's concept of entelechy. Despite the implications of free will in Burke's theory, he finds that frequently humans (however free) subject themselves to near-deterministic compulsions supplied by their own terminologies. These logical (or logological) compulsions are easily carried to the extreme or to psychotic levels. The term psychotic entelechy refers to *the tendency of some individuals to be so desirous of fulfilling or bringing to perfection the implications of their terminologies that they engage in very hazardous or damaging actions.* The terrorist threats are here. The world's fate rests in the hands of moderate Muslims, not extremist Muslims, Christians, Jews, or secularists. Moderate Muslims must move to cure the psychotic entelechy that has gripped much of their religion.

Notes

[1] "Saudis May Ask U.S. to Leave, *Washington Post* Says" *Yahoo News* 1/18/02. Available: http://dailynews.yahoo.com/h/nm/20020118/ts/attack_saudi_report_dc.html (1/18/02).

[2] "Frontline: Interview with Osama bin Laden" 5/98. Available: http://www.pbs.org/wgbh/pages/frontline/shows/binladen/who/interview.html (10/1/01).

[3] "Frontline" 5/98.

[4] Gareth Smyth, "Wipe Israel From Map, Says Iran's President," *Financial Times* 10/26/05. Available: http://news.ft.com/cms/s/14cc1ccc-465b-11da-8880-00000e2511c8.html.

[5] "Bin Laden's Sole Post-September 11 TV Interview Aired," *CNN.com/U.S.* 2/1/02. Available: http://www7.cnn.com/2002/US/01/31/gen.binladen.interview (2/2/02).

[6] "Frontline" 5/98.

[7] "Frontline" 5/98.

[8] "Sole TV Interview" 2/1/02.

[9] "Frontline" 5/98.

[10] "Frontline" 5/98.

[11] "Suicide Bombers: Why Do They Kill Themselves and Others, and What Does Islam Say About Their Actions?" Available: http://islam.about.com/library/weekly/aa051801a.htm (5/29/02).

[12] George W. Bush, "State of the Union Address," 1/29/02, Available: http://www.washingtonpost.com/ac2/wp-dyn/A58285-2002Jan29?language=printer (1/30/02).

[13] "Suicide Bombers."

[14] "Suicide Bombers."

[15] "Sympathy for U.S. in Mosque Pulpits," *USA Today* 10/2/01. Available: http://www.usatoday.com/news/nation/2001/09/14/mosque-pulpits.htm (11/7/01).

[16] Richard N. Ostling, "If It Holds, New Muslim Unity Could Remake America's Religious Landscape," *Religious Studies News, AAR Edition* 16, no. 3 (2001): 8.

[17] James D. Tabor, "Introductory Remarks," *Religious Studies News* 10, no. 3 (1995): 3.

[18] Louis Finkelstein, ed. *The Jews: Their History*, 4th ed. (New York: Shocken Books, 1970), 144. It is probable that Jesus' disciple Judas, since he is surnamed "Iscariot" (*iskariôtês*), was one of these "Sicarii." Another disciple, Simon "the Zealot" (Luke 6:15, Acts 1:13), should be identified as a member of the Zealot party.

[19] "Muslim Group Takes Responsibility for 9-11: 'We Are So Sorry,'" *World Tribune.com* 9/10/04. Available: http://216.26.163.62/2004/me_islam_09_10.html (9/11/04).

Chapter 5

Muslims, Christians, & Jews *Versus* Secular Psychotic Entelechies

To dispel any notion among readers that this book is a unidirectional attack on the world's religions, this chapter examines some major psychotic entelechies being advanced by non-religious people and the agreements among these three world religions opposing those psychotic entelechies.

Lutheran Hour Ministries reports:

> Under attack for his opposition to moral, religious, and social evils, Mohammed fled to Medina from his native Mecca in 622 A.D. . . . Nearly 20% of the world's people are followers of Islam. . . . There are almost 150 branches of Islam, but they can be divided into two main groups: The SUNNI (about 83% and the SHIA (about 16%) groups.[1]

Mohammed, like Moses and Jesus, was an opponent of immorality. The moral codes of Christians, Jews, and Muslims are quite similar. They derive from a common source. The three religions agree that there is one God (the God of Abraham) and that coveting, lying, stealing, fornication, and murder are wrong. Furthermore, there are strong elements of each religion that sense dangerous entelechies in several issues discussed in this chapter. This is true despite the fact that Christians and Jews do not believe that the Koran is a collection of divine revelations, just as "Muslims believe that . . . Jewish and Christian scriptures have been corrupted and are no longer reliable, or are superseded by the Qur'an, and hence no longer necessary."[2] Even though they often disagree regarding which texts may be considered inspired, certain Moslem, Christian, and Jewish groups have united in opposing some psychotic entelechies.

Since psychotic entelechy refers to *the tendency of some individuals to be so desirous of fulfilling or bringing to perfection the implications of their terminologies that they engage in very hazardous or damaging actions*, we may consider the Unabomber Theodore Kaczynski. He was motivated by (secular) anti-technologism. Kaczynski killed people in his anti-technologistic entelechy. Religions oppose the murderous methods by which Kaczynski sought to enforce his anti-technologistic views, but religions are not heavily involved (with the exception of the Amish religion) in either promoting or opposing technologism. Much more severe problems, however, have resulted from secular psychotic entelechies: abortion, the AIDS epidemic, drug abuse, and the death and destruction resulting from alcoholic beverages, among others.

AIDS and the Political Correctness Entelechy

One powerful contemporary secularist entelechy that masquerades as a quasi-religious entelechy is political correctness. I mentioned in Chapter 1 an expert on "diversity training" who remarked in an interview that no religion is superior and none are inferior. The problem I associated with this view in the earlier chapter is that it makes Jim Jones' People's Temple, Gene Applewhite's Heaven's Gate, Osama bin Laden's al-Qaida version of Islam, and David Koresh's Branch Davidians all equal in validity to values-driven Christianity, peaceful Islam, and morals-based Judaism. Many times, following the values of world religions would have saved individuals and societies from needless danger and destruction. Political correctness, on the other hand, is an entelechy infused with the fear of making any value judgments (except, of course, the value judgments of political correctness). It stems from the combination of a Postmodernist view that neither truth nor right-and-wrong exist (Relativism) and a Naturalist philosophy (something discussed later in this chapter).

According to political correctness, one must be extremely careful not to suggest that any cultural values or behaviors are in any way superior to those of any other culture. As a result of the political correctness entelechy, it is still difficult to point out that in the early stages of the AIDS epidemic promiscuous male homosexual intercourse was the primary method of transferring the disease. AVERT, the international AIDS charity reports on its web site:

> Already, more than **twenty million** people around the world have died of AIDS-related diseases. . . . [A]lmost 40 million . . . are now living with HIV, and most of these are likely to die over the next decade or so. . . . [I]n 2004 alone, 4.9 million people were newly infected with HIV.
> It is disappointing that the global numbers of people infected with HIV continue to rise, despite the fact that effective prevention strategies already exist.[3]

Although the website does not so state, the earliest available prevention strategies were sexual behavior codes from the Bible that prohibit both homosexual behavior and heterosexually promiscuous behavior. Why were these strategies left out of most literature on the problem? Are they considered politically incorrect because they come from the Bible? Instead, band-aid approaches such as the use of condoms while continuing promiscuous homosexual and heterosexual behaviors became the politically correct cure for the problem.

According to the AVERT website, eight cases of an aggressive form of Kaposi's Sarcoma (KS) in young gay men in New York in March 1981 and five cases of Pneumocystis carinii pneumonia (PCP) in five men in Los Angeles in June 1981 began the general awareness of AIDS in the United States. Dr. Curran of the Center for Disease Control (CDC) states in July 1981: "[N]o cases have been reported to date outside the homosexual community or in women."[4] Most of the world's major religions oppose the very types of behaviors that spawned this epidemic. Even drug use and the shared needles that perpetuated the AIDS epidemic are opposed by the world's major religions. In December 1981, according to AVERT, "the first cases of PCP were reported in injecting drug users."[5] If secular society had opposed the behaviors that started and perpetuated the epidemic as much as the world's major religions did, the AIDS epidemic would not have been as severe. Instead, secular society offered politically correct tolerance of most varieties of sexual behavior, but disregard for religious values. AVERT reports: "[By November 1982] a number of AIDS organizations were already producing safer sex advice for gay men."[6] The key politically correct phrase here is "safer sex." The psychotic entelechy that permitted the AIDS epidemic to grow was and is primarily political correctness.

By the end of 1982, concern for the blood supply and hemophiliacs was rising.[7] The epidemic had moved beyond the efficacy of religious strategies. In March 1983, "Haitian entrants to the United States" were included among those identified as high-risk groups. AVERT reports: "[T]he inclusion of Haitians as a risk group caused much controversy. Haitian Americans complained of stigmatization, officials accused the CDC of racism."[8] Once again, fear of political incorrectness—this time, connecting the problem with a racial group--threatened to muffle the voice of reason.

Religious values were not the cause of this pandemic, but, if practiced, religious values could have minimized the pandemic. Yet, politically correct American society has become so fearful of permitting the expression of religious values in public settings such as schools that schools tend to become values-free zones. School shootings such as the Columbine incident occur. Molestations and rapes occur. Drug traffic flourishes. Qualified teachers refuse to teach in some school districts. Why? It's too dangerous. Political correctness has spawned psychotic entelechy. Practitioners of political correctness would do well to question their own infallibility and the infallibility of their philosophy.

Abortion and the Materialist, Naturalist, and Humanist Entelechies

In my earlier work, *Implicit Rhetoric: Kenneth Burke's Extension of Aristotle's Concept of Entelechy*, I write: "The modern abortion debate involves terminology, essence, the temporizing of essence, narrative, drama, identification, and action."[9] Chapter 5 of that book is devoted to demonstrating that the abortion debate may be analyzed in terms of the Burkean pentad. The terminology drives the drama. Essentially, two abortion dramas are competing for acceptance. One abortion drama uses the term "fetus" to refer to what the other abortion drama calls "unborn child." Although the Latinate term "fetus" has not always carried with it the "disposable" connotation, it is less emotionally charged in current vernacular than the terminology "unborn child." I point out in Chapter 5 of *Implicit Rhetoric* that the primary arguments for abortion come from Materialist, Naturalist, and Humanist philosophies. Burke states: "A philosophy is an 'entelechy'" (ATH 107n). Philosophies offer basic perspectives of reality that, when elaborated, result in the recommendation of everyday actions. These everyday actions resulting from philosophic perspectives are the *teloi*, or the perfected results. If those perfected results of the philosophies are hazardous or damaging, the philosophies have become psychotic entelechies.

Materialist Philosophy

Materialist philosophy is related to Aristotle's Material Cause. Aristotle's use emphasizes the material from which an entelechy develops. For example, the material cause of a granite sculpture is the piece of granite from which the sculpture is carved. The material cause of an apple tree is the basic cellular structure that already exists in an apple seed. A Materialist philosophy emphasizes only (or at least primarily) the material involved. Pertaining to the abortion debate, a Materialist philosophy would not focus on the fetus as an agent. That specific focus would indicate the existence of an Idealist philosophy. A Materialist philosophy would not focus on abortion as an agency or method of birth control. That focus would be indicative of a Pragmatist philosophy. Instead, a Materialist philosophy would focus on the fetus as material that has not yet become a true organism.

When women in the pro-choice movement proclaim in defense of the abortion option, "It's my body," they are proclaiming a Materialist philosophy. The fetus is seen not as a separate organism, but as material that is part of the woman's body. This is a secular Materialist philosophy. What if the fetus, though, is not actually part of the woman's body? What if the fetus is a separate living organism, altogether? DNA evidence might be considered. Genetic science demonstrates that the mother's DNA and the DNA of the fetus are not identical. They are two separate bodies, though admittedly connected. Of course, this variety of Materialist philosophy may be either secular or religious.

As an example of religious Materialist philosophy, Jeffery L. Sheler suggests that some Jewish movements view the fetus as the "material" from which a human is formed:

> Conservative and Reconstructionist [Jewish] movements generally consider abortion a matter of individual conscience . . . a position with roots in ancient Jewish writings. The Talmud suggests that the fetus is not fully a person but, rather, is "as the thigh of its mother." Nonetheless, it is worthy of protection as a potential human being.[10]

While this view tends to lead toward a "disposability" connotation, these two Talmudic descriptions of the fetus as "the thigh of its mother" and as "a potential human being" are contradictory. A mother's thigh is not a potential human being. The genetic advances of modern science demonstrate that the mother's thigh and the fetus are not composed of identical DNA. A thigh might be disposable; a human being is not. What, then, if the view expressed in the Talmud that a fetus is "as the thigh of its mother" is wrong? Religiously sanctioned destruction of "potential human being[s]" sounds like psychotic entelechy. I am not asking Jews to reject the Talmud, here. Jews understand that not all views expressed in the Talmud are correct; various competing views are expressed in the Talmud.

Naturalist Philosophy

Burke, unlike Aristotle, equates Materialist philosophy with his pentadic term "scene." He understands a Materialist to be one who is concerned only with the motivation that the scene in which an act occurs contributes to the completing of the act. This view of Materialist philosophy is not an exact equivalent of Aristotelian Materialist philosophy as described above. Naturalist philosophy, however, is a good example of a purely Materialist philosophy in a Burkean sense. Burke comments: "Naturalism dropped the principles of personality and action from the *scene*." (GM 80). Naturalist philosophy so thoroughly emphasizes the scene in which something happens, it leaves no room for the concept of action whatsoever. What happens is not an act because there is no "purpose" to the happening. What happens is sheer motion. There is no agent performing an act because an agent has free will; in a purposeless scene, what happens is simply determined by the various factors of the scene.

If a Naturalist views a fetus from a scenic circumference that eliminates all agents (GM 81), there are no moral issues connected with abortion. But, then there are no moral issues at all from a thoroughly Naturalist perspective. Burke complains that Naturalism is a "movement towards the dissolution of drama . . . [which drops] the principles of personality and action from the *scene*" (GM 79-80).

What if Naturalist views of scene are incorrect? What if there really is a God? What if humans are agents and do possess free will? What if there really is, as Burke asserts, human action—not just non-purposive motion? What if morality should apply? Naturalists are not infallible. They should take care that their philosophy does not result in psychotic entelechy.

Humanist Philosophy

Humanists back away from purely Naturalist views and claim that agents and action do exist. The exclusive agents involved in the creation and development of a fetus for Humanists, however, are those humans whose action resulted in conception--as in Burke's citation of Aristotle: "[T]he father [is] a cause of the child . . ." (GM 228). Leaving God out of the Scene, they may claim that humans as the sole "agents" possess the free will and right to either allow a potential human to live or to choose not to. Burke comments: "[I]n proportion as Naturalism dropped the principles of personality and action from the *scene*, Humanism compensatorily stressed their presence in men as *agents*" (GM 80).

Returning to religious philosophies, Sheler writes: "Professor Virginia Ramey Mollenkott . . . argues that . . . 'God foreknew that Adam and Eve would misuse their power to choose . . . We should follow our Creator's example by giving each other more moral elbow room.'"[11] Mollenkott is arguing that humans should be the agents who make such (life-and-) death decisions. In *Implicit Rhetoric*, I respond to Mollenkott's argument:

> The argument for granting more free will works better from a Humanist perspective than from a scriptural perspective. Assuming that humans are the only agents, one might indeed be prone to grant humans the free will to kill not only their unborn offspring but also their recently born offspring (as is currently happening to baby girls in Communist China), their totally dependent elderly, and their infirm— unless society grants the right to life to some of these categories of individuals. Since humans would be the ultimate agents in such a system, humans could set whatever restrictive codes they wish to set. These restrictive codes could theoretically allow the killing of

individuals of a different race (as in Nazi Germany), individuals of a different religious tradition (as in Northern Ireland), individuals of a different level of technology and civilization (as in the Native American-European American clashes), or even individuals with whom other humans simply have arguments. Humans would be the final arbiters of all restrictive codes. And, due to the politically correct value that opposes all ethnocentrism, no culture could impose its restrictive codes upon any other culture.

From a scriptural perspective, however, Professor Mollenkott has managed to allude to the very proof that abortion might better be outlawed. She correctly notes that in scripture, God gives humans the right to choose (to "misuse their power"). She neglects to mention, however, that in scripture God also gives *laws*, such as the one which Adam and Eve broke. She further neglects to mention that in scripture God imposes punishment upon the breaking of those laws. Those who approach the abortion issue by selecting a circumference of Scene which emphasizes the action of the Judeo-Christian God may well turn to authoritative scriptures for those restrictive codes which that God may impose upon human action.[12]

Moslems, Christians, and Jews

Roman Catholicism, Islam, Evangelical Protestants, and some Jewish groups sense danger in the Materialist, Naturalist, and Humanist abortion entelechies. Sheler observes: "[T]he Roman Catholic Church and Evangelical Protestants have been highly visible in opposing abortion."[13] The Islamic world has also been a strong opponent of abortion on a global scale, as have Orthodox Jews. Without a strong alliance between Islam and the Catholic Church, abortion would be much more rampant worldwide than it currently is. Discussing basic Jewish and Christian morality, a very early Christian text, the *Didache*, states: "*Thou shalt do no* murder . . . thou shalt not murder a child by abortion nor kill them when born."[14] What if the *Didache* is right?

Abortion rights activists may legitimately turn the tables and ask the "what if" question in the instance of the *Didache* quotation. What if the *Didache* is wrong and abortion is not actually murder? What if a mother's life is endangered by carrying her pregnancy to full term, thus forcing her into a situation that takes her life? Is that not psychotic entelechy? What if an abortion opponent so strongly believes abortion is wrong that s/he murders an abortion doctor? Is that not psychotic entelechy? The argument is persuasive. Some pro-life advocates will accept abortion for certain purposes, such as to save the life of the mother. Sheler writes:

> The Mishna, a compilation of Jewish law from the third century A.D., explicitly approves of therapeutic abortions if the mother's life is endangered. . . . Orthodox Jews today allow abortions only in strictly defined cases involving the health and survival of the mother.[15]

Approval of abortion under such circumstances seems consistent with biblical laws which while condemning murder (Deuteronomy 5:17) permit self-defense (Exodus 22:2).

Some secular abortion rights activists have been able to show flexibility in their positions (as some pro-life advocates have). Both houses of Congress passed the partial-birth abortion bill with bipartisan support. The senators and representatives agreed that the line needs to be drawn somewhere. Some secularists draw the line much earlier—at viability (that point in a pregnancy at which the fetus could survive outside the womb). That line continues to move closer and closer to conception, due to progress in medical technology. What if abortion occurs at a time the fetus was viable? Does that constitute murder?

Other secularists have suggested that life should be protected only after quickening, based on classical secular sources such as Aristotle. Although many think of quickening as that point in a pregnancy at which the mother feels "movement (or *kinêsis*)" in her womb, such an interpretation is not classical. Aristotle distinguishes between the seed [*sperma*] of plants and the sperm [*sperma*] of humans. While Aristotle might understand the seed of plants to be a "first grade of" entelechy, he would require the combined ovum and sperm in order to have entelechy or life in humans. At conception, when growth of the embryo begins (one type of *kinêsis*), Aristotle would classify the entity as entelechy. The life has begun.

It was common for the Greeks to locate the beginning of human life in "quickening [*zôopoiein*, meaning literally 'to make alive']." It is clear that the Greeks connected *zôopoiein* with *kinêsis*.[16] Aristotle's use of *kinêsis* includes "growth." Furthermore, it seems strange that Aristotle would bother to mention the *sperma* and the *katamênia* (or menstrual flow [containing ovum]) as being causes of entelechy unless he considered their combination to be the beginning of *entelecheia*.

Classical secularists should ask themselves: What if Aristotelian teaching is that quickening, or the beginning of life, happens at conception? Would the taking of life after that point constitute murder? The real crux of the issue of abortion is: Does the act of abortion constitute murder?

One of the reasons Judeo-Christian leaders hold such divergent views is that the Bible is silent on this issue. Not a single biblical passage discusses an elective abortion. Why is this true? There are several suggested possibilities. Paul D. Simmons suggests the Apostle Paul regarded abortion as a matter of faith, grace, and Christian freedom. Disagreeing, James L. Nash suggests that abortion was not a problem among early Christians. It was a dangerous option for women and simply wasn't practiced among Christians.[17] An explanation of the silence of the Old Testament on the subject is that abortion flies in the face of one of the greatest Old Testament values--God's covenant with Abraham to give him an uncountable offspring (Genesis 13:16, 15:5). Why would a culture that considered multiple offspring to be evidence of the blessing of God even entertain thoughts of abortion? There is certainly no reason, just because of the Bible's silence on the issue, to attribute to any ancient Jewish writer (the Apostle Paul included) a pro-abortion stance in any respect. While the Bible is silent on the issue of abortion, it certainly is not silent on the matter of fetal existence. Many texts suggest a human existence, and even personality, prior to birth.[18]

Even though all these questions remain, an avoidance of psychotic entelechy does not require a definitive answer to the question of whether abortion is murder. Psychotic entelechy is *the tendency of some individuals to be so desirous of fulfilling or bringing to perfection the implications of their terminologies that they engage in very hazardous or damaging actions*. Abortion is definitely hazardous and damaging to the fetus/unborn child. President Ronald Reagan adopted the position that since we do not know for certain whether or not an embryo or fetus is a human, it is better to err on the side of life.

While Humanists may completely overlook religious considerations in the matter, most Humanists still oppose murder on Humanistic grounds. Is it necessary for Humanists to decide at what point the fetus becomes human? Not in order to avoid psychotic entelechy. Humanists simply need to be able to doubt a little of their own infallibility.

Both Naturalists and Humanists are distraught to find that Theists such as Muslims, Catholic and Evangelical Protestant Christians, and

Orthodox Jews) refuse to accept the entelechy Naturalists and Humanists propose. Likewise Theists, convinced that all abortion is murder, quite easily equate the thousands of annual abortions with the entelechy of the murder of Jews by Hitler. The abortion doctor, the Planned Parenthood counselors, *etc.* become the equivalent of Hitler and his henchmen. The methods of abortion become the moral equivalent of gas chambers, firing squads, *etc.* Theists who hold to these views are not inclined to be patient. Clinics are bombed. Abortion doctors are killed. These are the acts of psychotic entelechy. Only a few pro-life Theists follow this course of action, however. On the other hand, the thousands of abortions that occur annually appear to result from a much more dangerous psychotic entelechy. With Reagan, Theists, Naturalists, and Humanists would all do well--since error is possible--to err on the side of life.

Alcohol Consumption and Cultural Entelechies

Today, Muslims, Mormons, and many Evangelical Christians oppose the drinking of alcoholic beverages. Is drinking a psychotic entelechy? In 1919 so many Americans believed drinking was wrong this nation passed Prohibition--the Eighteenth Amendment to the U.S. Constitution. Consider how much popular support is required to pass any constitutional amendment. The United States was a Christian nation and, due largely to the efforts of Christians, Prohibition was passed. Even such an avowedly heavy drinker of alcoholic beverages as Kenneth Burke admits that Prohibition had good effects. In a 1982 interview, he was asked: "Did you ever take any drugs?" Burke replied:

> Nothing but alcohol. I think what saved me was prohibition. All that [expletive deleted] stuff. Every night I got sick so I got rid of it. I wasn't proud. If I'd kept my liquor, I'd been gone a long time ago. . . . My body wouldn't put up with it. . . . When I look back over my life, and all the hours I've spent under alcohol, I think that's my lostness.[19]

In the 1920s, the biblical teaching concerning alcohol was an issue not only in America but also worldwide. In 1920, the German scholar V. Zapeltal published a journal article on wine in the Bible. In 1922, the German scholar E. Busse published a journal article on wine in the Old Testament. In 1923, the German Jewish scholar J. Döller published a journal article on wine in the Bible and the Talmud. In 1926, German scholars J. Hempel, H. Schmidt, and E. Zurhellen-Pfleiderer published scholarly articles on Mysticism and alcohol, alcohol in the Old Testament, and alcohol in the New Testament, respectively, in the German book, *Die Alkoholfrage in Religion.* In 1927, I. W. Raymond published *The Teaching of the Early Church on the Use of Wine and Strong Drink* in English. I cite these works from the 1920s not to suggest that all these studies were anti-drinking but to show that alcohol use in the Church (and in Judaism) was a worldwide issue in that decade. Even in Germany, where some claim alcohol consumption has always occurred without anyone questioning the morality of the practice, several studies delved into the issue. Suggestions that no one questioned the morality of the practice are not accurate.

In 1933, fourteen years after it was passed, Prohibition was repealed. Prohibition was considered too difficult to enforce. Since the repeal of prohibition, public acceptance of drinking in the U.S. has been rising. Many Evangelical Christians, the citizens so essential to the crusade to prohibit the use of alcoholic beverages, now typically try to justify drinking by using biblical proof texts (as some Christians had used proof texts to justify slavery in the nineteenth century). Even so, some counties in the U.S. still have local prohibition laws. All states have modified prohibition laws. Such laws prohibit minors from drinking alcohol.

The establishment of a legal drinking age in a state (typically age eighteen or age twenty-one) clearly implies that American culture continues to see dangers in alcoholic beverage consumption. Drinking impairs driving ability. From one-third to two-thirds of all traffic fatalities in the United States are alcohol-related. Alcohol causes liver damage. It is used frequently to facilitate rape or sexual abuse. It is blamed for irresponsibility at work. It is the culprit in much spouse and child abuse. It destroys families. It kills brain cells. According to life insurance specialist Brendan McKenna:

> There is no doubt that heavy drinking can lead to health problems. According to the Society of Actuaries, abusing alcohol can take an average of 10 to 15 years off your life. The most frequent cause of premature death from alcoholism is heart disease, followed by cancer, accidents and suicide. . . . While alcohol has the potential to damage every organ in the body, certain conditions, such as chronic

inflammation of the pancreas or nonspecific liver problems, are often strongly associated with alcohol use.[20]

Alcohol consumption qualifies as a psychotic entelechy.

On the other hand, the drinking public is always thirsty for news that might tend to suggest that "moderate drinking" is good for a person. Psychotics always tend to seek out information that confirms their psychoses. Some studies suggest, for example, that drinking alcohol is helpful in the battle against heart disease. Associated Press writer Janet McConnaughey writes:

> As little as half an alcoholic drink a day can reduce the risk of heart attacks, whether the beverage of choice is beer, red wine, white wine or liquor, new research shows. . . . "[F]requency of use seemed to be what reduced the subsequent risk of a heart attack," said Dr. Kenneth Mukamal of Harvard University Medical School, who led the study.
> Those who drank at least three days a week had about one-third fewer heart attacks than did nondrinkers. . . . Those who imbibed only once or twice a week had only a 16 percent lower risk of a heart attack.
> Some studies have indicated that alcohol raises the level of "good" cholesterol and also thins the blood, warding off the clots that cause heart attacks. . . . Mukamal speculated that regular, moderate drinking is beneficial because it helps keep the blood thinned. . . . The study was published in Thursday's *New England Journal of Medicine*. . . . Mukamal and other doctors emphasized that the study applies only to moderate drinkers. The dangers of heavy drinking are well established and include alcoholism, drunken driving, and damage to the liver and brain. Studies have also found that women who have two or more drinks a day are 41 percent more likely to develop breast cancer . . . than women who do not drink. . . . Doctors have long believed that red wine explains the so-called French Paradox — the fact that the French have fewer heart attacks than Americans even though their food is richer. But the new study adds to the evidence that it is the alcohol itself, and not something found only in red wine, such as red pigment, that is good for the heart.[21]

Welch's, the company known for producing grape juice and jelly, disagrees with that last assessment. Welch's conducted studies of its own that indicate that claims made regarding the medical benefits of drinking alcoholic wine are true also for unfermented grape juice. According to their studies, the so-called medical benefit appears to be in the grape, not in the alcohol.[22] Although Mukamal suggested that alcohol *may* help keep the blood thinned, this very result can be obtained by using a small dose of aspirin. As an individual who had a sudden, rapidly increasing cholesterol problem myself, I had a discussion with my cardiac specialist regarding wine. He informed me that I was precisely the type of individual who might benefit from wine consumption, according to medical research. I needed a much higher good cholesterol score. He asked if I drank alcohol. I stated that I did not. He responded, "Then I would not recommend it for you." He said that the health negatives of alcohol consumption far outweigh any possible health benefit, according to the research. Dr. Gary Francis, director of the coronary intensive care unit at the Cleveland Clinic, concurs with my doctor: "I don't think any doctor would advise a patient to start drinking to prevent heart disease .... Certainly we don't want to exchange one public health problem for another."[23] MSN's Health & Fitness website listed as one of its Top Ten Smart Foods (according to *Psychology Today*) "Red Wine, or, better yet, Grape Juice":

> Drinking red wine in moderation increases longevity. But since alcohol slows down the brain's ability to function properly, grape juice may be a smarter beverage choice. New research . . . shows that Concord grape juice significantly improves short term memory . . . . It's not just the heavy dose of antioxidants. Joseph believes that grape juice increases . . . the neurotransmitter dopamine.[24]

Incidentally, I began drinking Welch's grape juice, shortly thereafter. My good cholesterol score quintupled.

So, if even individuals, such as I, who might benefit from drinking wine, are advised by our doctors not to do so, why has there been such a drastic abandonment of the anti-drinking position? We live in a time when our society is recognizing the problems of alcohol, when brewers are producing alcohol-free beers, when MADD and SADD are raising the level of consciousness of our culture regarding the dangers of this substance. We live in an age when our president, George W. Bush, is a teetotaler. Why, then, is even Evangelical Christianity now backing away from its historic stance?

The answer lies in a cultural entelechy. Alcohol consumption is a secular cultural practice. As Americans noted during Operation Desert Storm, the culture of Saudi Arabia does not accept the drinking of alcoholic beverages. The Saudis are predominantly Muslim. The

Mormon religious culture also opposes the drinking of alcoholic beverages. It is strange that the culture that once produced the Eighteenth Amendment to the U.S. Constitution--the Church--is not only abandoning its position on the issue, but it has also become a voice in favor of drinking alcohol. Scriptures have been reinterpreted to support the drinking of alcohol. Have the dangers changed? What if Muslims and Mormons are right and the increasingly alcohol-consuming Evangelical Church is wrong? In the spirit of recalcitrance, I now revisit those scriptures. I reexamine the scriptural evidence for and against drinking and offer a recalcitrant Christian perspective on this issue.

Drinking in the Bible

There are several biblical principles related to the drinking issue. I discuss those principles individually:
Principle #1--There was no reliable method to avoid some fermentation in biblical times. There were no refrigerators. If Christians would ask modern Muslims to differentiate between the Christians of the Crusades and modern Christians, Christians should be willing to differentiate between the technological scenes of biblical times and now. Even if those in biblical times had wanted desperately to avoid fermentation, the issue was moot. Avoidance was impossible. It is likely that any wine consumed some days after the grapes were pressed contained some alcoholic content. Even in the 1920's, conservative scholars were not blind to the scriptural evidence that suggests that some alcoholic consumption took place. According to conservative scholar Burton Scott Easton (writing in 1929):

> In the climate of Pal[estine] fermentation begins almost immediately, frequently on the same day for juice pressed out in the morning, but never later than the next day. At first a slight foam appears on the surface of the liquid, and from that moment, according to Jewish tradition, it is liable to the wine-tithe (*Ma'aseroth* 1:7). The action rapidly becomes more violent, and while it is in progress the liquid must be kept in jars or in a vat, for it would burst even the newest and strongest of wine skins (Job 32:19). Within about a week this violent fermentation subsides, and the wine is transferred to other jars or strong wine skins (Mark 2:22 and [parallels]), in which it undergoes the secondary fermentation.[25]

As Easton indicates, grape juice qualifies as wine from the moment a slight foam appears on the surface of the liquid. Most Americans are not aware that the term "wine" in the Greek means grape juice (regardless of any level of fermentation it may have reached). However, the biblical languages also, at times, distinguish between "new" (or relatively unfermented) wine and "old" (fermented) wine. Jesus' parable of the wine skins clearly indicates that Jesus took the fermentation process for granted and seems to indicate that he viewed this fermentation process innocently. He does not implicitly or explicitly condemn the fermentation process. He states, "No one pours new wine into old wine skins, lest the new wine burst the skins and run out and the skins be ruined. But new wine should be put in fresh wine skins" (Luke 5:37-38). For God to have issued a commandment in biblical times such as "Thou shalt not allow wine to ferment" would have made no sense. We do not make moral commands that are impossible to fulfill.[26] As the song from the 1960s says, "It's impossible . . . to teach a baby not to cry; it's just impossible." Hence, we do not command babies, "Thou shalt not cry." Obviously, no moral commandment to stop fermentation could be made in biblical times, but that is not the situation today. Moderns have the technology to actually stop the fermentation. Moderns have no excuse for drinking fermented beverages as biblical characters did.

Principle #2--Since it was impossible to stop the fermentation of wine in biblical times, precautions were taken to avoid the negative consequences of drinking fermented wine. For example, in his parable of the wine skins, Jesus associates *his* message not with old (fermented) wine but with new (relatively unfermented) wine.

New wine is an important association for the Church as well. In Acts 2:13, Luke (the author of Acts) reports a comment made by individuals in Jerusalem on the day of Pentecost. Observers had noticed the Christian leaders speaking God's word boldly. Some said, "They had too much new wine!" Peter interpreted the crowd's comment to suggest that the Christians were drunk (Acts 2:15). Peter denies the charge, of course, but it seems strange that the crowd would accuse the Christians of drunkenness from overindulging in "new wine." Clearly, "old wine" would be more capable of getting someone drunk! Perhaps, the crowd already knew that the Christians drank only "new wine." The comment from the crowd could be taken as a joke about the Christians. Knowing that they drank only new wine, the crowd would have known that the Christians would not be drunk; the crowd would have been using ironic humor and ridicule. Or, perhaps the crowd actually charged the Christians with being drunk on "wine." In that case Luke, the premier church historian, would certainly know what type of wine the Christians drank. Perhaps Luke was, in his historical account, stipulating what beverage the early Christians consumed. At the very least, no one can claim either that Christians were drunk or that Christians drank strongly fermented wine, based on this account.

Comparing the church with the Essenes—a first century Jewish group--who wrote the Dead Sea Scrolls, a meal similar to the Lord's Supper is found. The meal is described in the scroll of the *Messianic Rule*. The Messiah blesses the bread and wine before anyone partakes. The scroll makes explicit reference to the wine--it is always "new wine." The Church may well be borrowing some understanding of "Communion" from the "Common Table" of the Essenes.

Some suggest that the wine Jesus made from water at the marriage feast in Cana of Galilee was fermented (John 2:1-10) because the table manager pronounced this wine the best. There is no such indication in the Bible. Instead, the best grade of wine, according to Easton was the very first squeezing of the new grape crop:

> It is a general principle of wine making . . . that "the less pressure the better the product"; therefore the liquid that flowed at the beginning of the process, esp. that produced by the mere weight of the grapes themselves when piled in heaps, was carefully kept separate from that which was obtained only under heavy pressure. A still lower grade was made by adding water to the final refuse and allowing the mixture to ferment.[27]

John is probably issuing a disclaimer against the possibility that some easy miracle was performed--mixing the grape refuse with the water in the jars. What Jesus made was the best grade of wine. It makes sense that Jesus would have created wine as God creates it *fresh--unfermented*.

Does it matter that even fresh wine (new wine) may have at times contained some alcoholic content? It is not true that Evangelical Christians have always opposed the consumption of small quantities of alcohol in foods. Dill pickles, ketchup, and mustard all have some alcoholic content. Although I do not drink alcoholic beverages, I do eat pickles, ketchup, and mustard. Therefore, even as a teetotaler, I probably consume about as much alcoholic content as did a typical

Jewish Christian in the New Testament period who drank wine. I say this not only because of the "new wine" stipulation, but also because of the next principle.

Principle #3--By the New Testament period, wine was almost always highly diluted. Most Jews of the period could not afford to drink much wine each day. The wealthy were typically the ones who were singled out for the charge of drunkenness. Only they could afford to drink wine without restraint. Yet, wine was consumed by most Jews at every meal. The only way most Jews could afford to drink wine at each meal was to generously dilute the wine with water. Easton comments:

> In [Old Testament] times wine was drunk undiluted, and wine mixed with water was thought to be ruined (Isa[iah] 1:22). . . . At a later period, however, the Gr[eek] use of diluted wines had attained such sway that the writer of 2 Macc[abees] speaks (15:39) of undiluted wine as "distasteful" (*polêmion*). This dilution is so normal in the following centuries that the Mish[nah, the Jewish tradition of laws at around the time of Jesus,] can take it for granted and, indeed, R[abbi] Eliezer even forbade saying the table blessing over undiluted wine (*Berakhoth* 7:5). The proportion of water was large, only one-third or one-fourth of the total mixture being wine (*Niddah* 2:7; *Pesahim* 108b).[28]

When Paul counsels Timothy (I Timothy 5:23) to no longer drink "water alone, but use a little wine for [his] stomach's sake," Paul is not recommending alcoholic beverages to Timothy. Although there may have been some alcoholic content involved (as with ketchup and mustard), Paul was recommending wine greatly diluted with water (using just "a little wine"). However, the real reason Paul was addressing the issue of wine with Timothy was that Timothy was apparently attempting to live as a Nazirite. The Nazirite principle is the next principle I consider.

Principle #4--Much of the confusion over the question of wine in the New Testament stems from the failure of Christians to understand the Nazirite principle in the early Church. In a messianic prophecy accepted by all Jews at the time of the New Testament, Isaiah predicts: "A twig shall shoot forth from the stump of Jesse and a 'Branch' from his roots shall produce fruit" (Isaiah 11:1). Christians understand this to mean that Jesus (the Messiah) would come from the family of David and his father Jesse. But some Jews also saw another implication in this messianic prophecy. The word translated "Branch" is the Hebrew word *netzer*. This word is from a Hebrew root similar to the word *nazir* which is translated "Nazirite."

The linguistic evidence related to how easily the two words may be connected is discussed by H. H. Schaeder in the *Theological Dictionary of the New Testament*.[29] Schaeder also connects these words with the term "Nazarene." Matthew takes pains to explain that Jesus being called a "Nazarene" fulfills a prophecy. However, Matthew does not state where that prophecy is found. The most logical explanation is that Matthew refers to the Isaiah 11:1 prophecy and that his audience was expecting a *netzer*. Since Jesus was not a *Nazirite*, Matthew explains that the prophecy is fulfilled by Jesus being a *Nazarene*.

This explanation of the *netzer* prophecy is, however, not sufficient for some of Jesus' critics. Matthew 11:18-19 and Luke 7:33-34 report the insatiability of Jesus' critics who were looking for a Nazirite messiah. Jesus complains that John the Baptist came as a Nazirite (Luke 1:15), neither eating grapes nor drinking wine (grape juice), but the critics rejected him as messiah, claiming that he had a demon. Jesus, on the other hand, was not a Nazirite, yet the critics rejected him as their messiah, claiming that he was a wine drinker.

The sixth chapter of the Old Testament book of Numbers describes the qualifications of a Nazirite. A Nazirite must abstain from all grape products--grapes, raisins, grape juice/new wine, old wine, vinegar, grape seeds, and grape skins. Furthermore, a Nazirite is not allowed to cut his hair or to touch a dead body. John the Baptist fit these requirements; Jesus did not--hence, Jesus' frustration with his critics. Eating grapes, raisins, etc., was not morally wrong, but it was outlawed for Nazirites. Readers today often do not understand that the issue that caused the charge of "wine bibber (literally, wine drinker)" to be leveled against Jesus had nothing to do with *alcoholic* content; it had to do with *grape* content.

Scholars generally agree that Timothy's persistence in drinking only water was based upon his view that Christians were to be Nazarenes/Nazirites. Paul simply informed him that it was not necessary for Christians to be Nazirites. Nevertheless, several in the early church did strive to be Nazirites. Paul advises the Romans in 14:21 to eat no meat and to drink no wine if it makes a brother stumble. It is possible that the weaker brother thought that wine was forbidden to followers of the Nazarene. Paul says it is not forbidden but he does not want to drink grape juice (wine) it if it causes someone to stumble.

Principle #5--Perhaps the most important principle in the New Testament relating to the drinking issue is the condemnation of drunkenness and of drinking wine that should be discarded. In I Corinthians 5:11, Paul lists drunkenness with six other sins that should cause Christians to be excommunicated. Those Christians who drink usually accept the view that drunkenness is a sin. They claim that they are drinkers but not drunkards. However, rare is the drinker who does not, on occasion, become drunk. Perhaps the drunkenness occurs only once per month or twice per year or only on special occasions. This analogy may be drawn: Besides drunkenness, Paul lists sexual immorality as a sin that deserves excommunication. Who is sexually immoral? Does the person who is sexually immoral only "once per month or twice per year or only on special occasions" qualify?

In Ephesians 5:18, Paul instructs the disciples not to be drunk with wine in which is *asôtia*. The word *asôtia* literally means "unsavability." Jews threw away wine that had become unsavable (strongly fermented). Only soldiers and construction workers drank the strongly fermented variety. Easton reports, "[I]n the wines of Pal[estine] acetous fermentation, changing the wine into vinegar, was likely to occur at any time."[30]

Mark 15:23 states that Jesus was offered wine mingled with myrrh on the cross, but he refused it. John 19:28-30 reports that immediately before dying Jesus asked for something to drink. All that was offered to him was wine vinegar on a hyssop sponge. John indicates that he "received" the vinegar before dying. The exact amount Jesus received in John's account is unclear, but that *soldiers* drank vinegar and would have had some with them at the crucifixion is in line with earlier comments.

In *Berachoth* 6:3 of the Mishnah, Rabbi Judah rejects the possibility of saying a blessing over "sour wine" (vinegar): "We do not say a blessing over any food which has the character of a curse."

The requirements for being an elder, deacon, or woman leader in the church in I Timothy and Titus all suggest abstaining from wine that causes drunkenness. The adjective *nêphalios* which is translated "sober" by the King James Version in I Timothy 3:11, but is a requirement for being a bishop in I Timothy 3:2, for the women of I Timothy 3:11, and for the elders of Titus 2:2 literally means "holding no wine."[31]

Unlike Abraham's nephew Lot in the Old Testament, not a single New Testament church leader is depicted as getting drunk. Furthermore, there is no evidence that any early church leader drank anything other than new wine. Even though fermentation was unstoppable in New Testament times, many precautions were taken to avoid the negative consequences--drinking only new wine, diluting all wine with water, throwing away wine that became unsavable, forbidding wine usage for any church leader, and excommunicating any Christian engaging in drunkenness.

Christians who promote the drinking of alcoholic beverages today do not do so because: (1) it helps families stay together, (2) it helps people keep their jobs, (3) it makes people healthier, (4) it keeps people alive on the highways, *etc.* So, why do they search the scriptures so diligently to find passages that allow for drinking? The Bible calls it "legalism." Legalism is consistently condemned by both Jesus and Paul (Mark 7:8-13, Rom. 2:26-29, 2 Cor. 3:2-6). Christians who promote the drinking of alcoholic beverages today do not consider the "spirit of the law"; that surely would suggest that drinking alcohol is destructive. Instead, they seek to find in the "letter of the law"--written at a time when refrigerators capable of stopping fermentation and automobiles capable of killing did not exist--some indication that God accepts the drinking of alcohol. As my recalcitrance has shown, Christians have not even been particularly good at understanding the letter of the law. This is because they are not looking for the correct interpretation of the letter of the law. They are looking for an excuse—something that will fit neatly into their psychosis.

Cultural Psychotic Entelechy

I call the Christian motivation in this instance psychotic entelechy. It is not a religious psychotic entelechy; it is a secular psychotic entelechy. In the instance of drinking, the entelechy is cultural and pertains to socializing. The drinking of alcoholic beverages has become so firmly entrenched in society that it is easier for Christians to go along with the entelechy and rationalize their actions. Even though they use the Bible to rationalize, they are not seeking a religious entelechy so much as they are seeking a salve for their consciences.

To illustrate how a cultural entelechy operates, I cite the following from my book, *The Seven Cs of Stress: A Burkean Approach*:

> If I walk up to a business associate and stretch out my open right hand to him, it is not necessary for me to explain to him what he should do.

He reaches out and grasps my right hand in his right hand. His grip is not too limp--firm but not too firm. He shakes my hand for approximately one second and lets go. This action may be accompanied by some small verbal greeting such as, "How are you?" How did he know to do all of that? His culture taught him. I simply assumed that he would respond in precisely the manner he did. These cultural behaviors are implicit, not explicit.

Notice also that my business associate's implicit behaviors were a set--he grasps, he grips, he shakes, he releases, and he verbally greets. What if my associate does not know my culture? What if he does not grasp my hand when extended? I feel community stress: Does he not consider me a friend? Is he snubbing me? What if his grip is too firm? I may have both community stress and corporal stress: Is he trying to harm me or seem superior to me? What if his grip is too limp? I may think: This weak individual is not my equal. What if he continues to grasp my hand longer than one second? I may have community stress: What message is he sending me? I may feel I need to pull away from him.

. . .

All humans greet one another, but your culture teaches you how this should be done. Obviously, in American male business culture the greeting occurs as a handshake in the manner I have described. But, American male business culture is only one culture. In American female culture, individuals greet each other, too. But, outside of business contexts, the handshake is not as common among females as it is among males. The hug is more common in American female culture, but there is a set of implications about how that hug will be practiced. In some cultures, the appropriate greeting is a kiss. But you must know the implicit set. It may be a kiss on each cheek; it may be a series of three kisses (from cheek to cheek to cheek); it may be a kiss on the hand, a kiss on the forehead, a kiss on the neck, a kiss on the lips. In some cultures, the appropriate greeting is a bow, but know the set. The bow may be accompanied by eye contact or by averting the gaze. It may be accompanied by folding your hands together in front of your neck and chest or by a circling gesture of one hand. The bow may be at the neck or at the waist or even with a knee to the ground (kneeling). Cultural expectations are such that the violation of one element of the set may cause community stress (misinterpretations, and hence discord).[32]

While the cultural entelechy of greeting with handshakes, kisses, *etc.* is not psychotic, the cultural entelechy of drinking of an alcoholic beverage is psychotic. Drinking alcoholic beverages belongs to the entelechy of socializing. The vast majority of socializing situations in

Western civilization include drinking as a part of the cultural set. Yet, by drinking, *some individuals . . . engage in very hazardous or damaging actions.* The socializing process has a beginning, middle, and an end. All entelechies do. Included in socializing process is the drinking of alcohol on the part of those who would socialize. Drinkers give no thought to the dangers of their behavior because they are driven not by logic and reasoning but by the power of an entelechy. Just as David Koresh and Osama bin Laden may have thought they were innocently following the dictates of the messages they received from God, the drinkers think they are innocently following the dictates of messages they have received from their cultures. But drinking has dangers: drunk driving, liver damage, heart disease, rape, molestation, abuse, loss of work, destruction of families, impaired judgment, *etc.*

Muslims condemn drinking. The Koran states: "O believers, wine . . . [is] an abomination, some of Satan's work; so avoid it; haply so you will prosper. Satan only desires to precipitate enmity and hatred between you in regard to wine" (I.142).

The Jewish Bible warns against drinking: "Wine is a mocker and beer a brawler; whoever is led astray by them is not wise" (Proverbs 20:1 NIV). The Mishnah rejects the possibility of saying a blessing over vinegar because one should not bless a curse (*Berachoth* 6:3).

Mormons condemn drinking. Based originally on the Word of Wisdom received by church founder and prophet Joseph Smith: "[T]he minimum standard the church now teaches . . . is no alcohol, tobacco or recreational drugs including (relatively recently) all caffeinated drinks."[33]

Many Christians continue to condemn drinking. I have in this chapter discussed virtually all of the New Testament passages pertaining to this issue. While arguments can be made rationalizing the consumption of alcoholic beverages on the basis of the Bible, recalcitrant arguments can also be offered that point in the opposite direction.

So, where are we? Let's return to "What if."

What if Catholics, Evangelical Christians, Muslims, and Orthodox Jews are wrong about promiscuous sexual behavior and abortion? Would their error negatively affect society? To this extent: Those who engage in promiscuity and abortion might feel more guilt than they currently feel. If religious people manage to make abortion illegal again, some who still opt for abortion will arrange for illegal abortions with some serious health risk. What if Mormons, Evangelical Christians, and Muslims are wrong about alcohol consumption? Would their error negatively affect society? To this extent: Those who engage in drinking alcohol anyway might feel some guilt. If religious people manage to make drinking illegal again (not a likely scenario, in light of our Prohibition experience), some who still opt for drinking alcoholic beverages will arrange for illegal alcohol purchases (as occurred during Prohibition) with some additional health risk. What if religions are wrong in opposing drug use? Would their error negatively affect society? To this extent: Those who engage in drug use may feel some guilt. If religious people manage to keep drug use illegal, some who still opt for using illegal drugs will arrange for illegal drug purchases with additional health and safety risks.

Conversely, what if Catholics, Evangelical Christians, Muslims, and Orthodox Jews are right about promiscuous sexual behavior and abortion? Would the error of secularists negatively affect society? Yes. Their error contributed to a worldwide AIDS epidemic that could have been controlled to a larger extent through the use of social pressure. Those who engage in abortion would correctly feel guilt. They would be guilty of an enormous number of wrongful deaths, worldwide. If religious people are right about the consumption of alcohol and other drugs, secularists who promote their use are responsible for a huge number of highway deaths, liver failures, wrecked households, rapes, and lost jobs.

The greater dangers in these issues exist if the religions are right-yet-their-counsel-is-ignored. The primary destructive psychotic entelechies in these issues are secular entelechies.

Notes

[1] "What is Islam?" Available: http://www.lhmint.org/whowillteach/what is_print.htm (9/26/05).
[2] "What is Islam?"
[3] "Aids Around the World." Available: http://www.avert.org/aroundworld.htm (10/4/05).
[4] "The History of AIDS 1981-1986." Available: http://www.avert.org/his 81_86.htm (10/4/05).
[5] "History" (10/4/05).
[6] "History" (10/4/05).
[7] "History" (10/4/05).
[8] "History" (10/4/05).
[9] Stan A. Lindsay, *Implicit Rhetoric: Kenneth Burke's Extension of Aristotle's Concept of Entelechy* (Lanham, MD: University Press of America, 1998), 111.
[10] Jeffery L. Sheler, "The Theology of Abortion," *U. S. News and World Report*, March 9, 1992, 55.
[11] Sheler, 55.
[12] Lindsay, *Implicit*, 115-116.
[13] Sheler, 54.
[14] J. B. Lightfoot, *The Apostolic Fathers* ed. J. R. Harmer (Grand Rapids, MI: Baker Book House, 1956), 123-124.
[15] Sheler, 55.
[16] Cf. Rudolph Bultmann, "zôopoieô," in *Theological Dictionary of the New Testament*, 9 vols., ed. Gerhard Kittel, tr. Geoffrey W. Bromiley (Grand Rapids, Michigan: Wm B. Eerdmans, 1964), 2:874.
[17] Sheler, 54.
[18] Lindsay, *Implicit*, 111-128.
[19] "Counter-Gridlock: An Interview with Kenneth Burke" *All Area*, vol 2 (Spring, 1983): 12.
[20] Brendan McKenna, "The Basics: Your Life Insurer is Counting Your Drinks," *Insure.com*.
[21] Janet McConnaughey, "Study: Frequent Drinking Can Help Heart," *Associated Press*, January 9, 2004.
[22] "Drinking Purple Grape Juice Significantly Reduced Oxidation of Bad Cholesterol, According to Study." Available: http://www.welchs.com (3/21/99).
[23] McConnaughey.
[24] "Eating for a Sharper Mind," *Psychology Today*. Available: http://articles.health.msn.com/id/100111228/site/100000000 (10/26/05).

[25] Burton Scott Easton, "Wine, Wine Press," in *The International Standard Bible Encyclopedia*, 5 vols., Ed. James Orr (Grand Rapids: Eerdmans, 1939 [originally published 1929]), 5:3087.

[26] Cf., Lindsay, *Implicit*, 4.

[27] Easton, 5:3087.

[28] Easton, 5:3087.

[29] H. H. Schaeder, "*Nazarênos, Nazôrios*," in *Theological Dictionary of the New Testament*, 9 vols., Ed. Gerhard Kittel, Tr. Geoffrey W. Bromiley (Grand Rapids, MI: Wm. B. Eerdmans Publishing, 1967), 4:878-879.

[30] Easton, 5:3087.

[31] O. Bauernfeind, "*nêphô, nêphalios, eknêphô*," in *Theological Dictionary of the New Testament*, 9 vols., Ed. Gerhard Kittel, Tr. Geoffrey W. Bromiley (Grand Rapids, MI: Wm. B. Eerdmans Publishing, 1967), 4:939.

[32] Stan A. Lindsay, *The Seven Cs of Stress: A Burkean Approach* (Orlando: Say Press, 2004), 37-38.

[33] Jim Catano, "Review of and Commentary on a Book Chapter on the LDS (Mormon) Church's Dietary Code Known as the Word of Wisdom," *Vegasource.com*. Available: http://www.vegasource.com/articles/cantano_review.htm (10/15/2005).

Chapter 6

A Brief History of Jewish, Christian, and Islamic Spiritual Gift Theology

In Chapter 1, I defined spiritual gifts as the receipt of messages from God. This chapter is concerned with tracing the history of those messages Jews, Christians, and Moslems believe they have received from God. I use the title-terminology not in the historiographical sense but in the sense that this is "history" as communicated from presumed spiritually gifted sources. The presumption is that much of the historic detail included would have relied on messages from God to certify its accuracy. Certainly, the Jewish Bible (the Christian Old Testament) accepts the premise that God spoke to and through certain individuals. That God spoke directly to Moses is the fundamental premise upon which Jewish Law is founded. The first five books of the Bible (Genesis, Exodus, Leviticus, Numbers, and Deuteronomy) are known as the Torah, the Hebrew word for Law. According to tradition, Moses is the essential author of all five books.

Genesis provides a rapid-fire account of more than two thousand years of human history prior to Israel's four hundred year sojourn in Egypt. Prior to the account of human history, Genesis offers a one-chapter account of the creation of heaven, earth, and the plant and animal kingdoms. Presumably, if Moses authored the creation and human history accounts, he would need some inspiration from God to certify that his account was accurate. Moses' account has God speaking directly to Adam and Eve, warning them not to eat of the Tree of the Knowledge of Good and Evil. Following their Fall, God interrogates them and communicates to them their respective punishments. To their children, God signifies his preference for the animal sacrifices (of Abel) to the vegetable sacrifices (of Cain). Then, God warns Cain not to kill his brother. After Cain murders Abel, God personally interrogates Cain and tells Cain of his punishment. Later, God speaks to Noah, instructing him to build an Ark. After the Flood, God provides Noah and his family a brief list of laws. Then, God does not appear to communicate with humans until he begins to communicate with Abram, whom God renames Abraham.

In the final three-fourths of Genesis, God communicates frequently with Abraham and his family. God makes covenants with Abraham, his son Isaac, and Isaac's son Jacob, whom God renames Israel. In addition to his son Isaac, Abraham has another son through surrogate marriage with Hagar, the handmaid of his wife Sarah. Nearly three thousand years later, the Prophet Mohammed will assert that Ishmael, this other son of Abraham, is the true heir of God's blessing. Such an assertion from a perspective nearly three thousand years removed would require that Mohammed be inspired by God to be certified historically accurate. Israel has twelve sons who become the patriarchs of the twelve tribes. One of those sons, Joseph, God takes special interest in, communicating with him through dreams. God has a special purpose in mind for Joseph, which takes Joseph to Egypt. His brothers sell him into slavery, but God causes him to rise to leadership in that land. Eventually, God uses Joseph's position of influence to rescue his father and his brothers' families from famine in the land of Canaan as they immigrate to Egypt. The entire account of Genesis, if authored by Moses, would require that Moses be inspired by God to be certified historically accurate. Moses' perspective was four hundred years removed from the most recent historical circumstances he reports on. The suggestion that Joseph may have written some accounts that Moses found in the Egyptian archives would argue for some historiographical accuracy, but none of the first five books make such an assertion.

Exodus begins with the Israelites still in Egypt four hundred years later. Now, the name of Joseph is long forgotten by the Egyptians and the Israelites have become an enslaved people. God raises up an Israelite named Moses, educates him in Pharaoh's palace, and eventually speaks to him through a burning bush, commanding him to lead the Israelites out of Egypt and back to the Promised Land (of Canaan). God infuses Moses with miraculous powers and, upon his successful campaign to lead the children of Israel out of Egypt, God gives Moses the Law on Mount Sinai. The various laws and instructions God gives to Moses are detailed in Exodus, Leviticus, Numbers, and Deuteronomy. These four books pertain to historical issues occurring during the lifetime of Moses. The exception to this observation is the final chapter of Deuteronomy, which discusses the death of Moses. The primary purpose of spiritual gifts theology in the final four books (of Moses) is to certify the accuracy of Moses' messages concerning the Law. The Law (Torah) comes from God.

After Moses, there is a lesser profusion of spiritual giftedness throughout Jewish history. God speaks to Moses' successor Joshua throughout his leadership career in retaking the Land of Canaan. He performs miracles through Joshua—such as causing the Walls of Jericho to fall. After Joshua's death, God inspires and speaks to various judges—Othniel, Deborah, Gideon, Samson, and others. These judges receive miraculous abilities and counsel from God as they defend and protect Israelites in battle.

Although Moses, following God's Law, institutes the priesthood, it is not until later that the High Priest becomes the primary vehicle for God to communicate with humans. After the time of the Judges, God speaks to Samuel, as a child, and calls him into the priesthood. God continues to communicate messages to Samuel throughout his career. Samuel, with God's direction, anoints the first Israelite king, Saul. Then, Samuel, with God's direction anoints King David to replace Saul. The anointing of Samuel as priest (and the sense in which Samuel's anointing also made him a prophet) combined with the anointing of David as King (and the sense in which David's anointing also made him a prophet) introduces a new era in God's communication with humans. The three anointed (messianic) offices—prophet, priest, and king— become God's primary mouthpieces for Israel. The Hebrew word meaning "anointed one" is "messiah." (The Greek word meaning "anointed one," incidentally, is "christ.")

King David, under inspiration from God, writes many psalms. His son King Solomon, with similar inspiration, writes many proverbs. Later kings and priests are not considered to have equal inspiration. Later prophets, however, become the voice of God to Israel. The prophet Nathan was a contemporary of David. Elijah, Elisha, Micaiah, Isaiah, Jeremiah, Ezekiel, and Daniel are the most famous prophets.

Other prophets whose writings are included in the Bible are: Hosea, Joel, Amos, Obadiah, Jonah, Micah, Nahum, Habakkuk, Zephaniah, Haggai, Zechariah, and Malachi. Pharisaic and Rabbinic Judaism and Christianity accept the premise that God spoke through these prophets. Other early Jewish groups such as Sadducees and Samaritans accepted only the inspiration of the Torah. Pharisaic and Rabbinic Judaism believes that God's activity of speaking through prophets, however, ended with the canonical prophets of the Jewish Bible. Ezra the scribe instituted a new way for God to speak to Israel—through reading the Torah aloud to the people. Even though the age of the prophets ended with the canonical Tanach (or Old Testament) for the Jews, Pharisaic and Rabbinic Judaism still allowed for the possibility that God might speak through infants and fools.

Pharisaic and Rabbinic Judaism also taught that God could speak through a Bat Qol (or "mysterious voice"). This type of communication is claimed by the early Christians on a few occasions. When Jesus was baptized, a voice from Heaven said: "This is my son, whom I love; with him I am well pleased" (Matthew 3:17 NIV). When Jesus was transfigured, his disciples were startled by a bright cloud. A voice from the cloud said: "This is my son, whom I love; with him I am well pleased. Listen to him" (Matthew 17:5 NIV). When Saul of Tarsus (who later became the Apostle Paul) was confronted on the road to Damascus, he was blinded by a light from heaven and heard a voice saying: "Saul, Saul, why do you persecute me?" Saul asks who is speaking and the voice responds: "I am Jesus, whom you are persecuting . . . . Now get up and go into the city, and you will be told what you must do" (Acts 9:5-6 NIV).

Christianity also believes that God continued to speak through the visitation of angels (as when Gabriel announced John's and Jesus' births) and through prophets and prophetesses such as Simeon and Anna (Luke 2:25-38) and especially through John the Baptist who lived at the time of Jesus. Christianity also teaches that God spoke through those (such as apostles and prophets) who had received spiritual gifts in the first generation of the church.

According to *Catholic.com*:

> Catholics hold that public or "general" revelation ended at the death of the last apostle (*Catechism of the Catholic Church* 66, 73), but private revelations can be given still—and have been, as Marian apparitions at such places as Fatima and Lourdes testify (*CCC* 67). Such revelations can never correct, supplement, or complete the Christian faith.[1]

Protestantism as defined by Martin Luther claimed that God's communication with humans ended with the canonical Old and New Testaments. Luther's mantra, *"sola scriptura,"* emphasized the point that even the Catholic Church in its various offices were not considered capable of credibly offering new messages from God.

Muslims believe God spoke through their great prophet Mohammed, hundreds of years after the time of Jesus:

> Islam began in Arabia in the 7th century A.D. Its founder and prophet, Mohammed, claimed to have received divine revelations, which were gathered into a collection called the Qur'an (or more commonly known as the Koran), the holy book of Muslims.[2]

As noted earlier, Orthodox Islam has always taught that Mohammed was the final prophet of God. An unorthodox Moslem sect, Farrakhan's group, has taught that "Allah appeared in the Person of Master W. Fard Muhammad" and that Elijah Muhammad was the final prophet instead of Mohammed of Arabia.[3]

Mormons believe God spoke and continues to speak through their prophets. Mormons place the scriptures received by their founder and prophet Joseph Smith—The Book of Mormon—on a par with the Old and New Testaments. The current president and prophet of the Mormon Church, Gordon B. Hinckley, authored a booklet entitled *What of the Mormons?* In the booklet, he claims that Mormons "are no closer to Protestantism than they are to Catholicism." This is particularly true with regard to continuing revelations:

> [C]ontinuing revelations are not exceptions to Mormon practice. "We believe all that God has revealed, all that he does now reveal, and we believe that he will yet reveal many great and important things"—this is the ninth article of faith for Mormons and is an official statement of doctrine.
>
> Hinckley notes that "Christians and Jews generally maintain that God revealed himself and directed chosen men in ancient times. Mormons maintain that the need for divine guidance is as great or greater in our modern, complex world as it was in the comparatively simple times of the Hebrews." Thus, revelation continues.[4]

Similar to the Mormons, charismatic Christians believe spiritual gifts, including prophecy, are available for Christians today. The primary difference between Mormons and Charismatics is that Mormons have fewer prophets than do Charismatics. A finite number of authoritative

Mormon prophets have arisen since the religion was founded by Joseph Smith in 1830. Assertions of early rampant Mormon spiritual giftedness exist, however: "The first Mormons were very charismatic. They spoke in tongues on a regular basis (weekly and sometimes daily). Prophecy by lay members was common as was healing by the laying on of hands."[5] Although widely experienced spiritual gifts existed early among Mormons, such wide-open theology has been curtailed at this point in history. By contrast, even to this day, countless prophets and prophetesses have arisen and continue to arise among charismatics. Indeed, every true Christian is believed to possess some spiritual gift, according to charismatics.

To most Pentecostals, the Charismatic Movement began in 1906, according to a website of the University of Virginia:

> [T]he history of the . . . Pentecostal tradition began with Charles Parham in Topeka, Kansas and/or at the Azusa revival led by William J. Seymour. . . . [O]ften neglected . . . are the number of more modest events that in some way set the stage for . . . Azuza.
>
> As early as 1831, in London, England, Edward Erving . . . led parishioners in a prayer . . . [that] resulted in them receiving the gift of tongues and prophecy. . . . [A]t Charles Finney's revivals, some of his followers began to re-think their Holiness definition of Holy Spirit baptism. During the 1870s . . . the notion of the baptism being more of an *anointing* rather than a cleansing (. . . the Holiness definition) was developed . . . .
>
> As the beginning of the 20th century approached . . . scattered incidences of people speaking in tongues and . . . gifts, signs and wonders [resulted] . . . .
>
> In . . . 1900, . . . Parham began the Bethel Bible College in Topeka . . . . [H]e required that [his students] investigate the 'baptism of the Spirit" . . . [and] the students immediately began to seek the baptism with the evidence of speaking with other tongues. . . .
>
> [I]n 1906 . . . in Los Angeles . . . African-American preacher William J. Seymour . . . opened the historic meeting . . . at 312 Azusa Street. . . . [T]housands sought to be baptized in the Spirit with the evidence of speaking in tongues and . . . other Holy Spirit manifestations.
>
> . . . Pentecostalism spread rapidly . . . becoming a major force in Christendom . . . noted for it's [*sic*] integration of both White and African-American Christian traditions.[6]

Brian Hughes, writing from a Catholic perspective, acknowledges the legitimacy of the current "official" Catholic "Charismatic movement, which is under the watchful eye and guiding hand of the Church's Magisterium," but writes at length about two fairly ancient charismatic movements that occurred prior to the Protestant Reformation, the Montanists and the Joachimists:

> One of the first, and certainly the most notorious of the early "enthusiast" challenges to Church authority, originated in Phrygia in the last years of the second century, and centered around the self styled prophet Montanus, who claimed to be the voice of the newly descended Paraclete, along with his two "prophetesses" Prisca . . . and Maxilla. . . . Eusebius is quoting an anonymous writer of the second century . . .
> "Montanus . . . became beside himself . . . in a sort of frenzy and ecstasy, he raved and began to babble and utter strange things . . . . Some . . . rebuked him as one . . . that was under the control of a demon . . . But others imagining themselves possessed of the Holy Spirit and of prophetic gifts."
> . . . The last remaining adherents of the sect were reconciled to the Catholic Church by St. Augustine in the fourth century.
> . . . Joachim of Flora was a Cistercian monk . . . who lived during the twelfth and thirteenth centuries. . . . Joachim never considered himself a prophet, merely a scriptural exegete. But some of his followers . . . speculated wildly about the nature of the "age of the Holy Spirit" to the point of predicting that . . . "everyone would possess the fullness of the Spirit."[7]

Pointing also to groups outside of Catholicism, such as the Camisards, the Brethren of the Free Spirit, Ranters, Quakers, Shakers, and the Mormons, Hughes sees the recent growth of charismatics in the Catholic Church as the result of many factors. The Camisards were French Protestant prophets of the seventeenth century. They prophesied, had visions, spoke in tongues, and advocated using armed force against the Catholic Church.

At the first of the eighteenth century, a Catholic group known as the Convulsionary Jansenists took refuge in the cemetery of St. Medard in Paris. There, a paralytic experienced "extremely violent movements." Individuals were falling and swallowing pebbles, glass, and live coals. There was groaning, singing, shrieking, and prophesying. One person hopped on one leg, proclaiming that his other (shorter) leg was growing.

These more ancient spiritual gifts theologies may have had some influence on the modern Charismatic Movement, but Hughes thinks the movement developed in the nineteenth century as speaking in tongues "spread rapidly to the various branches of the 'Holiness movement.'"[8] The teaching of Wesley (especially in the more traditional Wesleyan Methodist churches) of a "second experience of sanctification" metamorphosed into the Pentecostal "Baptism in the Holy Spirit." Until the 1960s, there were plenty of Pentecostal churches, but the movement had not generally infected other Christian denominations. Yet, by the Second Vatican Council, a form of spiritual gifts theology had become a part of the Catholic Church. By the end of the twentieth century, spiritual gifts theology had become a part of almost the entire Christian world. The University of Virginia website (mentioned earlier) reports:

> It was not until mid-way through the century that Pentecostal ideas and style began to surface in mainline Protestant churches . . . . Beginning officially in 1960, Dennis Bennett, priest over an Episcopalian congregation in Van Nuys, California announced that he had spoken in tongues. This movement soon spread into a network of independent charismatic churches and organizations which included Baptists, Lutherans, Presbyterians, Episcopalians, Methodists and Catholics, which all came to enjoy this outburst of speaking in tongues.[9]

My own religious heritage was one of the longer holdouts. I recall the upheaval that occurred as the Charismatic Movement became a part of my own local congregation. I had received my bachelor's degree from a Christian college, in 1971. During my years at the college, I met a few individuals who informed me that they had spoken in tongues. In the spirit of open-mindedness, I raised a question during a Church History course, taught by one of the founders of the college. The instructor had commented that I Corinthians 13:8 predicted a cessation of the spiritual gifts of prophecy and tongues. I suggested that the Greek terminology indicating cessation could have other meanings. My comments were met with outrage on the instructor's part. It was clear to me and to everyone else in the class that modern-day spiritual gifts were not considered valid by that college and my religious heritage. Actually, I agree with the noncharismatic views of the instructor.

Twenty years later, and seemingly out-of-the-blue to me, my local congregation, in 1992, conducted a spiritual gifts inventory as a part of a church growth plan for the congregation. Two other former elders of the church and I asked for a meeting with the current elders to discuss spiritual gifts theology. We three former elders resisted this introduction of spiritual gifts theology into our congregation. The current eldership wanted to videotape the encounter. The videotape records that the current eldership had decided in advance that they would not discuss the Bible in their meeting with us. Instead, the current eldership totally rejected our position. Nearly half the members left the church.

That event served as a wake-up call to me. In the years following that upheaval, I have noticed that, with very few exceptions, my entire religious heritage has been infected with spiritual gifts theology. Furthermore, in the last twenty years, I have visited congregations from a wide variety of other denominations. Virtually all of them accept spiritual gifts theology to some extent.

This situation is dangerous. I offered examples of the dangers in Chapter 2:

> In November of 1978, members of the People's Temple, led by Jim Jones and transplanted from San Francisco to South America, killed Congressman Leo Ryan and four others before committing mass suicide in their compound. In October of 1994, in Cheiry and Les Granges, Switzerland, forty-eight members of a Swiss cult called the Order of the Solar Tradition became victims of a mass murder-suicide. ... [T]he Swiss cult ... draws on Roman Catholicism and predicts the end of the world." In March of 1997, thirty-nine members of the Heaven's Gate cult in southern California shed their "vehicles" (earth-bound bodies) by committing mass suicide in order to hitch a ride on the chariot that was coming in the tail of the Hale-Bopp comet. Applewhite, the leader of the Heaven's Gate cult, identified somewhat with the Branch Davidians of Waco, Texas. ... In April of 1993, eighty-six persons died in a fire at the Branch Davidian compound after a fifty-one-day standoff with federal agents.

Various religions have found it necessary to argue for the cessation of spiritual gifts such as prophecy at various points throughout history. These religions have turned from expecting new messages from God to examining and interpreting their various canons of inspired scripture. Most current psychotic entelechies resulting from religion have resulted from the view that God continues to speak (and give new messages) to the spiritually gifted of each generation.

Notes

[1] "Distinctive Beliefs of the Mormon Church," *Catholic Answers*. Available: http://www.catholic.com/library/Distinctive_Beliefs_of_Mormon.asp (10/15/05).
[2] "What is Islam?" Available: http://www.lhmint.org/whowillteach/what is_print.htm (9/26/05).
[3] Richard N. Ostling, "If It Holds, New Muslim Unity Could Remake America's Religious Landscape," *Religious Studies News, AAR Edition* 16, no. 3 (2001): 8.
[4] "Distinctive Beliefs."
[5] J. Stapley reply to D. Bell, "Teach Me Some Church History #2," *The Millennial Star* 8/25/05. Available: http://www.millennialstar.org/index.php /2005/08/25/teach_me_some_church_history_2 (10/17/05).
[6] "Pentecostalism," *Religious Movements*. Available: http://religiousmovements.lib.virginia.edu/nrms/penta.html (10/17/05).
[7] Brian Hughes, "History of Charismatic Movement." Available: http://www.unitypublishing.com/Hist-of-Char.html (10/17/05).
[8] Hughes (10/17/05).
[9] "Pentecostalism" (10/17/05).

Chapter 7

An Examination of New Testament Spiritual Gift Theology

I have recommended that Muslims supply the recalcitrance to bin Laden's psychotic entelechy, as a Moslem website proposed: "Simply put, not only do Muslims need to join the war against terror, we need to take the lead in this war."[1] I agreed: "This psychotic entelechy can only be cured by Muslims like these." I noted, in the Waco case, that the cure is best administered by someone who shares normal standards with the psychotic:

> The negotiators who seemed to be most successful in gaining the trust of Koresh were biblical scholars--James Tabor and Philip Arnold. According to Tabor, these two scholars were genuinely concerned for the physical well being of cult members.[2]

Throughout my discussion of psychotic entelechy, I have maintained a Burkean principle:

> "For one can cure a psychosis only by appealing to some aspect of the psychosis. The cure must bear notable affinities with the disease: all effective medicines are potential poisons" (PC 126). Burke is . . . looking for those "normal standards" that even psychotics still possess.

> Once normal standards are located within the system of the psychotic, the process of discounting may begin.

Therefore, when it comes to the dangers posed by spiritual gifts theology in Christianity, I step forward. As an Evangelical Christian, I agree with most of the normal standards in this system. How could I ask Muslims to assume the real physical dangers of resisting bin Laden's brand of Islam, if I am unwilling to assume the cultural and social risks of resisting members of my own religion? Just as I offered recalcitrance to Evangelical Christians who increasingly embrace the entelechy of drinking alcoholic beverages in Chapter 5, I offer the following recalcitrance to Evangelical Christians who increasingly embrace the entelechy of modern-day Spiritual Gifts Theology.

Spirit=Angel=Word

Muslims do not refer to the Holy Spirit. (Yet, the Koran opposes a Trinity of God, Jesus, and Mary, rather than specifically a Trinity of God, Jesus, and Holy Spirit). For Muslims, God spoke to the Prophet Mohammed through the angel Jibril (= Gabriel). A similar method was used by God to speak to Abraham in the Old Testament and to Joseph, Mary, and Zechariah in the New Testament, among others. Angels spoke the word of God to humans in these instances, so the result was the same as if the humans receiving the word of God had been prophets. In discussing his confusion regarding the interchangeable use of the terms "spirit," "angel," and "word" by John, the author of the New Testament book of Revelation, G. B. Caird states:

> It is important for our understanding of John's kaleidoscopic imagery to notice that the seven stars do not mean in this letter [to Sardis] what they meant in the letter to Ephesus. There they were the angels of the churches, here they are the sevenfold Spirit of God; and since the Spirit, in speaking to the churches, addresses the angels of the churches, the two are clearly not to be identified. The one symbol does double service.[2]

Caird's "sevenfold Spirit of God" terminology should be examined more closely. Caird wants to make John's terminology stand for the Holy Spirit in a Trinitarian sense. Yet, it appears that John is defining the seven stars as the seven spirits of God in the letter to Sardis, whereas they are "angels" of the seven churches, earlier. Furthermore, there is that troublesome term "spirit" saying things "to the churches." I offer an explanation that makes sense out of John's interchangeable use of these terms that was available to John in the first century. In *Revelation: The Human Drama*,[3] I explain:

> George Kennedy credits Stoic grammatical studies for producing "the theory of tropes, which is first expressly mentioned in a rhetorical treatise by Cicero (*Brutus* 69)."[4] Burke, in his theorizing, narrows the list of tropes from the eight of the "grammatical treatises" to four master tropes--metaphor, metonymy, synecdoche, and irony (GM 503). . . . Of these four, Burke shows a marked preference for synecdoche.
>
> Burke claims that synecdoche is the key trope for handling matters of representation . . . . Burke . . . holds "that an anecdote, to be truly representative, must be synecdochic . . . or in other words, it must be a *part for the whole* . . . ." (GM 326, emphasis Burke's).
>
> . . . Even if John is not to be viewed as *consciously and deliberately* using a synecdochic art, by the time John wrote, synecdoche was an explicit trope used by rhetoricians. It may have been either an intuitive or a deliberate form of language use for John.[5] Certainly, Jews of John's time thought of God's word (a linguistic, not "physical" concept) from a synecdochic perspective.
>
> G. F. Moore links the terms of Caird's conundrum of the "seven stars" together quite easily. In his chapter entitled, "The Word of God. The Spirit," Moore states, "God's will is made known or effectuated in the world not only through personal agents (*angels*), but directly by his *word* or by his *spirit*" (emphases mine).[6] Here all three terms of Caird's puzzle fit neatly together. If the seven stars represent "angels," then "angels" are a part of the whole. If the stars "represent" "spirits of God," then spirits are a part of the whole. If "the spirit" is "say[ing]" things to the churches, then what "the spirit says" (or in other words, the word) is a part of the whole.
>
> For John, as for other Jews of his generation, a concept of a whole from which parts spring up and to which they return is the concept of the Nehar di-Nur (the "stream of fire"). Louis Ginzberg states: "Thus there are angels who spring up daily out of the stream Dinur (='stream of fire'; comp. Dan. 7.10); they praise God, and then disappear. Out of every word uttered by God angels are created."[7]

To put it more succinctly, angels equal spirits equal the spirit of God equals the word of God. God's spirit (the Holy Spirit) is God's method of speaking to humans. Any message delivered to humans from God would have to be considered miraculous, but Kenneth Burke makes a distinction between two types of messages (Word and word) that may come from God.

Word vs. word

In *Implicit Rhetoric*, I outline Burke's differentiation between "Word" and "word":

> In the first chapter of *Rhetoric of Religion* (hereafter, RR), Burke, referring to John's *Logos* hymn, draws analogies between "'words' (lower case) and 'The Word' (in capitals)" (RR 11). . . .
> Burke correctly sees . . . "equally relevant passages . . . such as the creative fiat of Genesis 1:3 ('And God said, Let there be light'), or Psalms 33:9: 'He spoke, and it was done; he commanded, and it stood fast'" (RR 11). Those steeped in Judeo-Christian culture may readily understand that the authoritative scriptures of their culture credit "Word"--*i.e.*, the utterance of God--with tremendous power.
> . . . Burke is suggesting that the theological distinctions between "word" and "The Word" . . . make a nice entry to discussions of the power to affect humans. . . .
> In Burke's third analogy in RR based upon the "Word" vs. "word" distinction, he identifies the primary ground upon which such a distinction can be made--the negative. . . . (that is, viewing the matter in terms of "action"), one should begin with the *hortatory* negative, the negative of command, as with the "Thou shalt not's" of the Decalogue. (RR 20)
> Clearly implied in any "Thou shalt not" is the element of free will or choice. . . .
> One distinction between "word" and "Word" may . . . be seen. "Word" affects motion; "word" affects action. Since Isaiah 55:11 claims that God's Word "will not return to [God] empty, but will accomplish what [God] desire[s] and achieve the purpose for which [God] sent it," it should be classified as that type of "Word" which affects motion. Yet, to the extent that any "word" attempts to motivate human conduct (in a situation where there is free will), that "word" is operating in the realm of action. Having this distinction in mind, I should point out that, although God's utterance is presented as "Word" in the case of the creative fiat, God's utterance might be understood as "word" in the case of the Decalogue. In the first instance, there is no implicit free will attributed to that which is created. In the second instance, humans to whom the Ten Commandments are directed are implicitly credited with free will.[8]

This distinction between Word and word applies to spiritual gifts theology. Capitalized Word refers to God's all-powerful control over nature. If God speaks to the waters and commands the waters to bring forth living things, as alluded to in John's Logos Hymn, the waters obey. Effectively, the power of capitalized Word is miraculous power. On the other hand, when God uses lower-case word, as in the Decalogue, He exerts no more power than the power of persuasion. Capitalized Word never fails to accomplish its purpose. Lower-case word frequently fails to accomplish its purpose. When Adam and Eve were instructed not to eat of the Tree of Knowledge of Good and Evil, God's persuasive word failed to accomplish its objective. Adam and Eve ate anyway. Nevertheless, the disobedience of Adam and Eve did not invalidate the truth or importance of God's command.

Spiritual gifts belong in one sense to the category of capitalized Word. When God tells Noah there will be a flood, a flood occurs. When God tells Abraham he will be the father of many nations, he has children in his old age. When God promises Moses he will free the children of Israel from Egyptian bondage, ten plagues on Egypt ensue. The waters of the Red Sea dry up; manna falls from heaven. When God tells Joshua the walls of Jericho will fall once they have marched the appropriate number of times around the city, the walls fall. When God tells David he will become king, history falls neatly into place.

In the New Testament, when God (through Gabriel) promises Mary that she will become pregnant as a virgin, the virgin birth occurs. This miraculous capitalized Word becomes prominent in the life of Jesus. He speaks the Word and water is changed to wine, a meal for one child feeds five thousand, storms at sea are calmed, and Lazarus is raised from the dead. When Jesus speaks capitalized Word, nature obeys.

On the other hand, Jesus frequently spoke lower-case word. He asked his disciples to stay awake and pray with him, but they slept anyway. In his sermon on the mount, he offered explicit and implicit hortatory negatives:

- Do not murder; do not be angry with your brother; do not call him a fool (Matthew 5:21-22).
- Do not commit adultery; do not look at a woman lustfully (Matthew 5:27-28).
- Do not divorce your wife except for the cause of fornication (Matthew 5:32)

- Do not break your oaths; do not swear at all (Matthew 5:33-36).
- Do not resist an evil person; do not turn away a borrower (Matthew 5:39-42).
- Do not hate your enemies (Matthew 5:43-44).
- Do not do your acts of righteousness before men, to be seen by them (Matthew 6:1-4).
- Do not pray on the street corners like the hypocrites (Matthew 6:5).
- Do not disfigure your faces when you fast (Matthew 6:16-17).
- Do not store up treasures on earth (Matthew 6:19).
- Do not worry (Matthew 6:25-34).
- Do not judge (Matthew 7:1).
- Do not give what is holy to dogs; do not cast pearls to swine (Matthew 7:6).

Clearly, his followers did not and have not always obeyed all of these hortatory negatives. Thus, his persuasion directed toward humans (or lower-case word) frequently fails. Nevertheless, his lower-case word is important. Its truth is not invalidated by virtue of the disobedience of his audience.

Spiritual gifts theology implies a miraculous empowerment (capitalized Word). It is not "natural" to think of God speaking to humans on a personal basis. His very act of speaking to humans is supernatural. On the other hand, spiritual gifts theology implies a persuasive or hortatory element (lower-case word). The messages God gives are often hortatory. Free will is implicit. Humans have the power to either obey or disobey any lower-case words (or commands). Hence, the Bible may make a distinction between individuals (such as the first deacons) who are "full of the Spirit" (Acts 6:3, 5) and individuals such as the apostles on the day of Pentecost who are "filled with the Spirit and began to speak in other tongues as the Spirit enabled them" (Acts 2:4). Those who are "full of the Spirit" are probably individuals who are very familiar with the teachings of God. Those who are "filled with the Spirit" are at that time actually in the process of *receiving* messages from God. In addition to using the mediation of angels and mysterious voices, God (in the New Testament period) used a variety of methods to communicate with humans. These methods are termed "spiritual gifts" by the apostle Paul. Yet, each method or gift was designed to provide communication from God.

An Examination of New Testament Spiritual Gifts Theology . 111

The spiritual gifts listed by the apostle Paul in three separate writings feature prophets prominently (Romans 12:6, I Corinthians 12:28, Ephesians 4:11). In the last two lists, prophets are listed second only to apostles. In the first list, apostles are not mentioned; prophets are listed first. Both apostles and prophets had miraculous powers. Their messages, whether written or spoken, were considered by the Church to have come from God just as surely as the messages of Moses, Elijah, and David did. The early Christians met weekly to devote themselves not to the Torah (as the Jews did in the Synagogue), but to the apostles' doctrine (Acts 2:42). Of the twenty-seven books in the New Testament canon, at least seventeen were thought to have been authored by apostles. The Book of Revelation was written by a prophet. Luke and Acts were both written by the evangelist Luke, and Mark is attributed to the evangelist John Mark. In the Ephesians 4:11 list, evangelists are mentioned as (spiritually) gifted immediately following apostles and prophets.

Hebrews and the three epistles of John were at one time thought to have been authored by the apostles Paul and John, respectively. None of the four epistles make the claim of apostolic authorship, however. Second and Third John claim to be written by "The Elder." If he is not the apostle John himself, the Elder is probably a prominent disciple of the apostle John. Given its Pauline elements, Hebrews may well have been written by a prominent disciple of the apostle Paul. James and Jude claim to have been written by Jesus' physical relatives: his brothers. All of the authors of New Testament books not authored by apostles or prophets could easily be authored by individuals who had other spiritual gifts. Paul seems to assert that he conveyed a spiritual gift of prophecy to Timothy at the time he laid hands on him to set him apart for eldership (I Timothy 4:14 and II Timothy 1:6). It is possible that the Elder of the epistles of John (if not the apostle John) also received a spiritual gift at his ordination as elder. The author of Hebrews claims to be a companion of Timothy (Hebrews 13:23). Hence, some think Paul is the author. If the author is not Paul, he may have received a spiritual gift from Paul as Timothy did. Jesus' brother James is depicted in Acts 15 as the presider among the apostles in Jerusalem. Paul lists James along with Peter and John as the pillars of the Jerusalem church (Galatians 2:9). Apparently, James had some form of inspiration, as his brother Jude may have.

The basis upon which Christians believe the books of the New Testament were inspired of God is that all books were written by

authors who had spiritual gifts. Various lists of spiritual gifts mentioned in the New Testament include:
- Apostles (I Corinthians 12:28-29, Ephesians 14:11),
- Prophets (Romans 12:6, I Corinthians 12:10, 28-29, 14:1-40, Ephesians 14:11),
- Evangelists (Ephesians 14:11),
- Teachers (I Corinthians 12:28-29, 14:6, Ephesians 14:11),
- Healers (I Corinthians 12:9, 28-29),
- Miracle workers (I Corinthians 12:10, 28-29),
- Pastors (Ephesians 14:11),
- Deacons/servants (Romans 12:7),
- Encouragers (Romans 12:8),
- Contributors to the needs of others (Romans 12:8),
- Leaders (Romans 12:8),
- Mercy givers (Romans 12:8),
- Helpers of others (I Corinthians 12:28),
- Administrators (I Corinthians 12:28),
- Revealer (I Corinthians 14:6)
- Messengers of wisdom (I Corinthians 12:8),
- Messengers of knowledge (I Corinthians 12:8, 14:6),
- Believers--with the gift of faith (I Corinthians 12:9)
- Speakers in tongues (I Corinthians 12:10, 28-30, 14:1-40), and
- Interpreters of tongues (I Corinthians 12:10, 30).

Also listed by Paul among the spiritual gifts in Romans 12:7, some of the early deacons on whom the apostles laid hands were apparently prophets, healers, and miracle workers, as well (Acts 7:56, 8:5-7, 13). Some of the abilities listed as spiritual gifts could be interpreted as the equivalent of typical aptitudes without respect to any miraculous abilities. Many teachers, pastors, servants, encouragers, contributors, leaders, mercy givers, helpers, administrators, and believers have existed throughout the history of mankind without respect to any specific spiritual giftedness. But, then, what would be the point of calling them spiritual gifts? The miraculous element is implicit in the way Paul discusses spiritual gifts. All spiritual gifts should be understood as the product of capitalized Word, even though the messages of those so gifted were frequently lower-case word.

While this miraculous principle is important to Christians to establish the authority of the New Testament, the church-wide universalization of the principle renders all Christians miracle workers. It suggests that any visions or voices a given Christian sees or hears come from God. This is dangerous. It has the potential of producing many situations similar to the following:

> A woman who tossed her young children off a pier into San Francisco Bay near Fishermen's Wharf . . . was booked on three counts of assault on a child with great bodily injury . . . . Lashaun Harris told authorities that voices had told her to throw her children into the water, the *San Francisco Chronicle* reported.[9]

Of course, most Christians who teach modern-day gifts theology will usually be able to distinguish between good and evil messages purportedly coming from God. The evil messages they will readily attribute to Satan. They will identify the messengers of evil as false prophets. But, will they always? What if a Christian experiencing voices with messages similar to those heard by Lashaun Harris believes s/he is being tested by God, as was Abraham when God asked him to sacrifice his son Isaac? How could that Christian afford to disobey God's message? Would such disobedience cause him or her to forfeit his or her relationship with God? His or her salvation? What if the entire theology of modern-day spiritual gifts is mistaken? There are good reasons to believe that it is. Christians will do well to obey the lower-case words of God as revealed in their scriptures. They should be less inclined to believe the capitalized Words they personally receive through miraculous inspiration.

Method of Conferring Spiritual Gifts

If spiritual gifts provide miraculous messages from God, it is important to know how they are conferred. In order to determine the method of conferral, a fundamental observation made by Kenneth Burke must be appreciated: The human "is the symbol-using (symbol-making, symbol-misusing) animal" (LSA 16). Burke expands:

> In school, as they go from class to class, students turn from one idiom to another. The various courses in the curriculum are in effect but so many different terminologies. . . . [T]he whole overall "picture" is but a construct of our symbol systems.
>
> . . .

> In referring to the misuse of symbols ... A fundamental resource "natural" to symbolism is *substitution*. For instance, we can paraphrase a statement; if you don't get it one way, we can try another way. We translate English into French, Fahrenheit into Centigrade, or use the Greek letter *pi* to designate the ratio of the circumference of a circle to its diameter. (LSA 5-7)

Each individual, regardless of how well that individual understands the language or culture into which he or she was born, has his or her own symbol system. No two individuals share the same symbol system. My symbol (or terminology) for a given phenomenon may or may not match yours. Burke states: "[T]here will be as many different world views in human history as there are people .... [N]o one's 'personal equations' are quite identical with anyone else's" (LSA 52). Yet, the phenomenon to which our different terminologies refer may be precisely the same.

On that basis, I assert that the phenomenon referred to by the apostle Paul as "spiritual gifts" may be referred to by other New Testament writers with different terminology. While never using the phrase "spiritual gifts," Luke points out in Acts: "The apostles performed many miraculous signs and wonders among the people. ... Crowds gathered ... bringing their sick and those tormented by evil spirits, and all of them were healed" (Acts 5:12, 16).

The Laying On of Apostles' Hands

In the early period of the church, seven deacons were chosen to assist the apostles. Luke states: "They presented these men to the apostles, who prayed and laid their hands on them" (Acts 6:6). Afterwards, one of those deacons, "Stephen ... did great wonders and miraculous signs among the people" (Acts 6:8). Another of the deacons, "Philip went down to a city in Samaria ... the crowds heard Philip and saw the miraculous signs he did .... [E]vil spirits came out of many, and many paralytics and cripples were healed" (Acts 8:5-7). Although Luke never refers to these special abilities of the apostles and deacons as "spiritual gifts," their abilities seem to be identical to the abilities of the healers and miracle workers in Paul's lists of spiritual gifts.

Although Philip baptized many Samaritans, Philip was the only Christian in Samaria capable of performing miraculous works. Luke states: "[T]he Holy Spirit had not yet come upon any of them; they had simply been baptized into the name of the Lord Jesus. Then Peter and John placed their hands on them, and they received the Holy Spirit" (Acts 8:16-17). One must assume that receiving the Holy Spirit in Luke's terminology means that the Samaritan Christians were capable of miraculous works, as was Philip. A sorcerer named Simon noticed the method by which these gifts were transferred: "When Simon saw that the Spirit was given at the laying on of the apostles' hands, he offered them money and said, 'Give me also this ability so that everyone on whom I lay my hands may receive the Holy Spirit'" (Acts 8:18-19). His request was denied.

The laying on of the hands of an apostle seems to be the method by which spiritual gifts were conferred in the apostle Paul's writings. In Romans 1:11, Paul tells the Romans: "I long to see you so that I may impart to you some spiritual gift." Why was it necessary for the apostle to see the Romans in order to confer spiritual gifts? Could he not just pray that they would receive spiritual gifts? Apparently not. Did they not automatically receive spiritual gifts upon being baptized? The Samaritans who were baptized by the deacon Philip did not receive spiritual gifts at baptism. The Roman church was in a unique position. Apparently, some Roman Christians *did* have spiritual gifts or Paul would not have written in the twelfth chapter of his epistle:

> We have different gifts, according to the grace given us. If a man's gift is prophesying, let him use it in proportion to his faith. If it is serving, let him serve; if it is teaching, let him teach; if it is encouraging, let him encourage; if it is contributing to the needs of others, let him give generously; if it is leadership, let him govern diligently; if it is showing mercy, let him do it cheerfully. (Romans 12:6-8)

Luke informs us that Jews and proselytes from Rome were in Jerusalem on the day of Pentecost (Acts 2:10-11). Some of these Romans were surely converted to Christianity by the apostles on that day. It is fair to assume that some of them received the laying on of the hands of apostles.

In Acts 19, Luke records another incident in which an apostle laid hands on some individuals and they received spiritual gifts. Paul discovered at Ephesus some disciples who had received only the baptism of repentance taught by John the Baptist, not Christian baptism. They were unaware of any Holy Spirit connection. Paul had them rebaptized in the name of Jesus. After the baptism, Luke reports: "When Paul laid his hands on them, the Holy Spirit came on them, and they spoke in tongues and prophesied" (Acts 19:6). Observing Luke's symbol system, the terminology he used in Acts 19--"receiving the Holy Spirit" and "the Holy Spirit coming on" individuals—is identical to the terminology he used in Acts 8:16-17, at which time the apostles Peter and John laid their hands on the first Samaritan Christians after their baptism. In the Acts 8 text, Simon the Sorcerer observed that (miraculous) gifts were given by the laying on of apostles' hands (Acts 8:18). Speaking in tongues is not clearly defined in the Acts 19 instance. Perhaps, it was similar to the spiritual gift of prophecy discussed by Paul in I Corinthians 12-14. Prophecy, which is also mentioned as a result of the laying on of Paul's hands in Acts 19, is definitely a spiritual gift.

Paul informs Timothy that Timothy's spiritual gift was conferred when Paul laid hands on him: "For this reason I remind you to fan into flame the gift of God, which is in you through the laying on of my hands" (II Timothy 1:6). Some have suggested, based on I Timothy 4:14, that spiritual gifts were conferred by the laying on of the hands of non-apostles. Paul tells Timothy: "Do not neglect your gift, which was given to you through prophecy by the laying on of the hands of eldership." The proposed interpretation suggests that the gift was conferred when the body of elders laid their hands on Timothy. While that interpretation of the text is possible, it is also possible that the text should be interpreted: The prophetic gift was conferred on Timothy when Timothy was set apart as an elder through the laying on of hands. II Timothy 1:6 argues strongly for this second interpretation. Paul clearly tells Timothy his gift was conferred when Paul laid hands on him.

If we accept this second interpretation, we do not have a single instance in the entire New Testament of someone receiving a "spiritual gift" except by the laying on of an apostle's hands. This observation, of course, does not apply to the conferral of the gift of apostleship. We will consider the method of conferring the gift of apostleship shortly. Before doing that, we look at another area of confusion: Does the "baptism with the Holy Spirit" refer to the conferring of a spiritual gift?

Baptism with the Holy Spirit

Luke, the author of Luke-Acts quotes John the Baptist, referring to the coming of Jesus: "I baptize you with water, but one mightier than I will come, whose sandals I am not worthy to untie. He will baptize you with the Holy Spirit and with fire" (Luke 3:16). Later, following Jesus' resurrection, Luke recalls this prophecy by quoting Jesus, addressing the apostles he had chosen, before his ascension: "Do not leave Jerusalem, but wait for the gift my Father promised, about which you have heard me speak. For John baptized with water, but in a few days, you will be baptized with the Holy Spirit" (Acts 1:4-5). That Luke understands that *the chosen apostles* (not to all Christians) were those to whom this promise of a baptism with the Holy Spirit is directed is clear from Acts 1:3 and 1:12-2:4.

The signs of the baptism with the Holy Spirit were:
- A sound like a rushing wind (Acts 2:2),
- The appearance of something like tongues of fire that separated and rested on each of the apostles (Acts 2:3), and
- The ability to speak in other tongues as the Spirit gave each apostle the ability (Acts 2:4).

This phenomenon is not identical to the spiritual gift of speaking in tongues as described by Paul. Luke describes the baptism with the Holy Spirit tongues phenomenon:

> Jews from every nation . . . came together in amazement, because each one heard [the apostles] speaking in his own . . . native language . . . Parthians, Medes and Elamites, dwellers of Mesopotamia, Judea and Cappadocia, Pontus and Asia, Phrygia and Pamphylia, Egypt and parts of Libya near Cyrene, visitors from Rome . . . Cretans and Arabs (Acts 2:5-11)

Conversely, in Paul's description of the spiritual gift of tongues, no one understands what is being said except for those who have the miraculous gift of interpretation of tongues. The language of tongues is not everyone's native language; rather, it is a completely foreign language to the hearers:

> Now, brothers, if I . . . speak in tongues, what good will I be to you? . . . So it is with you. Unless you speak intelligible words with your tongue,

> how will anyone know what you are saying? You will just be speaking into the air. . . . If then, I do not grasp the meaning of what someone is saying, I am a foreigner to the speaker, and he is a foreigner to me. . . . I speak in tongues more than you all, but in the church, I would rather speak five intelligible words to instruct others than ten thousand words in a tongue. (I Corinthians 14:6-19)

Furthermore, in Paul's description of the spiritual gift of tongues, there is no mention of sounds like rushing winds or visual tongues of fire.

The baptism with the Holy Spirit is not the gift of tongues. As Luke describes the phenomenon, it occurred only on the day of Pentecost and on one other occasion—at the conversion of the first Gentiles to Christianity. Luke is explicit:

> As I [Peter] began to speak, the Holy Spirit came on them [the Gentiles] as he had come on us [the apostles] at the beginning [Pentecost]. Then I remembered what the Lord had said: "John baptized with water, but you will be baptized with the Holy Spirit. (Acts 11:15-16)

Unfortunately, Luke does not specify all of the details of the phenomenon on this occasion, but he indicates that it was the same phenomenon that had occurred when the apostles were baptized with the Holy Spirit. On this occasion, however, we do know that there was speaking in tongues on the part of the gentiles and that the Jewish Christians understood their language: "The circumcised believers who had come with Peter . . . heard them speaking in tongues and praising God" (Acts 10:45-46). Had they been speaking in the spiritual gift of tongues, no one would have known that they were "praising God."

No other mention of a baptism with the Holy Spirit is mentioned in the entire New Testament, and no phenomenon with the three signs of the baptism with the Holy Spirit is described elsewhere under different terminology. The baptism with the Holy Spirit is not the method by which spiritual gifts were conferred in the New Testament. Spiritual gifts were conferred by the laying on of apostles' hands. So, the question arises: How does one become an apostle?

Requirements for Becoming an Apostle

According to the Revelation to John, Jesus praises the church at Ephesus for testing "those who claim to be apostles but are not" (Revelation 2:2). Revelation, however, does not spell out how false apostles are detected. Luke's writings identified the baptism with the Holy Spirit and the method by which spiritual gifts were conferred—by the laying on of apostles' hands. It is suitable, then, that we turn to Luke for information regarding how men became apostles.

In Acts 1:12-2:4 (a passage cited earlier to show that *the chosen apostles* were those to whom the promise of a baptism with the Holy Spirit was directed), Luke details the choosing of a new apostle to take the place of Judas Iscariot. He quotes Peter in listing the qualifications for the office:

> Therefore it is necessary to choose one of the men who have been with us the whole time the Lord Jesus went in and out among us, beginning from John's baptism to the time when Jesus was taken up from us. For one of these must be a witness with us of his resurrection. (Acts 1:21-22)

If, in order to be counted an apostle, one must have been a personal disciple of Jesus for at least three years and an eyewitness of his resurrected body, it seems impossible that a modern-day apostle could exist. Even Paul apparently had those who questioned his apostleship. Clearly, Paul was not a personal disciple of Jesus during his ministry from John's baptism to Jesus' ascension. He could, however, on the basis of his conversion experience on the road to Damascus, claim to be a witness of the resurrected Jesus. He asks rhetorical questions to the Corinthians: "Am I not an apostle? Have I not seen Jesus our Lord? Are you not the result of my work in the Lord? Even though I may not be an apostle to others, surely I am to you!" (I Corinthians 9:1-2). In his epistle to the Galatians, he offers his apostolic credentials as they pertain to the three-year discipleship issue:

> I want you to know, brothers, that the gospel I preached is not something that man made up. I did not receive it from any man nor was I taught it; rather, I received it by revelation from Jesus Christ. . . . When God . . . was pleased to reveal his Son in me so that I might preach him among the Gentiles, I did not consult any man, nor did I go

up to Jerusalem to see those who were apostles before I was, but I went immediately into Arabia and later returned to Damascus. Then after three years, I went up to Jerusalem to get acquainted with Peter and stayed with him fifteen days. (Galatians 1:11-18)

Paul claims here that he was indeed a personal disciple of Jesus, although he does not make clear how that instruction proceeded. Whether his specific mention of a three-year time period is significant or not is debatable.

To the Corinthians, he even claims to have learned specific details of Jesus' earthly life events directly from Jesus:

> For I received from the Lord that which I also passed on to you: The Lord Jesus, on the night in which he was betrayed, took bread, and when he had given thanks, he broke it and said, "This is my body which is for you; do this in remembrance of me." In the same way, after supper he took the cup, saying, "This cup is the new covenant in my blood; this do, as often as you drink it, in remembrance of me." (I Corinthians 11:23-25)

Paul asserts that he received this historical narrative from Jesus, not from others. Paul also points out that his apostleship is recognized by the other apostles: "James, Peter, and John, those reputed to be pillars, gave me and Barnabus the right hand of fellowship . . . . They agreed that we should go to the Gentiles, and they to the Jews" (Galatians 2:9). If Paul's apostleship is recognized only after some difficulty, we should certainly not lightly accept the apostleship credentials of anyone living today. It is relatively safe to say that there are no modern-day apostles. That being said, it is safe to say that, since spiritual gifts were conferred by the laying on of apostles' hands, there are no modern-day spiritual gifts. What then about that confusing "last days" prophecy of the prophet Joel?

Interpreting "The Last Days"

According to Luke, on the day of Pentecost, Peter cited a prophecy of Joel:

> In the last days, God says, I will pour out my Spirit on all people. Your sons and daughters will prophesy, your young men will see visions,

your old men will dream dreams. Even on my servants, both men and women, I will pour out my Spirit in those days, and they will prophesy. I will show wonders in the heaven above and signs on the earth below, blood and fire and billows of smoke. The sun will be darkened and the moon to blood before the coming of the great and glorious day of the Lord. And everyone who calls on the name of the Lord will be saved. (Acts 2:17-21)

The Mormons suggest that these last days are the ones in which the Mormon Church exists. They call their church The Church of Jesus Christ Latter Day Saints, alluding to this prophecy. Many modern-day charismatics believe that the last days may be today. If the Charismatic Movement began in the early twentieth century, perhaps that is when the last days began. What these interpreters do not take into account is the context into which Peter introduced this prophecy. The apostles were speaking loudly in various languages. The crowds in Jerusalem were trying to explain what was happening. Some suggested that the apostles were drunk. Peter refuted that suggestion and offered the Joel prophecy as the explanation of what was happening: "No, this is what was spoken by the prophet Joel: 'In the last days . . .'" (Acts 2:15-17). Peter's remarks would have made no sense unless the "last days" included the day of Pentecost on which Peter was speaking. It is not necessary to look for a last days outpouring of the Holy Spirit. It has already occurred. Those who believe the outpouring of the Holy Spirit cited by Peter should last until the end of time fail to take into account the cessation text in I Corinthians 13.

Spiritual Gifts Cessation "When the Perfect Comes"

Before concluding this examination of New Testament spiritual gifts theology, we should view what has come to be known as the "Love Chapter." Sandwiched between Paul's discussion of spiritual gifts in I Corinthians 12 and his discussion of spiritual gifts in I Corinthians 14, he tells his readers that love is superior to spiritual gifts. He says that after spiritual gifts have ceased love will remain:

> If I speak with the tongues of men and of angels, but have not love, I am a . . . clanging cymbal. If I have the gift of prophecy, and can understand all . . . knowledge, and if I have faith that can move mountains, but have not love, I am nothing . . . .

> Love never fails. But where there are prophecies, they will cease; where there are tongues, they will be silenced; where there is knowledge, it will vanish. For we know in part and we prophesy in part, but when that which is perfect is come, that which is in part will disappear . . . .
> Now these three things abide: faith, hope, and love. But the greatest of these is love. (I Corinthians 13:1-13)

The gift of tongues without love sounds terrible. The gifts of prophecy, faith, and knowledge without love are worthless. In fact, the gifts of prophecy, tongues, and knowledge will eventually cease, but the non-miraculous attributes of faith, hope, and love will abide. When will this cessation of some and continuation of others occur? When "that which is perfect is come."

Various interpreters have proposed interpretations for the "perfect." Charismatics have suggested that the "perfect" is the end of the world, the beginning of the new heavens and new earth. This is not likely. If the spiritual gifts vanish then, in what sense will faith and hope abide? Love will certainly abide, but in order for "faith" to continue, there needs to be some element of doubt in existence. What doubt will remain, if we know all things? It would make more sense for Paul to say that faith will cease, but knowledge will abide. Paul said just the opposite. Furthermore, what "hope" will remain after all humans have received their eternal reward? Faith and hope are related, according the writer of Hebrews: "Faith is the substance of things hoped for, the evidence of things not seen" (Hebrews 11:1). But, in eternity we will see clearly and know all things.

Some have suggested that the completion of the New Testament was the "perfect." Yet, compiling the New Testament canon took hundreds of years. Were the spiritual gifts still evident throughout those years? That would have continued the phenomena long after the generation following the death of the last apostle.

The Greek word translated "perfect" is *teleion*. Even Burke agrees: "In Greek . . . the word for 'perfect' is *teleios* . . ." (GM 261). The term is very closely related to the word *telos* and, by extension, to the word entelechy. Entelechy is part of the title of this book. *Telos* and entelechy are terms I have studied for years. This present volume is now the third scholarly book I have written on the subject of entelechy. I discuss the *telos-teleios-entelecheia* etymology thoroughly in my book *Implicit Rhetoric: Kenneth Burke's Extension of Aristotle's Concept of*

Entelechy. Simply put, entelechy is any process that has a beginning, middle, and end. The end or goal is the *telos*; it shows up as the second syllable of the word en-TEL-echy. A simple natural entelechy is the corn entelechy. A kernel of corn when planted begins an entelechy. That is, a process of growth begins as the kernel/seed sprouts roots, then a blade. The growth process continues until it reaches its *telos*. Its *telos* is the completion of the process and the resulting production of brand new kernels that look very much like the kernel that began this process. Once that *telos* or goal has been reached, we say that the process is complete or perfect or *teleios*. But then what happens? A new entelechy begins. Each of those kernels that were produced in the previous entelechy begins to sprout and produce its own entelechy. In other words, entelechies are often cyclical. The fact that we have reached one *telos*, and that that process is complete, or *teleios*, does not mean that the world has ended. I explain one part of the theological significance of *telos* on page 121 of *Revelation: The Human Drama*:

> An examination of the terms *telos* and, more frequently, its cognate verb, *teleô*, proves especially revealing. . . . John speaks of events that will happen when the thousand-year prison sentence of the dragon has been completed [*teleô*]. G. B. Caird sees a "serious problem" in "John's double eschatology." He recounts that scholars such as R. H. Charles have had trouble with the millennium discussed in chapter 20. But, Caird believes that "the dual fulfillment, with the intervening millennium, is a vital part of John's theology. He states: "The seventh bowl, which completes the wrath of God and brings about the collapse of Babylon is the end of an epoch, but it is in a different category from the dissolution of the physical cosmos which accompanies the final judgement (xvi.17-21; cf. xx.11)." Caird writes: "We return therefore to the question raised by the very first sentence of the Revelation. What did John think was 'bound to happen soon'? Certainly not the End, which was at least a millennium away."[10]

My point is that *teleios* does not signify the end of the world, only the completion of an entelechy. However we might be tempted to define the entelechy to which Paul refers, the safest bet is to understand it as the entelechy (or process) of disseminating spiritual gifts in the first generation of the church. The process of disseminating gifts would end when the last living apostle lays his hands on the last gift recipient before dying. This entelechy is not cyclical. The process is complete (*teleios*). It will not be repeated in the future. The recipient has no power to pass on the gift to anyone else. The New Testament contains no hint that anyone (other than an apostle) who possessed a spiritual gift could pass it on to someone else.

Conclusion

The examination of New Testament spiritual gifts theology in this chapter has proceeded along Evangelical Christian grounds. The purpose was to supply some recalcitrance to Evangelicals on this issue. Some New Testament scholars may be disappointed that no biblical criticism issues were raised in the discussion. Raising those issues would have been irrelevant. Evangelical Christians believe the New Testament is inspired of God.

Taking Paul at his word, a number of new methods for God to communicate with humans were introduced to the church in its first generation. Paul labels these methods spiritual gifts. Luke, while describing similar methods, does not use the spiritual gifts terminology. Nevertheless, Luke explicitly indicates the method by which the spiritual gifts were conferred—by the laying on of the hands of apostles. Paul seems to corroborate Luke's observation. He suggests that he needs to be physically present in Rome in order to confer some spiritual gift. He reminds Timothy that Timothy's gift was conferred when Paul laid his hands on him.

Taking Luke at his word, there are some fairly strict limitations on who could be considered an apostle. To be an apostle, one must be an eyewitness of the resurrected Jesus and a personal student of Jesus for some time. Paul struggles somewhat to assert his own apostolic credentials along those lines. If Paul faces difficulty in being counted among the apostles, how could a true apostle surface in the twenty-first century?

Following deductive reasoning, I assert the following:
- Major Premise: Spiritual gifts are only conferred by the laying on of apostles' hands.
- Minor Premise: There are no apostles living in the twenty-first century.
- Conclusion: There are no spiritual gifts in the twenty-first century.

So, what if I am wrong? What if there are modern-day spiritual gifts? What if God gives every Christian a spiritual gift? Then, there is no longer a strong need to study the Bible. God will find a way to speak to each of us. How can we tell which of our messages are truly from God, in the event different Christians have received different messages? The countless number of Christian denominations currently existing suggests that we have a monumental problem with this. Who can say that cult leaders have not received their messages from God? The number of Christian religious persuasions can only be limited by the number of those claiming to be Christians.

What if those who believe in modern-day spiritual gifts are wrong? Countless individuals will believe they are receiving messages directly from God. Many of those messages will be in line with traditional Christian messages, but some will not. It does not take the majority of Muslims to create worldwide chaos. It has not and will not take a majority of Christians to create future Waco's and Jonestown's. It only takes one misguided Christian who believes s/he has received a message from God to kill his/her children. Even if s/he kills his/her children by depriving them of medical care, because some spiritually gifted healer has told him/her s/he needs to display more faith, the result is the same. It only takes one misguided Christian to plant a bomb in an abortion clinic or to assassinate an abortion doctor. It only takes one misguided Christian to use deadly force to rid a community of prostitutes. What else can misguided Christians do, if they receive what they believe to be messages from God?

The New Testament has withstood two millennia of testing. Its messages are not inducive to great psychotic entelechy. Primarily, it teaches Christians to turn the other cheek, go the second mile, forgive repeatedly, and love their enemies. It teaches them that they should conquer as their Lord conquered, by selflessness and even martyrdom, but not by the sword. True, some Christians have used misguided interpretations that have resulted in slavery, anti-Semitism, and religious conflicts, but those are just interpretations. There is a difference between misinterpretation and the receipt of clearly dangerous messages from God. Unconstrained spiritual gifts theology provides the great danger from Christianity in the twenty-first century.

Notes

[1] "Muslim Group Takes Responsibility for 9-11: 'We Are So Sorry,'" *World Tribune.com* 9/10/04. Available: http://216.26.163.62/2004/me_islam_0 9_10.html (9/11/04).
[2] See page 28 of this text.
[3] G. B. Caird, *A Commentary on the Revelation of St. John the Divine*, a vol. of *Harper's New Testament Commentaries*, ed. Henry Chadwick (New York, Hagerstown, San Francisco, London: Harper & Row Publishers, 1966), 48.
[4] Stan A. Lindsay, *Revelation: The Human Drama* (Bethlehem, PA: Lehigh University Press of America, 2001), 70-72.
[5] George Kennedy, *The Art of Persuasion in Greece* (Princeton, NJ: Princeton University Press, 1963), 297. Kennedy continues: "A trope is a single word used in a novel way either because the idea to be expressed has no idea of its own (no 'proper' word) or for the sake of embellishment. The difference between a trope and a figure is parallel to the difference between barbarism and solecism: a figure, like a solecism, involves at least two words; a trope, like a barbarism, consists of only a single word: a metaphor is a trope, a simile is a figure. . . . Grammatical treatises display a basic set of eight tropes: onomatapoiia, katachresis, metaphora, metalepsis, synekdoche, metonymia, autonomasia, and antiphrasis."
[6] Cf. Kenneth Burke, "Poetics and Communication" in *Perspectives in Education, Religion, and the Arts* eds. Howard E. Kiefer and Milton K. Munitz (Albany: State University of New York Press, 1970), 402.
[7] G. F. Moore, *Judaism in the First Centuries of the Christian Era*, 2 vols. (Cambridge: Harvard University Press, 1927-30), I:414.
[8] Louis Ginzberg, *The Legends of the Jews*, 7 vols. (Philadelphia: The Jewish Publication Society of America, 5728-1968), V:21.
[9] Stan A. Lindsay, *Implicit Rhetoric: Kenneth Burke's Extension of Aristotle's Concept of Entelechy* (Lanham, MD: University Press of America, 1998), 1-6.
[10] Jordan Robertson, "Mom Arrested in Bay Area Children's Deaths," *Washington Post* 10/20/05. Available: http://www.washingtonpost.com/wp-dyn/content/article/2005/10/20/AR2005102000284 (10/20/05).
[11] Caird, 235-236.

Chapter 8

Motivation: Why Gifts Theology?

Why would so many Evangelical Christians advocate modern-day spiritual gifts theology if, as I suggest, such advocacy carries with it significant danger for society? Burke points out that nothing "causes" a person to advocate anything; rather, humans are "motivated" to advocate things. I provide a lengthy discussion of Burke's theory of motives in *Implicit Rhetoric*. Certain conclusions from that discussion are offered here to introduce my assignment of motives for gifts theology advocates. Motives are not identical to causes. Deterministic theories do not take this factor into account. Burke states:

> Determinism is a theory that the universe can make no mistakes. Not only is everything caused, but it is accurately caused. Alter the nature of the stimulus ever so little, and by the doctrine of determinism, you get a corresponding alteration of the response. . . . Once you introduce a point of view into the universe, however . . . a new factor enters. The point of view requires an interpretation of events, a reading of the recalcitrant factors favorable and unfavorable to the point of view. But an interpretation can be wrong. Hence, a point of view introduces the possibility of error. But where there is the possibility of a wrong interpretation, there is also the possibility of a right one. The freedom to err argues a freedom to be right. (PC 257)

Motives are, for Burke, the possibly-wrong-yet-possibly-right "interpretations" humans make to account for what takes place in human conduct. They are the explanations that are "assign[ed] for . . . acts" (PC 18). In speaking of "motives which people assign to their actions," Burke calls "motive . . . a term of interpretation" (PC 25). Again, he remarks:

> Our minds, as linguistic products, are composed of concepts (verbally molded) which select certain relationships as meaningful. These relationships are not realities, they are interpretations of reality . . . . (PC 35)

This chapter, then, contains my interpretation of reality. I am assigning motives to those who advocate spiritual gifts theology. In order to offer my interpretation and assign motives, I look at the spiritual gifts advocates from a variety of perspectives, or points of view. Burke supplies the five major perspectives for assigning motives in GM:

> We shall use five terms as generating principle of our investigation. They are: Act, Scene, Agent, Agency, and Purpose. In a rounded statement about motives, you must have some word that names the *act* (names what took place, in thought or deed), and another that names the *scene* (the background of the act, the situation in which it occurred); also, you must indicate what person or kind of person (*agent*) performed the act, what means or instruments he used (*agency*), and the *purpose*. (GM xv)

Part one of GM develops the point that all five of these terms, to which Burke refers together as the Pentad, motivate each other in terms of ratios. In other words, the scene in which an act takes place provides some motivation for the act. Briefly, this is how ratios work:

> Burke's "five terms would allow for ten" ratios: "([S]cene-act, scene-agent, scene-agency, scene-purpose, act-purpose, act-agent, act-agency, agent-purpose, agent-agency, and agency-purpose). The ratios are principles of determination" (GM 15).
>
> One could say that each term in a ratio "determines" (GM 15) what the other term in the ratio will be like, although Burke's use of the term "determines" here in no way commits him to a "deterministic" view when it comes to human action. Another way of putting this is to say

that the ratios are "principles of consistency" (GM 9) which bind each other together: "[S]cene, act, and agent also lead to reverse applications. That is, the scene-act ratio either calls for acts in keeping with scenes or scenes in keeping with acts . . ." (GM 9). Burke, in applying his representative anecdote--"drama" (GM 59-61)--to his analytical system appropriates an important "principle of drama" to his method: "that the nature of acts and agents should be consistent with the nature of the scene" (GM 3). He calls this principle of drama a "principle of consistency" (GM 3, 7, 9, 77).[1]

For the purpose of this chapter, I limit the ratios of importance to four, those containing the term act (scene-act, agent-act, agency-act, and purpose-act). I know what the act is for which I assign motives. The act under consideration is "advocating modern-day spiritual gifts theology." My questions pertain primarily to four issues:
- What scenes have motivated this act?
- What (types of) agents have motivated this act?
- What agencies have motivated this act?
- What purposes have motivated this act?

In discussing the terms of the Pentad in Part II of GM, Burke links each term with a philosophical language:

[S]urveying the entire field at a glance, let us state simply as propositions:
 For the featuring of scene, the corresponding terminology is materialism.
 For the featuring of agent, the corresponding terminology is idealism.
 For the featuring of agency, the corresponding terminology is pragmatism.
 For the featuring of purpose, the corresponding terminology is mysticism.
 For the featuring of act, the corresponding terminology is realism.
(GM 128)

Those philosophical languages supply the motives for individuals who advocate spiritual gifts theology. Burke offers the following caveat: "[T]here has been much borrowing of terms among the various philosophic schools, so that one cannot always take even key terms at their face value" (GM 129). Therefore, to avoid much confusion, I attempt to use the terms as Burke uses them. The step I take beyond

Burke, here, is to suggest that the term "Christian" may be attached to each of his philosophical languages to designate a specific motivation.

Act and Christian Realism

Why do many Evangelical Christians advocate modern-day spiritual gifts theology? One answer is that many Evangelicals have been persuaded that the best biblical scholarship requires their position. This motivation is primarily a Realistic motivation. Biblical statements are accepted by Evangelicals as facts. Facts may be combined syllogistically to establish truth. For Realistic Evangelicals, the truth must be advocated regardless of the consequences. I respect this position despite disagreeing with the conclusions advocated. Like those who feel compelled to advocate (modern-day spiritual gifts) what they perceive to be the truth, I am a Realist. We just have two different views of the truth. The belief that "there is truth" is what characterizes a Realist.

Plato was a Realist who believed that truth existed in a non-earthly realm of the ideal. His cave analogy illustrated his view that discovering truth was a matter of moving closer and closer to the light. Since all humans existed prior to birth in the ideal realm, they all know the truth but have forgotten it. Socratic questioning helps humans unforget the truth (*anamnēsis*).

Burke's association of Realism with "act" comes, however, from Plato's student Aristotle. He states, "In Aristotle, 'things are more or less real according as they are more or less *energeia*" (GM 227). Aristotle (and Burke) often uses *energeia* as a synonym for *entelecheia* (or entelechy). The primary distinction between the two terms is that *energeia* is a process (or act) that has the "work" it intends to accomplish implicit throughout the process; by contrast, entelechy is a process (or act) that has its "goal" implicit throughout the process. That goal may be a work or a change (*metamorphosis*) or a location toward which something is moving or growth toward maturity, *etc*. Aristotle, as contrasted with Plato, saw truth in the sensory world rather than in some otherworldly realm. Whatever actually existed in nature and was in some process of *kinēsis* was, for Aristotle, true reality.

The seventeenth century philosopher Rene Descartes was a Realist who is credited with founding Modernism. His methodological doubt suggested that Realists should doubt everything that could be doubted. Whatever is left is truth. Empiricists, following Descartes suggested that one could doubt everything that is not empirically verifiable. Unfortunately, even empirical evidence (sense-data) can be doubted, so empiricism died. Mathematics was the last stronghold of Modernism. When Kurt Gödel demonstrated that even mathematics could be doubted—because the whole system is nothing more than a tautology—Modernism effectively crumbled. In its place, Postmodernism arose. Postmodernism could be called a Realistic philosophy in that it makes a truth claim: typically, "there is no truth" or "there is relative truth." Burke is a Postmodern Realist, but he is not happy with either of these truth-related formulas.

Burke is not a Relativist. He is a perspectivist with neither the confidence of an Essentialist nor the pessimism of a Relativist. His epistemological stance is best represented by the word "perhaps" (CS xi). Burke's perspectivism is neither the truth-claiming attitude of a Modernist, nor the truth-disavowing attitude of the first variety of Postmodernists. In their own way, the Postmodern assertions that "there is no truth" or that "truth is unattainable" are truth-claiming assertions. In his essay, "The Rhetorical Situation," Burke quotes Norman O. Brown's remark that "there is no literal truth." Burke responds: "The sentence, on its face, is in dire trouble since there would be no point in his making the statement unless he wanted it to be taken literally, as 'true.'"[2] Burke is much happier with a Postmodern truth-related formula such as "there is probable truth."

When I write of Christian Realism, clearly it is not Postmodern Realism in the sense that "there is no truth" or "truth is unattainable." Likewise, Christian Realism is neither Empiricist nor Cartesian. Christian Realism is somewhat closer to Aristotelian Realism in that it is interested in the "purpose" of even natural entelechies—something that Nominalists and Naturalists would disavow. It is closer to Burke's Postmodern view that "there is probable truth." It is even closer to Platonic Realism in the sense that it views absolute truth as existing in otherworldly realms. We need, however, the term Christian Realism because it is certainly not identical with Platonic Realism or any other Realism discussed thus far. Christian Realism believes that there is truth and that such truth has been (and/or is still being) communicated to humans by God. Hence, Christian Realism believes that spiritual gifts have been given to humans. It is through these spiritual gifts that God has typically communicated with humans. All Evangelicals agree that the Old and New Testaments are among those messages communicated from God.

Since all Evangelical Christian Realists agree that the Bible is truth, any modern-day messages cannot express a truth that contradicts the truth in the Bible. Therefore, it is of utmost importance to Evangelicals that all truth be established in scripture. In the previous chapter I appealed to those Evangelicals who believed that modern-day gifts theology was based upon sound Bible-believing scholarship. I argued that they had missed some important biblical facts:
1. Spiritual gifts, according to the Bible, are conferred by the laying on of the hands of apostles.
2. The qualifications for becoming an apostle include being an eyewitness of Jesus' resurrected state and studying under Jesus as a personal disciple for an extended period of time.
3. The baptism with the Holy Spirit is explicitly spoken of as occurring on only two occasions with signs that are not identical to those of spiritual gifts.
4. The "last days" of Peter's Pentecost citation of Joel's prophecy refer to the point in time at which Peter spoke.
5. Paul promised that spiritual gifts would cease, but faith, hope, and love would continue.

My conclusion, based upon these Evangelical facts, is that spiritual gifts do not exist in the twenty-first century. Christian Realists must grapple with these issues. However, not all proponents of modern-day spiritual gifts are Christian Realists. Some are Christian Materialists.

Scene and Christian Materialism

Burke connects Scene with Materialism and, by extension, with Aristotle's material cause. Burke states:

> In Baldwin's *Dictionary of Philosophy and Psychology*, materialism is defined as "that metaphysical theory which regards all the facts of the universe as sufficiently explained by the assumption of body or matter, conceived as extended, impenetrable, eternally existent, and susceptible of movement or change of relative position." . . .
> Are not these citations enough to make it quickly clear that one gets a materialistic philosophy by featuring our term Scene?[3]

In GM, Burke remarks:

> In . . . Aristotle, you will observe that the "material" cause, "that from which (as immanent material) a thing comes into being, e.g. the bronze

of the statue and the silver of the dish," would correspond fairly closely to our term, *scene*. (GM 228)

In what senses, then, do scene and Materialism motivate the act of advocating modern-day spiritual gifts theology? The answer, quite ironically, is to be found in those senses in which the spiritual is transcended by the physical.

The first sense is quite crass. Some individuals advocate spiritual issues primarily for Materialistic rewards. Three biblical characters come immediately to mind—Balaam, Judas Iscariot, and Simon the Sorcerer.

The Old Testament prophet Balaam serves as an ancient example of a Materialistic spiritual gifts advocate. Entrusted by God with the gift of prophecy, Balaam was bribed repeatedly by a Moabite (non-Israelite) king Balak to prophesy against (*i.e.*, curse) Israel (Numbers 22-24, Deuteronomy 23:4-5, II Peter 2:15, Jude 11, Revelation 2:14). Balak's emissaries offered Balaam a fee for this service (Numbers 22:7). Balak personally offered to reward him generously (Numbers 22:17). He gave cattle and sheep to Balaam (Numbers 22:40). Balaam was willing to accept the material, and even used sorcery in an effort to find some way he could curse Israel prophetically (Numbers 24:1).

Judas Iscariot was, of course, the apostle of Jesus notorious for betraying Jesus for thirty pieces of silver (Matthew 26:14-56, Mark 14:10-50, Luke 22:3-53, John 13:2-30, 18:2-11). The gospel writers portray him as a crass Materialist. John's gospel reports an account of a woman who anointed Jesus' feet with expensive oil:

> But one of his disciples, Judas Iscariot, who was later to betray him, objected: "Why was this perfume not sold and the money given to the poor? It was worth a litra." He did not say this because he cared about the poor, but because he was a thief. As keeper of the money, he used to help himself to what was put into it. (John 12:4-6)

Simon the sorcerer, as reported in the previous chapter, noticed the method by which spiritual gifts were transferred: "When Simon saw that the Spirit was given at the laying on of the apostles' hands, he offered them money and said, 'Give me also this ability so that everyone on whom I lay my hands may receive the Holy Spirit'" (Acts 8:18-19). His request was denied. His motives were thoroughly condemned by the apostles.

Given these three examples, it is clear that some individuals are motivated by crass Materialism to advocate spiritual gifts theology. The non-Evangelical world certainly suspects, as do many Evangelicals, that some Evangelical religious leaders are so motivated. In Chapter 1, I cite an anecdote:

> In the 1970s, a woman I knew was watching the PTL Club. She heard Jim Bakker state that the Spirit had told him someone in the television audience needed to send a gift of $5000.00 to the ministry. She perceived that this message from the Holy Spirit was intended for her. She dutifully wrote a check for $5000.00 and sent it to the PTL Club. A few nights later, the Spirit told Bakker that the person who had sent $5000.00 before needed to send another $5000.00. The woman complied again. Unfortunately, she did not have the money in her checking account to cover either check. Both checks bounced, resulting in NSF fees.

My possibly-wrong-yet-possibly-right "interpretation" of Jim Bakker's motives is that he was being a Christian Materialist.

A second sense in which scene and Materialism motivate the act of advocating modern-day spiritual gifts theology pertains to Burke's borrowed definition of Materialists as those who regard "all the facts of the universe as sufficiently explained by the assumption of body or matter." It is difficult for one to be a Christian and to hold this view thoroughly. Spiritual gifts theology, however, offers a close approximation to Materialism. In spiritual gifts theology, abstract relationships with God are made concrete. It is unnecessary to worry whether one is saved when all one needs to do is present to oneself concrete physical (or material) evidence of one's salvation. Speaking in tongues does the trick. The individual can point to the concrete act of speaking in tongues as evidence that s/he has received the Holy Spirit.

Christians who accept the premise that all unforgiven sinners will spend eternity in Hell have a strong desire for some concrete material evidence that they have been forgiven. In the medieval Catholic Church, the statement of the church that an individual had been redeemed from purgatory was quite valuable—so valuable that great European cathedrals were built with the funds collected in the purchase of such assurances. With the rise of Protestantism, however, multiple voices began to be heard concerning how one knows if one has been truly redeemed. Some said individuals must earn their salvation through good works. Some said faith only was sufficient. Some said individuals must prove their repentance. Some said all that was needed was to pray a prayer in which Jesus is asked to come into the individual's heart. Some said a baby must be baptized (either by sprinkling or immersion) before it dies, or it would go to Hell. Others said babies are innocent; if they die, they go to Heaven. Some said sprinkling is not true baptism; the Greek word *baptizô* means to immerse. Others said God looks at the heart; so long as an individual is sincere, s/he will be saved. Some said God will save everyone. Others said God will save only a select few, perhaps only 144,000 in all of history. Some said baptism is sufficient. Others said individuals need a second act of grace. The result of these multiple voices is confusion in Christian culture.

American pluralistic values further aggravate the confusion. In the free market system of American Christianity, each denomination—yes, sometimes each individual congregation, and occasionally each group (or individual) within a given congregation—seeks to distinguish its brand of Christianity from all other brands of Christianity on the market. Churches use differentiation and positioning strategies to win adherents to their brand. The key selling proposition must be: My church is better than your church. Otherwise, why would individuals choose one church over another? Individual Christians must assume either great confidence in their own brand of Christianity or seek some concrete way of proving to themselves that they are among God's chosen ones.

Enter spiritual gifts theology. If an individual Christian can witness not just any miracle, but a miracle that materially demonstrates that God's Spirit is living within that individual, s/he will be greatly relieved. Burke explains it this way:

> The isolated mystic may appear at any time in history, since one man's experiences may be unique enough, sufficiently a "sport," to engross him with transitional concerns even in an era that has great fixity for most people—but mysticism *as a collective movement* belongs to periods marked by great confusion of the cultural frame, requiring a radical shift in people's allegiance to symbols of authority. (ATH 57-58)

If the confusion in American Christianity produced by rampant freemarket differentiation and positioning strategies were not enough, the beginning of the twentieth century—when the Charismatic Movement began—was marked by a huge shift in biblical scholarship. Not only

were the various denominations engaging in marketplace wrangling--
bent on demonstrating the superiority of their own specific versions of
Christianity—but biblical scholarship was adopting much more
Modernist approaches to the study of the Bible. Descartes had
recommended doubting everything that can be doubted, and biblical
scholarship was following suit. In academia, biblical scholars
systematically doubted:
- That the Bible was the word of God as opposed to human views,
- That the Creation account(s) in the Bible were scientifically defensible,
- That the history presented in the Bible was actual (not legendary),
- That Moses was the author of the first five books of the Bible,
- That the books of the Old and New Testaments were as ancient as they claimed to be,
- That the text of the Bible was untampered with over the years,
- That the Gospels presented a historical Jesus,
- That the books of the Bible were actually authored by those who claimed to author them,
- That even Paul was the author of all the books traditionally attributed to him,
- That the book of Revelation was written by one person at one time in history, or
- That the biblical prophecies were correct (For example, did Jesus and John predict an end that did not occur within their stated timelines?).

While the second half of the twentieth century saw resurgence in
Evangelical, or Bible-believing, biblical scholarship, the first half of the
century was a period of chaos for Bible-believing scholars. Many
Christians became opposed to scholarship, altogether. If they could not
prove to the scholarly world even that the Bible was reliable, they
would retreat from scholarship into a mystical relationship with God.

Purpose and Christian Mysticism

I have just demonstrated a close relationship between Christian
Materialism and Christian Mysticism. Burke agrees:

Motivation: Why Gifts Theology? 137

> [T]here is a point at which Mysticism and Materialism become indistinguishable. Both involve a narrowing of motivational circumference. Materialism accomplishes this by a deliberate elimination of purpose as a term . . . . Mysticism arrives at somewhat the same result unintentionally, by making purpose absolute, and thereby in effect transforming it into a fatality. (GM 291)

In the case of Materialism, Burke is thinking of such Materialistic philosophies as Naturalism in which the circumference (what one considers to be real in the world) is reduced to Nature alone; God is eliminated. The natural scene controls all motion; there is no action. Burke then observes that an extreme emphasis on purpose as in Mysticism also eliminates purpose from the realm of *human* action. The only action in the world is that in which God engages. Referring once again to the Baldwin dictionary, Burke defines Mysticism:

> Mysticism embraces "those forms of speculative and religious thought which profess to attain an immediate apprehension of the divine essence or ultimate ground of existence." . . . [I]t develops an ideal . . . "in which the distinctions of individuality disappear, and the finite spirit achieves, as it were, utter union or identity with the Being of beings." (GM 287)

While a purpose still exists for God as an agent in Christian Mysticism, there ceases, in a sense, to be a purpose in the human agent. The human is no longer an agent; s/he becomes only an agency through which God acts. The prophecy does not result through the will of the prophet, but through the will of God. The miracles are performed not because of the will of the miracle worker, but because God uses the miracle worker to effect a miracle. Likewise, the healer, the teacher, the evangelist are mere agencies.

Why would someone be motivated to dissolve into a mere agency? One answer makes sense: It allows the individual to abdicate personal responsibility. It is interesting that modern-day spiritual gifts advocates also believe strongly in modern-day demon possession. Whether one is merely the agency of God or merely the agency of a demon, one bears no personal responsibility for one's acts. Think of the most horrendous human criminal. If that person is demon-possessed, that person cannot help what s/he is doing. S/he is merely the agency of a demon.

There is little difference in the level of personal responsibility of one who is demon-possessed, the one who does a good work because s/he is an agency of God (*i.e.*, s/he is possessed of a spiritual gift), or the one who (viewed behavioristically) is merely behaving in accordance with the natural and/or environmental influences. All three individuals are "moving" deterministically. If I am not actually "acting," I am not responsible for my behavior. This is a motive for advocating modern-day spiritual gifts theology.

Our discussion of the Agent and Christian Idealism will demonstrate a contrast between Mysticism and Idealism in terms of the line suggested in the two preceding paragraphs, but before we move to a discussion of Idealism, it is important to note that Burke also connected the term "teleology" to purpose. Burke states:

> We must certainly give due consideration to the fact that the presence of a strongly purposive *ingredient* in the discussion of human motives is not in itself mystical. . . . Only when purpose becomes *total* does it fit our prescription for mysticism.
>
> Instruments are considered by Aristotle in teleological terms as their form is said to be derived from the end desired by their users. (GM 293)

Teleology is, etymologically speaking, the study of *telos* (or its plural, *teloi*). *Telos* may be translated as either purpose or end. Burke's reference to "instruments" suggests agency. Instruments are means to an end. When humans become the instruments by which God performs His acts, the humans are agencies. But, if experiencing spiritual gifts is considered the agency by which Christians secure their passage into Heaven, the *telos* is "getting into Heaven." This is where our discussion of Christian Mysticism began: If an individual Christian can witness not just any miracle, but a miracle that materially demonstrates that God's Spirit is living within that individual, s/he will be greatly relieved concerning the likelihood that s/he will spend eternity in Heaven rather than Hell.

Agent and Christian Idealism

If thoroughgoing Christian Mysticism effectively eliminates the human as agent, Christian Idealism celebrates the human as agent. Great Christian benefactors are Christian Idealists. Mother Theresa was an Idealist. Her behavior sprang from her very nature as an agent. While some Christians are motivated to advocate modern-day spiritual gifts theology by the sense that they are not responsible for their behavior, others are motivated to advocate the theology by the sense that the spiritual gift is the extension of themselves as agents. One of the definitions of Idealism Burke cites from the Baldwin dictionary is: "Any theory which seeks the explanation, or ultimate *raison d'être*, of the cosmic evolution in the realization of reason, self-consciousness, or spirit" (GM 171). Burke illustrates: "Henry James gives us a characteristically idealistic statement when referring to 'the artist's prime sensibility' as the 'soil out of which his subject springs' and which 'grows' the work of art" (GM 171). It is the artist's or agent's personal essence that motivates his or her acts.

One's personal spiritual gift may be viewed as one's essence. In my view, this is a quite common motive for advocates of modern-day spiritual gifts. Just as humans are prone to define themselves in terms of their occupations, these Christians are prone to define themselves in terms of their spiritual gifts. Humans are known to make comments such as:

- "Of course you can trust me; I'm a doctor."
- "I'm a mother; I care for innocent people."
- "As a salesman, I am a born communicator."

Likewise, in a typical "spiritual gifts inventory," respondents are asked to rate their agreement or disagreement on a Likert scale to statements such as:

- I enjoy providing for the needs of visitors.
- I feel led to visit sick, lonely or discouraged people and show kindness to them.
- I like to see that things are done in an orderly, efficient and responsible manner.[4]

Most spiritual gifts inventories are not really aptitude tests. They do not test aptitudes the way, for instance, an Algebra Aptitude Test does. They are not strong personality tests. They do not offer alternative courses of action from which to choose, based upon specific circumstances. They are personal interest tests, attitude tests, opinion tests; yet they give the illusion of producing social scientifically valid conclusions. Questions typically begin with:

- "I get/find satisfaction . . ."
- "I enjoy . . ."
- "I feel . . ."
- "I am willing/able . . ."
- "I like . . ."

- "I . . . see . . ."
- "I have a passion . . ."
- "I am passionately concerned . . ."
- "I am excited . . ."
- "I delight . . ."
- "I am good/skilled at . . ."
- "I am sensitive . . ."

Other questions clearly imply that spiritual gifts have definitely been bestowed (beginning with "Sometimes the Holy Spirit enables me to . . ." or being even more specifically explicit, such as "Through my prophetic utterances some have received God's guidance").

After taking the spiritual gifts inventory, the scoring of the inventory occurs. Then, the test-taker is assigned spiritual gift labels. The spiritual gift may be as uninteresting as "assisting" or "welcoming" or as impressive as "prophesying," "exorcising," "healing," or "miracle working." Each of the spiritual gifts is then defined for the test-taker. Whence the definitions come is undisclosed. There is no appeal to biblical texts to support the definitions. Perhaps, the definitions were supplied to the inventory developer by prophecy.

In terms of Idealism, however, any label attached to define one's essence helps one know how one will typically "act." The altercasting phenomenon illustrates the point. If a child is repeatedly told that s/he is a bad child and will probably end up in prison, this message becomes a self-fulfilling prophecy. If the same child is repeatedly told that s/he is a good child and will probably do great things for society, this message becomes a self-fulfilling prophecy. Conclusions drawn from even fake social scientific tests produce the same effects. When I was young, I took a Handwriting Analysis test at a state fair. A computer-generated result was given to me. I took all of the conclusions to heart and saw myself in terms of the adjectives the test had applied to me. Later, I saw the fine print: This test is unscientific. It is designed for entertainment purposes only. When in the eighth grade, I earned the highest score in my class on an Algebra Aptitude Test, I saw myself as one who would be adept at Algebra. I was very good at mathematics throughout high school (winning my High School Math Award) even though I was only an average math student in elementary school. The effect of labels on an agent is amazing.

Therefore, if some spiritual gifts inventory appears to offer social scientific conclusions that a given individual has the spiritual gift of teaching, that individual may very well perform acts that are consistent with that individual's concept of himself or herself as an agent. Never mind the fact that the same inventory will almost always indicate that everyone who takes it has some spiritual gift—even non-religious people! Yet my self-concept will often dictate my actions. Social scientist Frank R. Kardes cites Bem (1965, 1972): "According to self-perception theory, when beliefs and attitudes are relatively inaccessible, people form inferences about their beliefs and attitudes on the basis of their behavior and the context in which the behavior occurs."[5] Once my self-perception is established, my actions will tend to be consistent with my self-perception. This is also the essence of Burke's agent-act ratio.

If a believer really likes the self-perception a spiritual gift label affords him or her, s/he as a Christian Idealist will be inclined to advocate spiritual gifts theology. This might not be dangerous, if the believer has the gift of "serving" with the definition: "Seeing and doing detailed work necessary to the success of a church program or ministry." It might be dangerous, however, if the believer has the gift of "exorcising-delivering" with the definition: "Casting out or binding evil spirits" or the gift of "prophesying" with the definition: "Being inspired to declare the immediate word of God." I personally know a woman who believed she had these last two gifts. She called another person I know in the middle of the night with a request that he leave immediately to assist in an exorcism. She promised great sums of money to another person I know if he would assist her. She spent money and wrote checks based on money she prophetically knew the Lord would provide even though it was not in her accounts. She is currently undergoing psychiatric treatment.

Getting rid of spiritual gifts theology does not destroy Christian Idealism. The very label Christian is sufficient to motivate a wide variety of actions. The WWJD wristband Christian teenagers wear suggest that the teenagers are free agents and yet they are also willingly Christians. Their actions should be consistent with their nature as Christian agents. There is nothing wrong with discovering one's aptitudes, talents, skills, interests, and abilities. All of these personal attributes make up one's character as an agent. Christian Idealists have plenty of resources to understand their nature as agents without using the potentially dangerous labels of spiritual gifts theology.

Agency and Christian Pragmatism

When humans become the instruments by which God performs His acts, the humans are agencies. When experiencing spiritual gifts is taken by Christians as the sign that they are destined for Heaven, the spiritual gifts themselves become the agencies, the means to an end. But for what end(s) is the agency of "advocating spiritual gifts" a means?

One important end for which advocating spiritual gifts becomes the means is church growth. Peter Wagner has authored several books and articles describing how spiritual gifts theology helps churches grow. Since churches are primarily volunteer organizations, encouraging members to volunteer for the numerous tasks that must be completed and roles that must be filled becomes paramount. If all evangelism, teaching, giving, counseling, and service are performed by only a few individuals, the church cannot grow as quickly. Spiritual gifts inventories are administered to all members by the church leadership. The leadership, based upon the results of the inventories, assigns each member appropriate "gifts." These gifts are, practically (or pragmatically) speaking, roles that (according to the theology) God has personally assigned (through the Holy Spirit) to each Christian. How can a true Christian fail to follow-through on a task, job, or role that God personally assigned to him or her?

Never mind that modern-day spiritual gifts theology may not be scripturally defensible. For the Christian Pragmatist, the fact that "it works" is sufficient motivation for advocating spiritual gifts theology. And, apparently, it does work (although, not for every church). The very reason that so many mainline churches have followed Pentecostalism into modern-day spiritual gifts theology is that Pentecostalism has grown by leaps and bounds for over a century. If the Wall Street model is to be followed in American Christianity, the church that grows to be the largest wins! And, today's mega-churches, with weekly attendance and membership well into the thousands, attest to the efficacy of spiritual gifts theology as a means to accomplish church growth. Virtually all of the mega-churches use the theology.

On the other hand, use of the theology does not always achieve church growth. Frequently, the opposite result occurs. On pages 102 and 103, I described a personal experience:

> [M]y local congregation, in 1992, conducted a spiritual gifts inventory as a part of a church growth plan for the congregation. Two other former elders of the church and I asked for a meeting with the current elders to discuss spiritual gifts theology. We three former elders resisted this introduction of spiritual gifts theology into our congregation. The current eldership . . . had decided in advance that they would not discuss the Bible in their meeting with us. Instead, the current eldership totally rejected our position. Nearly half the members left the church.

Similar church arguments over spiritual gifts resulting in attendance drops and membership decimations have occurred elsewhere, but this is not the primary way church attendance and membership numbers have been negatively impacted by modern-day spiritual gifts theology.

By virtue of the very nature of spiritual gifts theology, church splits are a given. If one prophet in a church receives one message and another receives a contradictory message, divisions are inevitable. It is extremely naïve, given the denominationalized history of the Church, to expect otherwise. The quarrel scenario resulting from spiritual gifts theology dates back to the early Church. Paul writes more about spiritual gifts in I Corinthians than in any other New Testament book. In I Corinthians 1:10-3:23, Paul addresses the quarrels that have erupted:

> I appeal to you . . . that all of you agree and that there be no dissensions among you . . . . For it has been reported to me . . . that there is quarreling among you, my brothers. Each of you says, "I am of [the spirit of] Paul," or "I am of [the spirit of] Apollos," or "I am of [the spirit of] Cephas," or "I am of [the spirit of] Christ." Is Christ divided? Was Paul crucified for you? Or were you baptized in the name of Paul? . . . [A]s it is written, "Let him who boasts, boast of the Lord." . . . While there is jealousy and strife among you, are you not fleshly and ordinary men? When one says, "I am of Paul," and another, "I am of Apollos," are you not mere men? What then is Apollos? What is Paul? Servants through whom you believed, as the Lord assigned to each. I planted, and Apollos watered, but God gave the increase. . . . For all things are yours, whether Paul or Apollos or Cephas . . . and you are Christ's and Christ is God's.

In the New Testament period, apostles such as Paul had the authority to settle the disputes. When perceived differences arose among apostles, they convened a conference of apostles at Jerusalem (Acts 15) to settle issues. Before the Reformation, the Pope settled issues. But who settles the issues today? We may hold conferences within our respective denominations to settle issues. We may even grapple with issues of biblical interpretation in books, journals, and conferences. But, in the context of spiritual gifts theology, when one prophet asserts one thing and another prophet asserts quite another, who decides which prophet is a true prophet and which one is a false prophet? Members of the congregation vote with their feet. The church is split.

How, then, do mega-churches use modern-day spiritual gifts theology and avoid being splintered? They place the authority to determine who has what spiritual gift in the hands of the church leadership. The leaders write, administer, and interpret the spiritual gifts inventory. They maintain a strong hierarchy. They determine who accomplishes what task, assumes what role in the local church. This is quite pragmatic. It works. Christian Pragmatists are motivated to use modern-day spiritual gifts theology because it is a means to an end (church growth).

Conclusion

Motives are assigned. The motives we assign are possibly wrong, but that fact also argues that they are possibly right. When I attempt to assign motives to those who advocate modern-day spiritual gifts theology, I use Burke's Pentad. The Pentad offers five comprehensive perspectives for assigning motives. I have generally avoided assigning motives to specific individuals. Instead, by discussing Christian Realists, Christian Idealists, Christian Materialists, Christian Mystics, and Christian Pragmatists, I have presented a variety of ways individuals might be motivated. It is quite possible, even probable, that a given advocate of modern-day spiritual gifts theology will be motivated by more than one of these five motives.

To Evangelical Christian Realists, I appeal to your source of truth—the Bible. There are facts that should give you pause with regard to advocating spiritual gifts theology.

To crass Christian Materialists, I ask: Do you really want to be associated with the likes of Balaam, Judas Iscariot, and Simon the Sorcerer? Other Christian Materialists find the material evidence of miraculous gifts more satisfactory than abstract words and promises relative to a relationship with God. I would direct them to Hebrews 11, the faith chapter, and to Jesus' reminder that a wicked and adulterous generation seeks after a sign (Matthew 16:4).

To Christian Mystics, I point out that the second half of the twentieth century saw resurgence in Evangelical, or Bible-believing, biblical scholarship. The Cartesian Modernism that caused many to doubt the Bible has itself been doubted out of existence. Good reasons for believing in the Bible are being generated by scholars every day. The confusion that exists between the claims of various denominations produced a turn to Mysticism. But, spiritual gifts theology only exacerbates the problem. With modern-day spiritual gifts theology, every prophet has his or her own message. This will not reduce confusion.

To Christian Idealists, I suggest that getting rid of spiritual gifts theology does not destroy Christian Idealism. The very label Christian is sufficient to motivate a wide variety of actions. Christian Idealists have plenty of resources to understand their nature as agents without using the potentially dangerous labels of spiritual gifts theology.

To Christian Pragmatists, I assert that the Bible itself claims to be the most pragmatic approach. Second Timothy 3:15-17 states:

> [Y]ou have been acquainted with the sacred writings, which are able to instruct you for salvation through faith in Christ Jesus. All scripture is inspired by God and profitable for teaching, for reproof, for correction, and for instruction in righteousness, that the man of God may be complete, equipped for every good work.

Notes

[1] Stan A. Lindsay, *Implicit Rhetoric: Kenneth Burke's Extension of Aristotle's Concept of Entelechy* (Lanham, MD: University Press of America, 1998), 107.

[2] Kenneth Burke, "The Rhetorical Situation," in *Communication: Ethical and Moral Issues*, ed. Lee Thayer (London, New York, Paris: Gordon and Breach Science Publishers, 1973), 266.

[3] Kenneth Burke, "The Five Master Terms: Their Place in a 'Dramatistic' Grammar of Motives," *View* 3.2 (June, 1943): 50.

[4] John Turner, "Spiritual Gifts Inventory" Published by Vine Street Christian Church.

[5] Frank R. Kardes, *Consumer Behavior and Managerial Decision Making*, 2nd ed. (Upper Saddle River, NJ: Prentice Hall, 2002), 171.

Chapter 9

Perspectivism: The Eldership Approach

Burke recommends a perspectivist approach for dealing with the problem of psychotic entelechy. So does the New Testament. A parody of John 3:16 states: "For God so loved the world, He didn't send a committee." Anyone who has ever attempted to reach consensus with a group of peers understands the humor in the parody. Finding agreement among humans is stressful. I call the stress produced when dealing with other people Community Stress. In *The Seven Cs of Stress: A Burkean Approach*, I describe the primary options for dealing with Community Stress:

> One relief valve for community stress is the "tyranny" valve. Even entire nations have sometimes found that having a "tyrant" make all of the decisions relieves some community stress. Decisions are no longer an issue. It does not matter what our individual preferences may be. The only question is, "What does the tyrant say?" Of course, we sacrifice some free will in the process, but the community stress may be reduced. Just as nations tire of tyrants, so individuals long for such solutions as democracy and anarchy.
> The relief valve of democracy is often characterized by the four-letter word: VOTE. Sometimes this works. . . . [but] what if there is a tie? Who breaks the tie? This is even a problem in marriages. What if the husband wants one thing and the wife another? Who breaks the tie?

> Another democratic relief valve (that is in many respects superior to the four-letter word VOTE) is another four-letter word, which, incidentally, contains exactly the same letters, in a different sequence. I refer to the four-letter word VETO. It works many times when voting does not. ... Eventually ... a compromise is reached. This is how the veto operates. ...
>
> If tyranny sometimes works and democracy sometimes works, anarchy also works at times. In simplest terms, anarchy means, "nobody rules." There was a nineteenth century motto promoting church unity, which suggested: "In essentials, unity. In opinions, liberty. In all things, love." The second element of that catch phrase is a principle of anarchy. There may be instances in which each individual should have the latitude to decide for him or herself. When there is no compelling reason for everyone in the group to be doing the same thing, why not provide liberty/anarchy?[1]

When God speaks through a Jesus or Moses, the tyranny relief valve is activated. There is no room for perspectivism. Other perspectives are unnecessary. However, Jesus and Moses have not made themselves available in the twenty-first century to resolve disagreements. Most issues of biblical interpretation are best handled by committee, some form of democracy--preferably consensus. Nevertheless, voting and vetoing are not strongly recommended relief valves when it comes to biblical interpretation. Perspectivism is essential. The biblical term for perspectivism is eldership.

I completed my bachelor's degree at a Christian college, a school dedicated to producing salaried ministers for independent Christian Churches and Churches of Christ. While I was a student at the school, a concept as old as the New Testament became a fresh new discovery of many of the professors and students. "The Ministry of all Believers" became the slogan of not only the faculty and students of my *alma mater* but also of church leaders and professors nationwide. The biblical text from which this slogan was drawn is Ephesians 4:11-12: "And God gave some to be apostles, some prophets, some evangelists, some pastors and teachers, for the equipping of the saints for the work of ministry."

Many of the terms in this text were interpreted uncritically. For instance, "pastors" was interpreted as those who were called ministers in local churches and whose primary emphasis was counseling. "Evangelists" was interpreted as those preachers who traveled from church to church to conduct evangelistic meetings and those preachers whose primary emphasis was converting individuals to Christianity. "Teachers" was interpreted as those preachers who saw themselves primarily as biblical scholars and educators. When these terms were understood in these senses, the conclusion drawn was that such individuals were not to be termed "ministers," after all. The word "saints" was understood as all "Christians." The pastors, evangelists, and teachers were there to "equip" all Christians to be the "ministers."

In a most obvious manner, this new emphasis on the ministry of all believers produced a new identity crisis and search for identity among those who had studied for the professional "ministry." Furthermore, there was no consolation to be found in referring to the forefather of the independent Christian Churches and Churches of Christ, Alexander Campbell. Campbell himself was angry at the "clergy" system and refused to accept a salary for his "ministry." Ministerial students were faced with two facts:

1. They had spent years in college and seminary preparing for the ministerial profession alone—something that now appeared to be the province of all Christians.
2. The New Testament, despite the difficulties with the "ministry of all believers" slogan, still provided for the financial support of some church leaders.

A solution was immediately proposed, and came in almost the same breath as the cry for the universal ministry. It was difficult to remove the "minister" label from the salaried leaders in local churches, so they were subsequently termed "equipping ministers." Apostles, prophets, evangelists, pastors, and teachers were charged with the equipping ministry. Perhaps, this move was the small leak in the dam that led syllogistically to the acceptance of modern-day spiritual gifts theology among independent Christian Churches and Churches of Christ. I pointed out the problem in a 1976 article in a popular Christian publication:

> These five gifts are in fact in the same category as the spiritual gifts of I Corinthians 12, *et. al.* And, with the obvious exclusion of the gift of the "apostleship," *without exception*, those gifts were received only through the laying on of apostolic hands! It should then be abundantly clear that even this solution of the "equipping ministry" based on the Ephesians 4 text is no longer valid.[2]

An eldership approach is more biblical than an equipping ministry approach. Rather than using the biblical terminology of eldership, Christianity has generally opted for the past two millennia for clergy terminology. Roman Catholics call their salaried leaders clergy, priest, or father. Protestants call them pastor, reverend, preacher, or minister. Only a few denominations opt for the title elder. However, the Greek word for elder is *presbuteros*, so calling them presbyters would be biblical. Other Greek terms the New Testament applies to elders are *poimēn* (translated shepherd or pastor) and *episkopos* (transliterated bishop, or translated overseer). Language that approximates these terms is also biblical. The term pastor causes some confusion since the term appears in the Ephesians 4 list of gifts. And, even the term elder can be confusing, since Paul tells Timothy that Timothy had received a spiritual gift from Paul at the time Paul laid hands upon Timothy to set him apart for the eldership (II Timothy 1:6 and I Timothy 4:14).[3]

Nevertheless, elders are the only non-charismatic officeholders in the church for which the New Testament endorses financial support:

> Let the elders who rule well be considered worthy of double honor, especially those who labor in preaching and teaching; for the scripture says, "you shall not muzzle an ox when it is treading out the grain," and, "The laborer deserves his wages. (I Timothy 5:17-18).

Of course, the apostles were also given financial support in the New Testament church, even though Paul on occasion refused to accept it (I Corinthians 9:1-18). But, other than spiritually gifted individuals, the Bible only explicitly endorses financial support for elders.

Evangelical Christians agree that, in line with Martin Luther's *sola scriptura* dictum, church authority is vested in the Bible. But, whose interpretation of the Bible should Christians accept? Conscientious biblical interpreters such as Augustine, Ireneus, Luther, Wesley, Calvin, Campbell, and Billy Graham from all eras—past, present, and future— do not possess spiritual gifts. Their interpretations, while quite valuable, are not considered inspired, from an eldership perspective. Modern-day Christians, using an eldership approach, should search the scriptures and, like the Bereans of Paul's time, constantly test the concepts, ideas, notions, and interpretations of every credible biblical scholar. Those interpretations that seem to be the most correct should be tentatively accepted, as Christians continue to expand, weed out, and make additions to their understanding of the Bible.

Elders of the Jews

The Bible introduces this process in the concept of eldership. When I was involved in graduate studies under the tutelage of Henry A. Fischel, renowned Jewish scholar and head of Hebrew studies at Indiana University, I began to comprehend the full implications of the term eldership. The Greek word for eldership (*presbuteros*) with its cognates appears in the New Testament seventy-three times. In nearly one-half of those instances (thirty-five times), it refers to the "elders of the Jews." Twenty-two times it is used to denote Christian elders. The book of Revelation uses it twelve times to refer to the "twenty-four elders," a phrase that possibly includes both Christian and Jewish elders; and cognates are used four times to refer to old age itself.

From this data alone, it seems almost unmistakable that the Church borrowed the office from the Jewish system. What this means is that the New Testament eldership—the only noncharismatic office in the Church for which the New Testament encourages financial support—is essentially the same in character as the Jewish eldership.

What then was the Jewish eldership like? An elder of the Jews was among the best biblical scholars of his people. He was almost exclusively a biblical scholar. He had studied for years, usually as a disciple of another Jewish elder (a biblical scholar who had preceded him), often in "schools" such as the schools of Hillel or Shammai. He was generally aware of every major interpretation available for a given text. He could argue intelligently and persuasively for the validity of the interpretation he espoused. He was a representative of the Jewish point of view in an intensely philosophical culture. He and his colleagues interpreted the Jewish constitution (the Bible) for their countrymen. According to Luke 2:41-52, Jesus at the age of twelve discussed the Bible with some of these teachers at the Temple in Jerusalem: "After three days, they found him in the Temple, sitting among the teachers, listening to them and asking questions. All who heard him were amazed at his understanding and his answers."

These Jewish elders had no authority to pass new laws. Their place was merely that of scholarly interpreters of the law that they already possessed. Their general belief was that God's messages to humanity ended with the completion of what we know as the Old Testament, hundreds of years earlier. Although they admitted that God could still speak to humanity through children and "fools" (because of their moral innocence) or through a mysterious voice from heaven (*bat qol*), most of them had difficulty with the notion that the gift of prophecy continued to exist in their era. They were typically unwilling to accept either John the Baptist or Jesus as a prophet:

> Jesus entered the temple courts, and while he was teaching, the chief priests and the elders of the people came to him. "By what authority are you doing these things?" they asked. "And who gave you this authority?"
> Jesus replied, "I will also ask you one question. If you answer me, I will tell you by what authority I am doing these things. John's baptism—where did it come from? Was it from heaven, or from men?"
> They discussed it among themselves and said, "If we say, 'From heaven,' he will as, 'Then why didn't you believe him?' But if we say, 'From men,' we are afraid of the people, for they all hold that John was a prophet.
> So they answered Jesus, "We don't know." (Matthew 21:23-27)

Elders of the Church

The New Testament Christian eldership differed very little from the Jewish eldership. Of course, the Christian eldership accepted John as a prophet and Jesus as the Messiah. They also accepted the premise that in the last days Joel's prophecy of an outpouring of the Holy Spirit would occur (Acts 2:17-18). In contrast to the elders of the Jews, Christian elders in line with Peter's Pentecost pronouncement saw that outpouring (of spiritual gifts) as occurring at the beginning of the early church. Virtually all congregations in the New Testament period had prophets (and other spiritually gifted individuals) in their midst. Nevertheless, the early church also anticipated situations similar to the situation that prompted the Jewish eldership. There would be situations in the first generation church in which prophets and inspired teachers were unavailable to a local congregation. There would also be future generations of the church in which no spiritual gifts existed (I Corinthians 13:8). These situations cry out for a Christian eldership.

Although Paul's disciple, Timothy, had a spiritual gift, there is no evidence he could impart a spiritual gift to other Christians. Instead, Paul instructs Timothy concerning the laying on of hands of eldership (I Timothy 5:22, 3:1-7). Likewise, Paul instructs his "son in [the] faith" Titus to "appoint elders in every town, as I directed you" (Titus 1:5).

Some have observed that Paul's use of the phrase "elders in every town" may indicate that Paul was aware of the importance of perspectivism in developing a Christian eldership. Since elders (in line with the Jewish tradition) are not endowed with a spiritual gift, but are instead merely scholarly interpreters of the inspired messages that the church has received, their interpretations are possibly wrong. Nevertheless, Burke reminds us: "[W]here there is the possibility of a wrong interpretation, there is also the possibility of a right one. The freedom to err argues a freedom to be right" (PC 257). Having more perspectives available us increases the chance that one of them is correct.

While denominationalism has tended to force individuals into accepting a single set of interpretations, eldership would lay out all of the available interpretations of a given text. The individual Christian is allowed to search the scriptures and test the concepts, ideas, notions, and interpretations of every credible biblical scholar, to tentatively accept the best interpretations, and to continually adjust his or her understanding of the Bible. Of course, not every Christian is equipped to critically judge every interpretation.

The *ethos* of the various elders will influence the tentative decision-making of most Christians. What is it about some individuals that makes them trustworthier than others? There are essentially two elements in *ethos*. The first element is "expertise." Some elders have more expertise than others. Factors such as the academic credentials, the respect of other scholars, and the caliber of their publications may contribute to a perception of expertise. Here again, many Christians will be unaware of differences in academic credentials. They may not be aware of the difference between an M.Div. and a Ph.D. They may not know whether or not the university or seminary from which the elder received the degree is despised or respected. They may not know whether the publishing company and/or its process of peer review are respectable. They may not be able to appreciate the difference between articles published in major journals and those published in church newsletters. They may not be aware of the difference between participation in the Society of Biblical Literature and American Academy of Religion and other venues.

The second element of *ethos* is "active good will." Does the person to whom I am listening possess a large amount of good will toward me? I point out the following in *Persuasion, Proposals, and Public Speaking*:

Car repair shops sometimes have a bad reputation. I personally have taken my car to shops in order to ascertain the possible cost of a repair. Sometimes I have been told that it would cost hundreds of dollars only to discover later that the repair could be made for a few dollars. The offending shops do not have "active good will" toward me. I usually have my car repaired by a friend. However, there have been times that my friend was not sufficiently knowledgeable about the problem and how to repair it. I have paid at times for repairs that were not needed or that were not correctly completed. The best solution is to find a "friend" who possesses "expertise." Both of these elements are necessary for someone to possess strong *ethos*.[4]

Salespersons typically face difficulties with establishing *ethos*. They are often not well known to their prospects. Furthermore, since they are commissioned, it is assumed that they do not have "active good will" for the prospects. It is assumed that the salespersons are only concerned with making money. In a similar vein, critical scholars of the Bible often have little *ethos* for Evangelical Christians. It is assumed that they do not have active good will for Bible-believers; whereas, Evangelical scholars are perceived to have active good will for Evangelical Christians. Preachers strongly associated with a specific denomination or congregation may not be trusted, because it is assumed that they (in a fashion similar to salespersons) are only concerned with making converts to their church.

In addition to *ethos*, Christians will often be influenced by identification. I describe identification in *The Seven Cs of Stress*:

> Kenneth Burke, *Dramatism and Development* (Barre, MA: Clark University Press, 1972), 27-28 . . . points out, "we spontaneously identify with some groups or other . . . and . . . we spontaneously, intuitively, and often unconsciously, act upon ourselves." This spontaneous identification can be deliberately induced as when "a politician who, though rich, tells humble constituents of his humble origins." Secondly, it can operate antithetically, "as when allies who would otherwise dispute among themselves join forces against a common enemy" such as was the case in the Persian Gulf War of the early 1990's, Operation Desert Storm. But Burke claims, "The major power of 'identification' derives from situations in which it goes unnoticed." Burke's "prime example is the word 'we,' as when the statement that 'we' are at war includes under the same head soldiers who are getting killed and speculators who hope to make a killing in war stocks." In few situations does this third type of identification work more powerfully than in those situations where the terms "we"

and "you" are used by fans watching athletic competitions. Effectively, rooting for opposite teams in sports or opposite political parties in an election can produce tremendous stress.[5]

Lacking the ability to critically judge either the strength of a given biblical interpretation or the *ethos* of a specific interpreter, Christians will frequently revert to identification as a means of determining which interpreter is correct. As Burke suggests, this identification can be deliberately induced as when a specific scholar, though educated at Harvard and teaching at Duke, tells humble Midwesterners of his or her humble Midwestern roots. Secondly, the identification may be developed antithetically, as when Christians of all persuasions who would otherwise dispute among themselves join forces against Jewish or Moslem interpreters. But the prime example of identification is when it goes unnoticed in the term "we." The preface to a statement "We (meaning our church or religion) believe that . . ." is a staple of most religious discussions. Identification is implicit in the "we." "We" are inclined to believe those pronouncements and interpretations authored by prominent members of "our" denomination.

Despite the tendency of most Christians to rely on *ethos* and identification, *elders* should have or should develop the ability to critically consider the evidence and tentatively accept or reject interpretations based upon logic and textual evidence. Although elders themselves are also influenced by identification, conscientious exegetes should attempt put aside the tendency to provide an apologetic for their own denomination's views. With an open mind, they should examine the evidence put forth by other elders.

As opposed to the clergy concept, the elder's job is not to pass laws, to lead in ritual, to preach funerals, to perform marriages, to make calls on the sick (except when summoned—James 5:14), to forgive sins, to take confessions, etc. The elder's job is to study, to bring to bear every bit of scholarship that is at the elder's disposal, with a view to finding the most correct interpretation possible for a given biblical text.

The elder is never given any assurance of infallibility. Perhaps the suggestion of a multiplicity of elders in each city provides some cushioning against error in interpretation. A recognition of the dangers of certain interpretations as I have proposed in this volume might also provide some cushioning against dangerous errors in interpretation.

The lot that befalls the modern eldership is the task of biblical scholarship. They are not clergy, trustees, rulers, or hirers-and-firers.

They have no one to hire or fire since they are the only ones the New Testament directs the church to support. They are not elected according to majority vote like American politicians. God forbid that they would ever become politicians rather than honest conscientious exegetes (II Timothy 4:3).

Nevertheless, they might consider protecting themselves from being "hireling preachers" and therefore limited in their ability to declare openly the truths of God. It is expedient, like all other elders and scholars of the New Testament period—Paul in Corinth, for instance (Acts 18:3)—that they possess another craft or trade.

Conclusion

While writing this chapter, I was invited to contribute a chapter to an edited text proposed by Omar Swartz to Hampton Press for publication. The proposed volume title is *Transformative Communication Studies: Culture, Hierarchy, and the Human Condition*. In the proposal, Swartz notes:

> [T]he contributors consider the importance of uncertainty and contingency in the development of human potential. Rather than fearing uncertainty and contingency and allowing that fear to control us, contributors argue that we should find within these conditions the source of our humanity, the strength to question and the will to resist.

It is in a similar spirit that I offer this volume on psychotic entelechy, and this chapter on eldership. The strength of eldership is found in its uncertain and contingent nature. Eldership does not fear that uncertainty and contingency.

An eldership approach recognizes that while the Bible may be inerrant, interpretations of the Bible are another matter. Multiple perspectives are useful when interpreting biblical texts. Conscientious biblical interpreters such as Augustine, Ireneus, Luther, Wesley, Calvin, Campbell, and Billy Graham from all eras—past, present, and future— do not possess spiritual gifts. Their interpretations, while quite valuable, are not considered inspired, from an eldership perspective.

The Church borrowed the office from the Jewish system. What this means is that the New Testament eldership—the only noncharismatic office in the Church for which the New Testament encourages financial support—is essentially the same in character as the Jewish eldership.

Perspectivism: The Eldership Approach 157

An elder of the Jews was among the best biblical scholars of his people. He was almost exclusively a biblical scholar. He had studied for years, usually as a disciple of another Jewish elder. He was generally aware of every major interpretation available for a given text. He could argue intelligently and persuasively for the validity of the interpretation he espoused. Jewish elders had no authority to pass new laws. Their place was merely that of scholarly interpreters of the law that they already possessed.

Christian elders, while considering an additional corpus of inspired material (the New Testament) are like the Jewish eldership in that they have no assurance of infallibility in their interpretations. There is an indication in Paul's letter to Titus that multiple elders in each city are preferred. It is true that multiple perspectives should provide some cushion against gross error in interpretation. When elders recognize their own fallibility, uncertainty and contingency become important factors. When considering the dangers of spiritual gifts theology, such uncertainty and contingency helps the church avoid psychotic entelechy.

Notes

[1] Stan A. Lindsay, *The Seven Cs of Stress: A Burkean Approach* (Orlando: Say Press, 2004), 35-36

[2] Stan A. Lindsay, "Restore Eldership," *The Christian Standard* (August 22, 1976), 12.

[3] See my discussion of this matter on pages 111 and 116.

[4] Stan A. Lindsay, *Persuasion, Proposals, and Public Speaking* (Orlando: Say Press, 2004), x-xi.

[5] Lindsay, *Stress*, 5.

Conclusion

I use the term psychotic entelechy to refer to *the tendency of some individuals to be so desirous of fulfilling or bringing to perfection the implications of their terminologies that they engage in very hazardous or damaging actions.* Psychotic entelechy has been around for a long time. People, psychotically invested in the belief that God has spoken to them, have at times been very destructive.

Around 1200 B.C., if the fifth century B.C. playwright Aeschylus is to be believed, the Greek king Agamemnon, following the dictates of the Delphic oracle, sacrificed his daughter, Iphigenia, to Greek gods.

In 950 B.C., Jewish and Canaanite worshippers of the god Molech sacrificed their children by burning them to death.

In 30 A.D., Jesus Christ was crucified. There is evidence that his coreligionists participated in accomplishing the task. His followers were subsequently persecuted and killed. Religious convictions played a role in the destructive behavior. Luke Timothy Johnson writes:

> In the first generation, furthermore, the messianists were a persecuted sect. Some non-messianist Jews certainly sought to extirpate the cult. Jesus was executed. Subsequent leaders of the movement were arrested, imprisoned, stoned, killed. Whether this was all the direct work of Jews is irrelevant, because in the eyes of the messianists they were to blame. . . . Even if I Thess 2:14-16 is an interpolation, it is early evidence for the messianists' perception of Palestinian and diaspora persecution from Jews. Together with Paul's statements about

his own activity (Gal 1:13; Phil 3:6; I Cor 15:8; I Tim 1:12-13) and experience (2 Cor 11:23-29), and the evidence of Acts (5:17-18; 6:12-13; 7:58; 8:3; 9:1-2; 13:50; 14:19; 17:5; 18:12; 23:12-15), as well as that of Josephus . . ., the simple statement of my text may be allowed to stand as historically accurate. . . . The fact of such persecution is also acknowledged by D. R. A. Hare.[1]

Between 500 and 900 A.D, in what is now Mexico, the ancient Mayans sacrificed their noblest children to the gods.

During the Crusades, Christians killed many Jews and Muslims.[2] Muslims also killed many Christians. In 1290, England expelled Jews. In 1320, France expelled Jews. In 1492, Jews were killed and expelled from Spain.

From 1933 to 1945, Adolph Hitler, claiming to act on behalf of God, murdered an estimated six million Jews in Europe in what has been termed the Holocaust. Burke cites Hitler's slogan: "I am acting in the sense of the Almighty Creator: *By warding of Jews I am fighting for the Lord's work*" (*The Philosophy of Literary Form*, hereafter PLF, 198).

From 1900 to the present day, Christians who believe in faith healing have denied their children access to medicines and medical procedures that might have prolonged their lives. They did this in order to demonstrate their faith in the spiritual gifts of their "healers." In the same vein, best-selling crime writer Patricia Cornwell blasted Scientologist actor Tom Cruise who dismissed psychiatry and asserted that medication used to treat mental disorders is an attempt to suppress people. Cornwell claims that Cruise's beliefs could endanger the lives of young fans who worship the megastar.[3]

In November of 1978, members of the People's Temple, led by Jim Jones and transplanted from San Francisco to South America, killed Congressman Leo Ryan and four others before committing mass suicide in their compound. Jones believed he had received messages from God.

In April of 1993, eighty-six persons died in a fire at the Branch Davidian compound, in Waco, Texas, after a fifty-one-day standoff with federal agents. David Koresh, leader of the Branch Davidians, believed he was the Christ referred to in the book of Revelation.

In October of 1994, in Cheiry and Les Granges, Switzerland, forty-eight members of a Swiss cult called the Order of the Solar Tradition became victims of a mass murder-suicide. According to Alexander G.

Higgins of the Associated Press, "the Swiss cult . . . draws on Roman Catholicism and predicts the end of the world."[4]

In March of 1997, thirty-nine members of the Heaven's Gate cult in southern California shed their "vehicles" (earth-bound bodies) by committing mass suicide in order to hitch a ride on the chariot that was coming in the tail of the Hale-Bopp comet. Applewhite, the leader of the Heaven's Gate cult, identified somewhat with the Branch Davidians of Waco, Texas.

On September 11, 2001, Osama bin Laden directed nineteen Moslem men to commit suicide in a terrorist attack on New York City and Washington, D.C., murdering thousands. If the terrorists were not convinced that the Koran taught that they would definitely go to paradise upon completing this deed, they probably would not have willingly killed themselves and others. Since September 11, 2001, more than 3000 additional deadly terror attacks have been carried out by Islamic terrorists.[5]

In October 2005, Lashaun Harris tossed her young children off a pier into San Francisco Bay near Fishermen's Wharf. She told authorities that voices had told her to throw her children into the water.[6]

In November of 2005, Dawn Serrena Young of Eugene, Oregon told police that she killed her 17-month-old daughter, Ruby, to protect the baby from spirits. She said the spirits were talking to her and abusing her daughter. Young's friend, Rosemary Childs, said Young was trying to get away from her spiritual past. Recently, she had explored both Buddhism and Christianity. Said Childs: "She had mentioned that she had some deities that she was taking care of."[7]

Of course, religions are not the only sources of psychotic entelechy. In 1859, Charles Darwin published his book *On the Origin of Species by Means of Natural Selection, or The Preservation of Favoured Races in the Struggle for Life*. The "secondary" title for the work is particularly disturbing. Darwinist theories of evolution contributed strongly to racial supremacy views. Darwinist views devalued the lives of members of some races and the victims of some illnesses:

> Following Darwin's publication of the *Origin* his cousin Francis Galton applied the concepts to human society. . . . In 1883, after Darwin's death, Galton began calling his social philosophy *Eugenics*. In the twentieth century, eugenics movements gained popularity in a number of countries . . . then were stigmatized after their usage in the rhetoric of Nazi Germany in its goals of genetic "purity." . . . In 1944 the American historian Richard Hofstadter applied the term "Social

Darwinism" to describe . . . nations competing for survival . . . . These ideas became discredited by association with racism and imperialism.[8]

From 1978 to 1995, Theodore Kaczynski (the Unabomber) sent mail bombs to various people, killing three and wounding 29. He was motivated by psychotic entelechy as it relates to anti-technologism. Kaczynski was fighting against what he perceived as the evils of technological progress.[9]

Since 1983, more than twenty million people around the world have died of AIDS-related diseases. More than 40 million are now living with HIV, and most of these are likely to die over the next decade or so. In 2004, 4.9 million people were newly infected with HIV.[10] Another 4.9 million were infected in 2005 with HIV.[11] The earliest available prevention strategies were sexual behavior codes from the Bible that forbid both homosexual behavior and heterosexually promiscuous behavior. The psychotic entelechy that permitted the AIDS epidemic to grow was and is primarily political correctness. Biblical morality and sexual behavior codes are routinely dismissed in politically correct circles.

In 1996, 2,315 youth died in alcohol-related crashes. Motor vehicle accidents kill more teenagers and other young adults than any other cause, according to the Center for Disease Control. According to the National Highway Traffic Safety Administration, more than 39 percent of such fatalities involving persons aged 15 to 20 are alcohol related crashes. Every year, 1,400 college students die as a result of alcohol-related accidents.[12] Nearly one-third of high school students binge drink at least once each month.[13] About 40 percent of college students are binge drinkers. The consequences include "death, injury, assault, unprotected sex, drunken driving, vandalism, suicide, and academic problems."[14] The psychotic entelechy that produced this problem is cultural. Alcohol is viewed as an inseparable part of adult socialization.

In 1919 so many Americans believed drinking was wrong this nation passed Prohibition--the Eighteenth Amendment to the U.S. Constitution. The United States was a Christian nation and, due largely to the efforts of Christians, Prohibition was passed. Muslims typically condemn drinking. The Koran states: "O believers, wine . . . [is] an abomination, some of Satan's work; so avoid it; haply so you will prosper. Satan only desires to precipitate enmity and hatred between you in regard to wine" (I.142). The Jewish Bible warns against

Conclusion 163

drinking: "Wine is a mocker and beer a brawler; whoever is led astray by them is not wise" (Proverbs 20:1 NIV). The Mishnah rejects the possibility of saying a blessing over vinegar because one should not bless a curse (*Berachoth* 6:3). Mormons condemn drinking. Based originally on the Word of Wisdom received by church founder and prophet Joseph Smith: "[T]he minimum standard the church now teaches . . . is no alcohol, tobacco or recreational drugs including (relatively recently) all caffeinated drinks."[15]

Since the Roe v. Wade decision, 46,000,000 unborn babies have been killed by abortion.[16] The Roman Catholic Church and Evangelical Protestants have been among the most visible opponents of abortion.[17] The Islamic world has also been a strong opponent of abortion on a global scale, as have Orthodox Jews. Without a strong alliance between Islam and the Catholic Church, abortion would be much more rampant worldwide than it currently is. The psychotic entelechy that permitted abortion to grow is primarily political correctness. Views that disagree with the politically correct view that promiscuous teen sexual behavior is acceptable are frequently suppressed. For example: "Miss America 2003, Erika Harold, . . . said pageant officials . . . ordered her not to talk publicly about sexual abstinence, a cause she advocated to teenage girls in Illinois."[18]

Why Do People Engage in Psychotic Entelechy?

While Darwinism is not technically a religion, it functions in a similar manner. Like Creationism, Darwinism functions as a metanarrative, explaining the story of life. It, therefore, supplies something close to an entelechy. It has a beginning, a middle, and almost an end. The end or *telos* of Christian Creationism is clear--a New Heavens and New Earth, purged of all sin, illness, pain, and death. The *telos* of Darwinism is somewhat more elusive. The question is: At what point will evolution cease? Will life forms ever reach a point at which the perfect life form has evolved? No, probably not. Therefore, Darwinism as a natural process is not a true entelechy. It does not have a clearly defined *telos* toward which the process is moving. As I explain in the next paragraph, however, Darwinism as a "philosophy" is an entelechy. The Darwinist "process" is philosophically tied to the notion that some species (or races) have evolved beyond other species (or races). Hence, Darwinism is probably largely responsible for Hitler's Nazi Germany and the Holocaust. This is not to say that Islamic and Christian anti-

Semitism played no role in Hitler's decisions and destruction. Islamic and Christian anti-Semitism certainly contributed to the Holocaust just as, years earlier, Jewish anti-Christian behavior and attitudes contributed to the development of Christian anti-Semitism.

Darwinism is a Naturalist philosophy. I point out in Chapter 5 of *Implicit Rhetoric* that the primary arguments for abortion come from Materialist, Naturalist, and Humanist philosophies. Burke states: "A philosophy is an 'entelechy'" (ATH 107n). Philosophies offer basic perspectives of reality that, when elaborated, result in the recommendation of everyday actions. These everyday actions resulting from philosophic perspectives are the *teloi*, or the perfected results. If those perfected results of the philosophies are hazardous or damaging, the philosophies have become psychotic entelechies.

Burke comments: "Naturalism dropped the principles of personality and action from the *scene*." (GM 80). Naturalist philosophy so thoroughly emphasizes the scene in which something happens, it leaves no room for the concept of action whatsoever. What happens is not an act because there is no "purpose" to the happening. What happens is sheer motion. There is no agent performing an act because an agent has free will; in a purposeless scene, what happens is simply determined by the various factors of the scene. If a Naturalist views a fetus from a scenic circumference that eliminates all agents (GM 81), there are no moral issues connected with abortion. But, then there are no moral issues at all from a thoroughly Naturalist perspective.

Burke, unlike Aristotle, equates Materialist philosophy with his pentadic term "scene." He understands a Materialist to be one who is concerned only with the motivation that the scene in which an act occurs contributes to the completing of the act. This view of Materialist philosophy is not an exact equivalent of Aristotelian Materialist philosophy. Naturalist philosophy, however, is a good example of a purely Materialist philosophy in a Burkean sense. Pertaining to the abortion debate, a Materialist philosophy would not focus on the fetus as an agent. That specific focus would indicate the existence of an Idealist philosophy. A Materialist philosophy would not focus on abortion as an agency or method of birth control. That focus would be indicative of a Pragmatist philosophy. Instead, a Materialist philosophy would focus on the fetus as material that has not yet become a true organism. When women in the pro-choice movement proclaim in defense of the abortion option, "It's my body," they are proclaiming a Materialist philosophy. The fetus is seen not as a separate organism, (or biological entelechy) but as material that is part of the woman's body. This is a secular Materialist philosophy. What if the fetus, though, is not actually part of the woman's body? DNA evidence suggests that it is not. Abortion, then, as a very destructive behavior, becomes the *telos* of a Materialist psychotic entelechy.

Burke points out the power of Materialism as a philosophy in his essay, "The Rhetoric of Hitler's Battle":

> Every movement . . . must have some spot towards which all roads lead. . . . Hitler . . . decided that this center must be not merely a centralizing hub of *ideas*, but a mecca geographically located . . . . So he selected Munich, as the *materialization* of his unifying panacea. . . . [A] movement must also have its devil. . . . [T]his policy was exemplified in his selection of . . . the "international Jew" . . . . This *materialization* of a religious pattern is, I think, one terrifically effective weapon of propaganda . . . . (PLF 192-194).

Humanists back away from purely Naturalist views and claim that agents and action do exist. The exclusive agents involved in the creation and development of a fetus for Humanists, however, are those humans whose action resulted in conception--as in Burke's citation of Aristotle: "[T]he father [is] a cause of the child . . ." (GM 228). Leaving God out of the Scene, they may claim that humans as the sole "agents" possess the free will and right to either allow a potential human to live or to choose not to. Burke comments: "[I]n proportion as Naturalism dropped the principles of personality and action from the *scene*, Humanism compensatorily stressed their presence in men as *agents*" (GM 80). The psychotic entelechy in a Humanist approach to the abortion issue is exposed when, by extension, we point out: If humans are the final arbiters of life and death, one might indeed be prone to grant humans the free will to kill not only their unborn offspring but also their recently born offspring (or to perform any forms of child abuse, for that matter), and to kill their totally dependent elderly and their infirm.

The cultural entelechy of drinking an alcoholic beverage is psychotic. Drinking alcoholic beverages belongs to the entelechy of socializing. The vast majority of socializing situations in Western civilization include drinking as a part of the cultural set. Yet, by drinking, *some individuals . . . engage in very hazardous or damaging actions.* The socializing process has a beginning, middle, and an end. All entelechies do. Included in socializing process is the drinking of alcohol on the part of those who would socialize. Drinkers give no thought to the dangers of their behavior because they are driven not by logic and reasoning but by the power of an entelechy. Just as David Koresh and Osama bin Laden may have thought they were innocently following the dictates of the messages they received from God, the drinkers think they are innocently following the dictates of messages they have received from their cultures.

Why Emphasize Spiritual Gifts?

If, as I have indicated,
- Darwinism contributed to the murder of 6,000,000 Jews in the Holocaust,
- Alcohol consumption is the number one killer of young people on the highways,
- Abortion has taken the lives of 46,000,000 unborn since 1973, and
- AIDS has killed 20,000,000,

why have I emphasized spiritual gifts in this book? The answer pertains to a principle I outlined in Chapter Two. Clearly, the insertion of two biblical scholars into David Koresh's psychotic entelechy offered Koresh someone other than the devil with whom to negotiate. The genuine concern of the scholars and their willingness to listen to the views of Koresh apparently made an impact. When Koresh wrote to federal negotiator (and Koresh's lawyer) DeGuerin, he commented, "As soon as I can see that people, like Jim Tabor and Phil Arnold have a copy [of my book] I will come out . . . ."[19] The language Koresh uses seems to imply trust and appreciation for the two scholars. By using negotiators who were detached from the evil government entity, a trusting negotiation was made possible.

Having identified myself as an Evangelical Christian, I have lost *ethos* for Darwinists, Materialists, Naturalists, and Humanists. My words may have little impact on advocates of those philosophies. Yet, hopefully, other Evangelical Christians will identify with me. Perhaps, my words will be received with open minds on this subject. I should be far more capable of supplying recalcitrance to religious people than to nonreligious people. Even so, as I have indicated, my influence as a religious person does not necessarily extend to Muslims. To stop the

Conclusion

march of tragedy on a worldwide scale, rational Muslims must have the courage to take the initiative. At least one Moslem group agrees:

> Only moderate Muslims can challenge and defeat extremist Muslims. We can no longer afford to be silent. If we remain silent to the extremism within our community then we should not expect anyone to listen to us when we complain of stereotyping and discrimination by non-Muslims; we should not be surprised when the world treats all of us as terrorists; we should not be surprised when we are profiled at airports.
>   Simply put, not only do Muslims need to join the war against terror, we need to take the lead in this war.[20]

This psychotic entelechy can only be cured by Muslims like these. My efforts, on the other hand, are directed toward solving the type of psychotic entelechy with which I may have some capability.

Like Darwinism, Materialism, Naturalism, and Humanism, the psychotic entelechy of spiritual gifts theology is philosophical in nature. The dangerous behavior results from deductive reasoning. The basic syllogism has the major premise: God speaks to humans through spiritual gifts. The minor premise is: I have a spiritual gift. The conclusion follows: God speaks through me. Of course, many other conclusions have been established syllogistically prior to this, such as: God's communication is perfectly true, One should always do exactly what God says, *etc.*

Since the entire psychotic entelechy rests on the reliability of every premise in the syllogistic development, rebutting a single premise is often all that is necessary. Stephen Toulmin's extension of the syllogism is useful here. The following brief explanation is from my book *Persuasion, Proposals, and Public Speaking*:

> Stephen Toulmin builds upon the syllogism. . . . He suggests that the three elements of the syllogism are not enough. He offers six elements. His first three elements--data, warrant, and claim--are similar to the three parts of the syllogism. . . . However, Toulmin does not allow us to stop here. He provides three more elements--rebuttal, backing, and qualifier. . . . A "rebuttal" may be offered against any data, warrant, claim, or backing. It usually begins with the word "unless." . . . "Backing" is the answering of a rebuttal. It usually starts with the word "but."
>
> . . .

This process of data, warrant, claim, rebuttal, and backing continues until all argumentation is exhausted. Then, we add the "qualifier." The qualifier is usually an adverb such as "probably," "possibly," "absolutely," *etc.*, which indicates the relative strength of the claim after all arguments are considered.[21]

Consider the following example:
- **Major Premise/Warrant**: Humans should do whatever God commands.
- **Minor Premise/Data**: God commands everyone in the People's Temple to drink cyanide-laced Kool-Aid.
- **Conclusion/Claim**: We (in the People's Temple) should drink the Kool-Aid.

It would be difficult to rebut the *warrant*,[22] but we might rebut the *data* as follows:
- **Rebuttal**: (God commands everyone in the People's Temple to drink cyanide-laced Kool-Aid) *unless* Jim Jones is not a true prophet.

Or, we might rebut the claim as follows:
- **Rebuttal**: (We should drink the Kool-Aid) *unless* it contradicts another command of God, such as one not to commit suicide.

The problem with the first rebuttal is that there is an easy backing available:
- **Backing**: (God commands everyone in the People's Temple to drink cyanide-laced Kool-Aid unless Jim Jones is not a true prophet) *but* we all so strongly believe him to be a prophet that we left our homes in the United States to follow him to South America.

Perhaps, a decent backing for the second rebuttal would be:
- **Backing**: (We should drink the Kool-Aid unless it contradicts another command of God, such as one not to commit suicide) *but* God might miraculously save us from death as he saved Isaac from being sacrificed by Abraham.

Another backing for the second rebuttal is:
- **Backing**: (We should drink the Kool-Aid unless it contradicts another command of God, such as one not to commit suicide) *but* the Bible says in Mark 16:17-18, "[T]hese signs will accompany those who believe: . . . when they drink deadly poison, it will not hurt them at all . . . ."

This backing may be rebutted thus:
- **Rebuttal**: (We should drink the Kool-Aid unless it contradicts another command of God, such as one not to commit suicide but the Bible says in Mark 16:17-18, "[T]hese signs will accompany those who believe: . . . when they drink deadly poison, it will not hurt them at all . . . .") *unless* that verse of Mark does not actually belong in the Bible.

As most versions of the Bible will point out, Mark 16:9-20 is not found in the earliest manuscripts of Mark. Those verses are also missing in other ancient textual witnesses. A *qualifier* is needed for the backing, such as ". . . but the Bible *possibly* says in Mark 16:17-18 . . . ."

After considering all rebuttals and backings, we might assign an appropriate qualifier:
- **Claim plus Qualifier**: We should *possibly* drink the Kool-Aid.

If, instead of "possibly" we used the qualifier "probably" or "certainly," our attempt to supply recalcitrance to the members of the People's Temple would be unsuccessful. Even "possibly" is not a very happy qualifier. It would be far better if we were able to use the qualifier "not":
- **Claim plus Qualifier**: We should *not* drink the Kool-Aid.

My goal in this book has been to move certainly's to probably's or possibly's or not's, as they relate to psychotic entelechies. Since that is the case, the most strategic (and, at the same time, weakest) premise in spiritual gifts theology is the following:
- **Major Premise/Warrant or Claim**: Spiritual Gifts are available to modern-day Christians.

I have attempted to rebut that warrant:
- **Rebuttal**: (Spiritual Gifts are available to modern-day Christians) *unless* they were only transferred by the laying on of Apostles' hands, as observed by Simon in Acts 8:18-19.
- **Rebuttal**: (Spiritual Gifts are available to modern-day Christians) *unless* they ceased, as predicted by Paul in I Corinthians 13:8.
- **Rebuttal**: (Spiritual Gifts are available to modern-day Christians) *unless* the "last days" in which, as Joel prophesied, the Holy Spirit would be poured out on all flesh (as cited by Peter in Acts 2:17-21) refer, as Peter says, to Peter's lifetime, not ours.

I personally conclude that the correct qualifier to apply to this claim is "not":

- **Major Premise/Warrant or Claim plus qualifier**: Spiritual Gifts are *not* available to modern-day Christians.

Nevertheless, even "probably" or "possibly" should be enough of a qualifier to encourage us to avoid some of the dangers of spiritual gifts theology. If church leaders teach that Spiritual Gifts are "possibly" or even "probably" available to modern-day Christians, it leaves enough doubt in the equation that it may defuse the dangerous behavior that waits at the *telos* of some message "possibly" received from God.

In January 2006, Israeli Prime Minister Ariel Sharon suffered a massive stroke. Televangelist Pat Robertson strongly implied that his stroke was punishment from God because Sharon had given away part of the Holy Land.[23] A few days later, Ray Nagin--the African-American mayor of hurricane-ravaged New Orleans--promising to rebuild the city as a "chocolate" (he clarified: "African-American") city, proclaimed that "surely" God had sent the hurricanes to America to punish the country for engaging in war in Iraq.[24] These two statements, which were very offensive to many people, could have been rendered less offensive had the speakers injected a qualifier such as "possibly" or even "probably." Instead, Nagin used the qualifier "surely."

What if?

I recommend the "what if" treatment to avoid the dangers of psychotic entelechy. Whenever dangerous or damaging results will be produced by any behavior, try asking yourself: What if I am wrong?

- What if bin Laden's interpretation is wrong and the moderate Moslem interpretation of the Koran is right?
- What if the "unbelievers" and "evildoers" the Koran commands Muslims to fight and kill are NOT Christians or Jews—two groups the Koran also identifies as people of the Book?
- What if Mohammed meant only to fight against pagan unbelievers and evildoers, which is what Mohammed did himself?

- What if bin Laden's tactic of suicide bombing innocent bystanders is not martyrdom, but "insolently transgressing beyond bounds"?
- What if the fetus is not actually part of the woman's body?
- What if the fetus is a separate living organism, altogether?
- What if Naturalist views of scene are incorrect?
- What if there really is a God?
- What if humans are agents and do possess free will?
- What if there really is, as Burke asserts, human action—not just non-purposive motion?
- What if morality should apply?
- What if the *Didache* is right when it says, "Thou shalt not murder a child by abortion nor kill them when born"?[25]
- What if a mother's life is endangered by carrying her pregnancy to full term, thus forcing her into a situation that takes her life?
- What if an abortion opponent so strongly believes abortion is wrong that s/he murders an abortion doctor?
- What if abortion occurs at a time the fetus was viable? Does that constitute murder?
- What if Aristotelian teaching is that quickening, or the beginning of life, happens at conception?
- What if Muslims and Mormons are right and the increasingly alcohol-consuming Evangelical Church is wrong?
- What if Catholics, Evangelical Christians, Muslims, and Orthodox Jews are right about promiscuous sexual behavior and abortion?
- What if those who believe in modern-day spiritual gifts are wrong?
- What if a Christian experiencing voices with messages similar to those heard by Lashaun Harris believes s/he is being tested by God, as was Abraham when God asked him to sacrifice his son Isaac?
- What if one misguided Christian believes s/he has received a message from God to kill his/her children.
- What if a misguided Christian kills his/her children by depriving them of medical care, because some spiritually gifted healer has told him/her s/he needs to display more faith?

- What if one misguided Christian plants a bomb in an abortion clinic or to assassinate an abortion doctor?
- What if one misguided Christian uses deadly force to rid a community of prostitutes?
- What if Jim Jones is not a true prophet?
- What if doing what a prophet commands contradicts another command of God, such as one not to commit suicide.
- What if spiritual gifts were only transferred by the laying on of Apostles' hands, as observed by Simon in Acts 8:18-19.
- What if spiritual gifts ceased, as predicted by Paul in I Corinthians 13:8.
- What if the "last days" in which, as Joel prophesied, the Holy Spirit would be poured out on all flesh (as cited by Peter in Acts 2:17-21) refer, as Peter says, to Peter's lifetime, not ours.

We all need the courage to doubt our own opinions from time to time.

Notes

[1] Luke Johnson, "The New Testament's Anti-Jewish Slander and the Conventions of Ancient Polemic," *The Journal of Biblical Literature* (1989), 108:424.

[2] Mark Albrecht, "Martin Luther and the Jews," a Middler Church History paper, November 19, 1982.

[3] Alexa Baracaia, "Author blasts Cruise's beliefs," *This is London*, 14 December 2005, Available: http://www.thisislondon.co.uk/showbiz/articles/21183785?version=1 (12/14/05).

[4] Alexander G. Higgins, "48 in Swiss Religious Sect Die," *Journal and Courier*, 6 October 1994, sec. A.

[5] "This Week in Islam." Available: http://www.thereligionofpeace.com/default.htm (10/11/05).

[6] Jordan Robertson, "Mom Arrested in Bay Area Children's Deaths," *Washington Post* 10/20/05. Available: http://www.washingtonpost.com/wp-dyn/content/article/2005/10/20/AR2005102000284 (10/20/05).

[7] "Mother says she killed daughter to protect child from 'spirits,'" *Herald.com*, 14 December 2005. Available: http://www.montereyherald/news/13403604.htm?template (12/4/2005)

[8] "Charles Darwin," *Wikipedia*. Available: http://en.wikipedia.org/wiki/Charles_Darwin (1/9/06).

[9] "Theodore Kaczynski," *Wikipedia*. Available: http://en.wikipedia.org/wiki/Theodore_Kaczynski (1/9/06).

[10] "Aids Around the World." Available: http://www.avert.org/aroundworld.htm (10/4/05).

[11] Kamil Zaheer, "Record New HIV Cases in '05: UN," *Reuters* 21 November 2005. Available: http://reuters.myway.com/article/20051121/2005-11-21T132928Z_01_KNE9629 (11/21/05).

[12] Regina Stone, "Group's Ads to Fight Alcohol Abuse," *Tallahassee Democrat* 10 April 2002.

[13] Janelle Carter, "Underage Drinking is on the Rise," *Yahoo! News* 26 February 2002. Available: http://story.news.yahoo.com/news?tmpl=story&cid=514&u=/ap_o.../teen_drinkin (2/26/02).

[14] Richard Morgan, "Report on Alcohol Use Criticizes 'Culture of Drinking' on Campuses," *The Chronicle of Higher Education* 9 April 2002. Available: http://chronicle.com/daily/2002/04/2002040903n.htm (4/9/02).

[15] Jim Catano, "Review of and Commentary on a Book Chapter on the LDS (Mormon) Church's Dietary Code Known as the Word of Wisdom," *Vegasource.com*. Available: http://www.vegasource.com/articles/cantano_review.htm (10/15/2005).

[16] "Abortion in the United States: Statistics and Trends," National Right to Life home page. Available: http://nrlc.org/abortion/facts/abortionstats.html (1/16/06).

[17] Jeffery L. Sheler, "The Theology of Abortion," *U. S. News and World Report*, March 9, 1992, 54.

[18] George Archibald, "Miss America Silenced," *Washington Times* 9 October 2002.

[19] Koresh, "Letter," 3.

[20] "Muslim Group Takes Responsibility for 9-11: 'We Are So Sorry,'" *World Tribune.com* 9/10/04. Available: http://216.26.163.62/2004/me_islam_0 9_10.html (9/11/04).

[21] Stan A. Lindsay, *Persuasion, Proposals, and Public Speaking* (Say Press, 2004), xiii-xiv.

[22] Actually, it would be possible in some religions, such as the ancient Greek religion, to rebut the warrant as follows:

> **Rebuttal**: (Humans should do whatever God commands) *unless* the god is intentionally misleading us.

[23] "Robertson Blamed Sharon Stroke on Policy of 'Dividing God's Land,'" *Media Matters for America* 5 January 2006. Available: http://mediamatters.org/items/200601050004 (1/21/06).

[24] Brett Martel, "New Orleans Mayor Ray Nagin: God Mad at America, but Also at Blacks," *Sign On San Diego.com* 16 January 2006. Available: http://signonsandiego.printthis.clickability.com/pt/cpt?action=cpt&title=SignOnSanDiego (1/21/06).

[25] J. B. Lightfoot, *The Apostolic Fathers* ed. J. R. Harmer (Grand Rapids, MI: Baker Book House, 1956), 123-124.

BIBLIOGRAPHY

Works by Kenneth Burke

Burke, Kenneth. *Attitudes Toward History.* 3rd ed. Berkeley, Los Angeles, London: University of California Press, 1984. (Abbreviated: **ATH**)

---. *Attitudes Toward History.* 2 vols. New York: The New Republic, 1937.

---. *The Complete White Oxen.* Berkeley, Los Angeles, London: University of California Press, 1968. (Abbreviated: **CWO**)

---. *Counter-Statement.* Berkeley, Los Angeles, London: University of California Press, 1968. (Abbreviated: **CS**)

---. "Dramatism." In *Communication: Concepts and Perspectives.* edited by Lee Thayer. 327-360. Washington, D.C.: Spartan Books, 1967.

---. *Dramatism and Development.* Barre, MA: Clark University Press with Barre Publishers. (Abbreviated: **DD**)

---. "The Five Master Terms: Their Place in a 'Dramatistic' Grammar of Motives." *View* 3, no. 2 (1943): 50-52.

---. "Freedom and Authority in the Realm of the Poetic Imagination." In *Freedom and Authority in Our Time.* edited by Lyman Bryson, Louis Finkelstein, R. M. MacIver, and Richard McKeon. 365-375. New York and London: Harper & Brothers, 1953.

---. *A Grammar of Motives.* Berkeley, Los Angeles, London: University of California Press, 1969. (Abbreviated: **GM**)

---. *Language as Symbolic Action: Essays on Life, Literature, and Method.* Berkeley, Los Angeles, London: University of California Press, 1966. (Abbreviated: **LSA**)

---. "On Catharsis or Resolution, with a Postscript," *Kenyon Review* 21 (1959): 337-375.

---. "On Human Behavior Considered 'Dramatistically.'" In *Permanence and Change: An Anatomy of Purpose.* 2nd ed. 274-294. Indianapolis: The Bobbs-Merrill Company, Inc., 1975.

---. "On Stress, Its Seeking." In *Why Man Takes Chances: Studies in Stress-Seeking.* edited by Samuel Z. Klausner. 75-103. Garden City, NY: Doubleday, 1968.

---. "Othello--An Essay to Illustrate a Method." In *Perspecives by Incongruity.* edited by Stanley Edgar Hyman. 152-195. Bloomington: Indiana University Press, 1964.

---. *Permanence and Change: An Anatomy of Purpose*. 2nd ed. Indianapolis: The Bobbs-Merrill Company, Inc., 1975. (Abbreviated: **PC**)

---. *The Philosophy of Literary Form: Studies in Symbolic Action*. 3rd ed. Berkeley, Los Angeles, London: University of California Press, 1973. (Abbreviated: **PLF**)

---. "Poetics and Communication." In *Perspectives in Education, Religion, and the Arts*. edited by Howard E. Kiefer and Milton K. Munitz. 401-418. Albany: State University of New York Press, 1970.

---. "Questions and Answers about the Pentad." *College Composition and Communication* 29 (1978): 330-335.

---. "The Rhetorical Situation." In *Communication: Ethical and Moral Issues*. edited by Lee Thayer. 263-275. London, New York, Paris: Gordon and Breach Science Publishers, 1973.

---. *A Rhetoric of Motives*. Berkeley, Los Angeles, London: University of California Press, 1969. (Abbreviated: **RM**)

---. *The Rhetoric of Religion*. Boston: Beacon Press, 1961. (Abbreviated: **RR**)

---. "Rhetoric--Old and New." In *New Rhetorics*. edited by Martin Steinmann, Jr. 59-76. New York: Scribner's Sons, 1967.

---. "Rhetoric, Poetics, and Philosophy." In *Rhetoric, Philosophy, and Literature*. edited by Don M. Burks. 15-33. West Lafayette, IN: Purdue University Press, 1978.

---. *The Selected Correspondence of Kenneth Burke and Malcolm Cowley 1915-1981*. edited by Paul Jay. Berkeley and Los Angeles: University of California Press, 1990.

---. "Theology and Logology (Abstract)." *Journal of the American Academy of Religion* 47 (1979): 298.

---. *Towards a Better Life*. Berkeley, Los Angeles, London: University of California Press, 1982. (Abbreviated: **TBL**)

Works about Kenneth Burke

Appel, Edward C. "Kenneth Burke: Coy Theologian." *Journal of Communication and Religion* 16 (1993), 99-110.

Booth, Wayne C. "The Many Voices of Kenneth Burke, Theologian and Prophet, as Revealed in His Letters to Me." In *Unending Conversations: New Writings by and about Kenneth Burke* edited by Greig R. Henderson and David Cratis Williams (Carbondale: Southern Illinois University Press, 2001), 179-201.
Burke, Kenneth. *On Symbols and Society.* edited by Joseph R. Gusfield. Chicago and London: University of Chicago Press, 1989.
Burks, Don M. "Dramatic Irony, Collaboration, and Kenneth Burke's Theory of Form." *Pre/Text* 6 (1985): 255-273.
---. *Rhetoric, Philosophy, and Literature: An Exploration.* West Lafayette, IN: Purdue University Press, 1978.
"Counter-Gridlock: An Interview with Kenneth Burke." *All Area*, vol 2 (Spring, 1983): 12.
Cowley, Malcolm. "Prolegomena to Kenneth Burke." In *Critical Responses to Kenneth Burke.* edited by William R. Rueckert. 247-251. Minneapolis: University of Minnesota Press, 1969.
Donoghue, Denis. "American Sage." *The New York Review* 26 (September, 1985): 39-42.
Foss, Sonja K., Karen A. Foss, and Robert Trapp. *Contemporary Perspectives on Rhetoric.* 2nd ed. Prospect Heights, IL: Waveland Press, 1991.
Griffin, Leland M. "A Dramatistic Theory of the Rhetoric of Movements." In *Critical Responses to Kenneth Burke.* edited by William R. Rueckert. 456-478. Minneapolis: University of Minnesota Press, 1969.
Hart, Roderick P. *Modern Rhetorical Criticism.* Glenview, IL and London: Scott, Foresman/Little, Brown, 1990.
Howell, Wilbur Samuel. *Poetics, Rhetoric, and Logic.* Ithaca and London: Cornell University Press, 1975.
Jennerman, Donald L. "Kenneth Burke's Poetics of Catharsis." In *Representing Kenneth Burke.* edited by Hayden White and Margaret Brose. 31-51. Baltimore and London: John Hopkins University Press, 1982.
---. "The Literary Criticism and Theory of Kenneth Burke in Light of Aristotle, Freud, and Marx." Ph.D. diss., Indiana University, 1974.
Lindsay, Stan A. "The Burkean Entelechy and the Apocalypse of John." Ph.D. diss., Purdue University, 1995.

---. *A Concise Kenneth Burke Concordance*. Orlando: Say Press, 2004.

---. *Implicit Rhetoric: Kenneth Burke's Extension of Aristotle's Concept of Entelechy*. Lanham, MD: University Press of America, 1998.

---. *Persuasion, Proposals, and Public Speaking*. Orlando: Say Press, 2004.

---. *The Seven Cs of Stress: A Burkean Approach*. Orlando: Say Press, 2004.

---. *The Twenty-One Sales in a Sale*. Grants Pass, OR: Oasis Press/PSI Research, 1998.

Nichols, Marie Hochmuth. "Burkeian Criticism." In *Essays on Rhetorical Criticism*. edited by Thomas R. Nilsen. New York: Random House, 1968.

---. "Kenneth Burke and the 'New Rhetoric.'" In *Contemporary Theories of Rhetoric: Selected Readings*. edited by Richard L. Johannesen. New York, Evanston, San Francisco, London: Harper and Row, 1971.

Rueckert, William H. *Critical Responses to Kenneth Burke*. Minneapolis: University of Minnesota Press, 1969.

---. *Encounters with Kenneth Burke*. Urbana and Chicago: University of Illinois Press, 1994.

---. *Kenneth Burke and the Drama of Human Relations*. 2nd ed. Berkeley: University of California Press, 1963).

---. "The Rhetoric of Rebirth: A Study of the Literary Theory and Critical Practice of Kenneth Burke." Ph.D. diss., University of Michigan, 1956.

Schiappa, Edward. "Burkean Tropes and Kuhnian Science: A Social Constructionist Perspective on Language and Reality." *Journal of Advanced Communication* 13 (1993): 401-422.

White, Hayden, and Margaret Brose, editors. *Representing Kenneth Burke*. Baltimore and London: John Hopkins University Press, 1982.

Winterowd, W. Ross. "Kenneth Burke: An annotated Glossary of His Terministic Screen and a 'Statistical' Survey of His Major Concepts." *Rhetoric Society Quarterly* 15 (1985): 145-177.

Abortion Resources

"Abortion in the United States: Statistics and Trends." National Right to Life home page. Available: http://nrlc.org/abortion/facts/abortionstats.html (1/16/06).
Archibald, George. "Miss America Silenced." *Washington Times* 9 October 2002.
Sheler, Jeffery L. "The Theology of Abortion." *U. S. News and World Report.* March 9, 1992, 54.

AIDS Resources

"Aids Around the World." Available: http://www.avert.org/around world.htm (10/4/05).
"The History of AIDS 1981-1986." Available: http://www.avert.org/his81_86.htm (10/4/05).
Zaheer, Kamil. "Record New HIV Cases in '05: UN." *Reuters* 21 November 2005. Available: http://reuters.myway.com/article/20051121/2005-11-21T132928Z_01_KNE9629 (11/21/05).

Alcohol Resources

Carter, Janelle. "Underage Drinking is on the Rise." *Yahoo! News* 26 February 2002. Available: http://story.news.yahoo.com/news?tmpl=story&cid=514&u=/ap_o.../teen_drinkin (2/26/02).
"Drinking Purple Grape Juice Significantly Reduced Oxidation of Bad Cholesterol, According to Study." March 1999. Available: http://www.welchs.com (3/21/99).
Easton, Burton Scott. "Wine, Wine Press." In *The International Standard Bible Encyclopedia* 5 vols. Edited by James Orr. Grand Rapids: Eerdmans, 1939 (originally published 1929), 5:3087.
"Eating for a Sharper Mind," *Psychology Today.* Available: http://articles.health.msn.com/id/100111228/site/100000000 (10/26/05).
McConnaughey, Janet. "Study: Frequent Drinking Can Help Heart." *Associated Press*, January 9, 2004.
McKenna, Brendan. "The Basics: Your Life Insurer is Counting Your Drinks." *Insure.com.*

Morgan, Richard. "Report on Alcohol Use Criticizes 'Culture of Drinking' on Campuses." *The Chronicle of Higher Education* 9 April 2002. Available: http://chronicle.com/daily/2002/04/2002040903n.htm (4/9/02).

Stone, Regina. "Group's Ads to Fight Alcohol Abuse." *Tallahassee Democrat* 10 April 2002.

American and World Political Resources

Bush, George W. "State of the Union Address" 1/29/02. Available: http://www.washingtonpost.com/ac2/wp-dyn/A58285-2002Jan29?language=printer (1/30/02).

"Charles Darwin." *Wikipedia*. Available: http://en.wikipedia.org/wiki/Charles_Darwin (1/9/06).

"God Told Me to Invade Iraq, Bush Tells Palestinian Ministers." *BBC.co.uk* 10/16/05. Available: http://www.bbc.co.uk/print/pressoffice/pressreleases/stories/2005/10_october/06/bush.shtml (10/6/05).

Martel, Brett. "New Orleans Mayor Ray Nagin: God Mad at America, but Also at Blacks." *Sign On San Diego.com* 16 January 2006. Available: http://signonsandiego.printthis.clickability.com/pt/cpt?action=cpt&title=SignOnSanDiego (1/21/06).

"National Day of Prayer and Remembrance." Available: http://www.holyfamilyhmb.org/US_Tragedy/Litany_and_Prayer/Islamic_Prayer/islamic_prayer.html (2/20/02).

"Prayer Service Speakers List." *Yahoo News* 9/14/01. Available: http://dailynews.yahoo.com/h/ap/20010914/us/prayer_service_list_2.html (9/19/01).

"Robertson Blamed Sharon Stroke on Policy of 'Dividing God's Land.'" *Media Matters for America* 5 January 2006. Available: http://mediamatters .org/items/200601050004 (1/21/06).

"Theodore Kaczynski." *Wikipedia*. Available: http://en.wikipedia.org/wiki/Theodore_Kaczynski (1/9/06).

"White House Denies Bush Claimed Divine Inspiration." *Breitbart.com* 10/17/05. Available: http://www.breitbart.com/news/2005/10/07/051007131357.nstalu7a.html (10/7/05).

Classical and Christian Resources

Albrecht, Mark. "Martin Luther and the Jews." Middler Church History paper. November 19, 1982.
Allen, James. *The First Year of Greek*. rev. ed. Toronto: MacMillan, 1931.
Aristotle. *De Anima*. translated by J. A. Smith. Oxford: At the Clarendon Press, 1931. Reprinted in *The Works of Aristotle Translated into English*. edited by W. D. Ross. Oxford: At the Clarendon Press, 1968.
---. *On Sophistical Refutations, On Coming-to-Be and Passing Away*. translated by E. S. Forster. Cambridge: Harvard University Press, 1955.
---. *Physica*. translated by R. P. Hardie and R. K. Gaye. In *The Basic Works of Aristotle*. edited by Richard McKeon. New York: Random House, 1941.
---. *Poetics*. translated by T. S. Dorsch. In *Classical Literary Criticism*. London: Penguin Books, 1965.
---. *The Rhetoric and the Poetics of Aristotle*. edited by Friedrich Solmsen. New York: Random House, 1954.
Bauernfeind, O. "*nêphô, nêphalios, eknêphô.*" In *Theological Dictionary of the New Testament* 9 vols. Edited by Gerhard Kittel. Translated by Geoffrey W. Bromiley. Grand Rapids, MI: Wm. B. Eerdmans Publishing, 1967, 4:939.
Bultmann, Rudolph. "*zôopoieô.*" In *Theological Dictionary of the New Testament*. 9 vols. edited by Gerhard Kittel. translated by Geoffrey W. Bromiley. 2:874-875. Grand Rapids, MI: Wm B. Eerdmans, 1964.
Caird, G. B. *A Commentary on the Revelation of St. John the Divine*. a vol. of *Harper's New Testament Commentaries*. Edited by Henry Chadwick. New York, Hagerstown, San Francisco, London: Harper & Row Publishers, 1966.
Clarke, Ruth Anne, and Jesse G. Delia. "Topoi and Rhetorical Competence." *Quarterly Journal of Speech* 65 (1979): 195.
Frisk, Hjalmar. *Griechisches Etymologisches Woerterbuch*. 2 vols. Heidelberg: Carl Winter Universitatsverlag, 1960.

Greeven, Heinrich. "*euchomai, euchê, proseuchomai, proseuchê.*" In *Theological Dictionary of the New Testament.* 9 vols. edited by Gerhard Kittel. translated by Geoffrey W. Bromiley. 2:775-784. Grand Rapids, MI: Wm. B. Eerdmans Publishing Company, 1964.

Homer. *The Iliad of Homer.* translated by Richmond Lattimore. Chicago and London: University of Chicago Press, 1961.

Johnson, Luke. "The New Testament's Anti-Jewish Slander and the Conventions of Ancient Polemic." *The Journal of Biblical Literature* (1989), 108:424.

Junior Classic Latin Dictionary. Chicago: Follett Publishing Co., 1960.

Kennedy, George A. *Aristotle On Rhetoric.* New York and Oxford: Oxford University Press, 1991.

---. *The Art of Persuasion in Greece.* Princeton, NJ: Princeton University Press, 1963.

Liddell, Henry George, and Robert Scott. Compilers. *A Greek-English Lexicon.* revised by Henry Stuart Jones. Oxford: At the Clarendon Press, 1968.

---. *A Lexicon Abridged from Liddell and Scott's Greek-English Lexicon.* Oxford: At the Clarendon Press, 1966.

Lightfoot, J. B. *The Apostolic Fathers.* edited by J. R. Harmer. Grand Rapids, MI: Baker Book House, 1956.

Lindsay, Stan A. "Restore Eldership." *The Christian Standard* (August 22, 1976), 12-14.

---. *Revelation: The Human Drama.* Bethlehem, PA: Lehigh University Press, 2001.

McKeon, Richard. *The Basic Works of Aristotle.* New York: Random House, 1941.

---. *Introduction to Aristotle.* 2nd ed. Chicago and London: University of Chicago Press, 1973.

Randall, John Herman, Jr. *Aristotle.* New York: Columbia University Press, 1960.

Ross, W.D. *Aristotle (A Complete Exposition of his Works & Thought).* New York: Meridian Books, 1960.

---. *Aristotle De Anima.* Oxford: At the Clarendon Press, 1961.

---. *Aristotle's Metaphysics.* 2 vols. Oxford: At the Clarendon Press, 1966.

---. *Aristotle's Physics.* Oxford: At the Clarendon Press, 1966.

---. *Metaphysica.* vol. 8 of *The Works of Aristotle Translated into English.* Oxford: At the Clarendon Press, 1966.

Schaeder, H. H. *"Nazarênos, Nazôrios,"* in *Theological Dictionary of the New Testament* 9 vols. Edited by Gerhard Kittel. Translated by Geoffrey W. Bromiley (Grand Rapids, MI: Wm. B. Eerdmans Publishing, 1967), 4:878-879.

Williams, C. J. F. *Aristotle's De Generatione et Corruptione.* Oxford: At the Clarendon Press, 1982.

Communication Resources

Berko, Roy M., Lawrence B. Rosenfeld, and Larry A. Samovar. *Connecting: A Culture-Sensitive Approach to Interpersonal Communication Competency.* 2nd ed. Fort Worth, TX: Harcourt Brace College Publishers, 1997.

Fisher, Jeanne Y. "A Burkean Analysis of the Rhetorical Dimensions of a Multiple Murder and Suicide," *Quarterly Journal of Speech* 60 (1974): 175-189.

Hart, Roderick P. *Modern Rhetorical Criticism.* Glenview, Illinois and London: Scott, Foresman/Little, Brown Higher Education, 1990.

Kardes, Frank R. *Consumer Behavior and Managerial Decision Making.* 2nd ed. Upper Saddle River, NJ: Prentice Hall, 2002.

Schiappa, Edward. Editor. *Landmark Essays on Classical Greek Rhetoric.* Davis, CA: Hermagoras Press, 1994.

Cult Resources

Baracaia, Alexa. "Author blasts Cruise's beliefs." *This is London* 14 December 2005. Available: http://www.thisislondon.co.uk/showbiz/articles/21183785?version=1 (12/14/05).

"Bible Scholar Claims Branch Davidian Disaster Could Have Been Avoided." *Religious Studies News* 10, no. 3 (1995): 3.

Higgins, Alexander G. "48 in Swiss Religious Sect Die." *Journal and Courier.* 6 October 1994, sec. A.

Koresh, David. "Letter from David Koresh to Richard DeGuerin [14 April 1993]." *Religious Studies News* 10, no. 3 (1995): 3.

Lardner, George, Jr. "U.S. Argues Idaho Can't Prosecute FBI Sniper: Case Stems From 1992 Ruby Ridge Siege." *Washington Post.* 14 March 1998, sec. A.

Miller, Mark. "Secrets of the Cult." *Newsweek.* 14 April 1997, 28-37.

"Mother says she killed daughter to protect child from 'spirits.'" *Herald.com* 14 December 2005. Available: http://www.montereyherald/news/13403604.htm?template (12/4/2005)

Robertson, Jordan. "Mom Arrested in Bay Area Children's Deaths," *Washington Post* 10/20/05. Available: http://www.washingtonpost.com/wp-dyn/content/article/2005/10/20/AR2005102000284 (10/20/05).

Tabor, James D. "Introductory Remarks." *Religious Studies News* 10, no. 3 (1995): 3.

Tabor, James D., and Eugene V. Gallagher. *Why Waco?: Cults and the Battle for Religious Freedom in America.* Berkeley, CA: University of California Press, 1995.

Islamic Resources

Abeidoh, Rawhi. "Focus-Bin Laden Adopts Saddam's Line in Fight Against U.S." *Yahoo News* 10/8/01. Available: http://uk.news.yahoo.com/011008/80/c7kw4.html (10/10/01).

Aboudi, Sami. "Defiant bin Laden Vows No Peace for U.S." *Yahoo News* 10/8/01. Available: http://uk.news.yahoo.com/011008/80/c713y.html (10/10/01).

Arberry, A. J. *The Koran Interpreted.* 2 vols. New York: MacMillan, 1955.

"Bin Laden's Sole Post-September 11 TV Interview Aired." *CNN.com/U.S.* 2/1/02. Available: http://www7.cnn.com/2002/US/01/31/gen.binladen.interview (2/2/02).

"Bin Laden Urges Pakistanis to Defend Islam-Jazeera." *Yahoo! News* 11/1/01. Available: http://dailynews.yahoo.com/htx/nm/20011101/ts/attack_binladen_letter_dc_4.html (11/1/01).

Dan, Uri, and Andy Geller. "Arafat on Hot Seat for Putting Down Protests." *NYPOST.COM* 10/11/01. Available: http://www.nypost.com/news/worldnews/33750.html (10/11/01).

Deeb, Mary-Jane. "A Closer Look at the Words of an Image Maker." *Washington Post* 10/28/01. Available: http://www.washingtonpost.com/ac2/wp-dyn/A6001420011Oct26?language=printer (11/13/01)

Drees, Caroline. "Bin Laden Speech Hits Right Chord." *Yahoo! News* 10/8/01. Available: http://uk.news.yahoo.com/011008/80/c7nfl.html (10/10/01).

"Full Transcript of bin Ladin's Speech." *Aljazeera.net* 11/1/04. Available: http://english.aljazeera.net/NR/exeres/79C6AF22-98FB-4A1C-B21F-2BC36E 87F61F.htm (1/24/05).

"Frontline: Interview with Osama bin Laden" 5/98. Available: http://www.pbs.org/wgbh/pages/frontline/shows/binladen/who/interview.html (10/1/01).

"Jihad Against Jews and Crusaders: World Islamic Front Statement." 2/23/98. Available: http://www.fas.org/irp/world/para/docs/980223-fatwa.htm (10/1/01).

Khan, Riaz. "Pakistanis Leave for Holy War." *Yahoo! News* 10/27/01. Available: http://dailynews.yahoo.com/h/ap/20011027/ts/attacks_holy_warriors_4.html (10/27/01).

Miller, John. "Interview: Osama bin Laden." *Frontline*. Available: http://www.pbs.org/wgbh/pages/frontline/shows/binladen/who/interview.html (10/1/01).

"Muslim Group Takes Responsibility for 9-11: 'We Are So Sorry.'" *World Tribune.com* 9/10/04. Available: http://216.26.163.62/2004/me_islam_0_9_10.html (9/11/04).

Ostling, Richard N. "If It Holds, New Muslim Unity Could Remake America's Religious Landscape." *Religious Studies News, AAR Edition* 16, no. 3 (2001): 8.

Reuters. "Bin Laden Fans Voice Online Admiration," *Yahoo! News* 10/10/01. Available: http://uk.news.yahoo.com/011008/80/c71f8.html (10/10/01).

Reuters. "Islamic Group Says Blair 'Legitimate Target.'" *Yahoo! News* 10/10/01. Available: http://uk.news.yahoo.com/011010/80/c8h17.html (10/10/01).

"Saudis May Ask U.S. to Leave, *Washington Post* Says" *Yahoo News* 1/18/02. Available: http://dailynews.yahoo.com/h/nm/20020118/ts/attack_saudi_report_dc.html (1/18/02).

Smyth, Gareth. "Wipe Israel From Map, Says Iran's President." *Financial Times* 10/26/05. Available: http://news.ft.com/cms/s/14cc1ccc-465b-11da-8880-00000e2511c8.html.

"Suicide Bombers: Why Do They Kill Themselves and Others, and What Does Islam Say About Their Actions?" Available: http://islam.about.com/library/weekly/aa051801a.htm (5/29/02).

"Sympathy for U.S. in Mosque Pulpits.'" *USA Today* 11/7/01. Available: http://www.usatoday.com/news/nation/2001/09/14/mosque-pulpits.htm (11/7/01).

"This Week in Islam." Available: http://www.thereligionofpeace.com/default.htm (10/11/05).

Webster, Philip, Christopher Walker, and David Charter, "Assad Ambushes Blair." *The Times* 11/1/01. Available: http://www.thetimes.co.uk/article/0,,2001370005200138049O,00.html (10/31/01).

"What is Islam?" Available: http://www.lhmint.org/whowillteach/what is_print.htm (9/26/05).

Jewish Resources

Di Sante, Carmine. *Jewish Prayer: The Origins of the Christian Liturgy.* translated by Matthew J. O'Connell. New York and Mahwah, NJ: Paulist Press, 1991.

Finkelstein, Louis, ed. *The Jews: Their History.* 4th ed. New York: Shocken Books, 1970.

Fischel, Henry A. *Rabbinic Literature and Greco-Roman Philosophy.* Leiden: E. J. Brill, 1973.

Fishman, Isidore. *Gateway to the Mishnah.* Hartmore, CT: Prayer Book Press, Inc., 1970.

Ginzberg, Louis. *The Legends of the Jews.* 7 vols. Philadelphia: The Jewish Publication Society of America, 5728-1968.

Moore, G. F. *Judaism in the First Centuries of the Christian Era.* 2 vols. Cambridge: Harvard University Press, 1927-30.

Mormon Resources

Catano, Jim. "Review of and Commentary on a Book Chapter on the LDS (Mormon) Church's Dietary Code Known as the Word of Wisdom." *Vegasource.com.* Available: http://www.vegasource.com/articles/cantano_review.htm (10/15/2005).

"Distinctive Beliefs of the Mormon Church." *Catholic Answers.* Available: http://www.catholic.com/library/Distinctive_Beliefs_of_Mormon.asp (10/15/05).

Stapley J. (reply to D. Bell). "Teach Me Some Church History #2." *The Millennial Star* 8/25/05. Available: http://www.millennialstar.org/index.php/2005/08/25/teach_me_some_chu rch_history_2 (10/17/05).

Pentecostal Resources

"Pentecostalism" *Religious Movements*. Available: http://religious movements.lib.virginia.edu/nrms/penta.html (10/17/05).
Hughes, Brian. "History of Charismatic Movement." Available: http://www.unitypublishing.com/Hist-of-Char.html (10/17/05).
Turner, John. "Spiritual Gifts Inventory." Published by Vine Street Christian Church.

INDEX

Note: Some entries that appear throughout the book--such as America, Burke, Christian, entelechy, gifts, God, Islam, Moslem, Muslim, prophecy, psychotic, religion, rhetoric, and spiritual--are not listed in the index.

abortion, 1, 3, 7, 70, 72-79, 91-92, 125, 163-166, 171-172
Abraham, 3, 40, 69, 78, 88, 96, 106, 109, 113, 168, 171
abstinence, 163
action, 1, 9, 13-14, 24-25, 27, 31, 40, 48, 59, 66, 70, 72-76, 78, 89, 91, 108, 128, 137, 139, 141, 145, 159, 164-165, 171
Afghanistan, 1, 38-39, 50, 57
Agamemnon, 7, 159
aggress/ion, 25, 38, 41, 43, 48, 60-61, 63-64, 71
agnosticism, 7
AIDS, 5, 65, 70-72, 92, 162, 166
alcohol, 3, 26, 70, 79-83, 85-87, 89-92, 106, 162-163, 165-166, 171
al-Qaida, 5, 44, 50, 65, 70
angel, 3, 98, 106-107, 110, 121
Antichrist, 25
anti-Semitism, 47, 125, 164
apocalyptic, 19, 28, 32
apostles' hands, laying on of, 100, 111-112, 114-116, 118-120, 123-124, 132-133, 149-150, 169, 172
Applewhite, Gene, 1, 5, 12-13, 70, 103, 161
archetype, 21, 30
Aristotle, 14, 66, 72-75, 77-78, 122, 130-132, 138, 164-165, 171

attitude, 8, 13, 27, 40, 131, 139, 141, 164
Augustine, St., 101, 150, 156
Babylon, 7, 19, 25-30, 32-33, 123
backing, 167-169
Bakker, Jim, 4, 134
Balaam, 133, 144
baptism, 100, 102, 115-119, 132, 135, 152 *See also* Definition of Holy Spirit Baptism
Bat Qol, 98, 151
Beast, 18, 21, 23, 25-26, 28-29, 32
beginning, 10, 22, 64, 77-78, 85, 100, 102, 118-119, 122, 135, 140, 152, 171
beginning, middle, and end, 10, 91, 123, 163, 165
benevolence, 4
Bible (-believing), biblical, 3, 5-6, 12, 17-21, 25, 28, 30-33, 40, 51-52, 63, 71, 77-80, 83-85, 89, 91, 95, 98, 100, 103, 105, 110, 124-125, 130, 132, 133 135-136, 140, 143-145, 148-151, 153-157, 162, 166, 168-169 *See also* scripture
bin Laden, Osama, 1, 5, 37-52, 55-56, 70, 91, 161, 166, 170-171
biological entelechy, 8-9, 14, 165

Branch Davidians, 5, 12, 17, 19, 22-24, 26-28, 30, 70, 86, 103, 160-161
bride, 18, 21-23, 28-29
Brown, Norman O., 131
Bush, George W., 1-2, 43-45, 49, 59, 82
castration, 13
Catholic, Roman, 3, 6, 12, 60, 76, 78, 91-92, 98-99, 101-103, 134, 150, 161, 163, 171
character/s, 11, 12, 84, 133, 141
China, Communist, 7, 75
Christ, 18-20, 22-23, 25, 97, 119, 143, 145, 159-160
circumference, 74, 76, 114, 137, 164
cluster, 18, 25, 27-28, 32, 34, 59
comic frame, 43
communication, 7, 11, 29, 31, 60, 97-99, 110, 156, 167
communism, 7, 75
complete, 9, 56, 59, 78, 98, 117, 123, 142, 145, 148, 154
compulsion, 11, 13-14, 25, 29, 59, 62, 66
conception, 75, 77, 78, 165, 171
consistency, 32, 77, 89, 129, 140-141
contingency, 156-157
crucifixion, 88, 143, 159
Cruise, Tom, 160
Crusades, 44, 52, 61, 83, 160
cultural (entelechy), 71, 79, 82, 89-91, 162, 165
Cyrus, 19, 26

Darwin, Charles, 7, 161-164, 166-167
deacon, 88, 110, 112, 114-115
death, 5, 7, 12, 26-28, 37, 49, 52, 59, 64, 70, 75, 80, 92, 97-98, 122, 159, 161-163, 165, 168
Deeb, Mary Jane, 45-47
definition of entelechy, 8-10
definition of Holy Spirit baptism, 100
definition of [hu]man, 9-10
definition of Idealism, 138-139, 140-141
definition of madness, 13
definition of Materialist/ism, 132, 134
definition of Mysticism, 137
definition of Pragmatism, 142
definition of Protestantism, 95
definition of psychotic entelechy, 13-14, 27, 31, 66, 70, 73, 78, 91, 159, 164-165
definition of Realism, 130-131
definition of speaking in tongues, 116
definition of spiritual gifts, 1, 95, 140
DeGuerin, Richard, 23, 26, 29, 33, 166
demon possession, 87, 101, 137
Descartes, Rene, 130, 136
destiny, 29, 62
determinism, 9, 14, 127
development, 8, 75, 156, 164-165, 167
Dewey, John, 11, 12
Didachē, 76, 171

differentiation, 108, 135
dignity, 100
discounting, 27, 31-34, 106
diversity, 5, 70
DNA, 73-74, 165
doubt, 2, 6, 17, 51, 78, 80, 122, 130-131, 136, 145, 170, 172 *See also* methodological doubt
dramatism, 10
drinking, 3, 5, 79-84, 87-92, 106, 162-163, 165-166
eldership, 20, 88, 102-103, 111, 116, 143, 147-157
Elijah, 97, 111   *See also* Muhammad, Elijah
end, 1, 6, 9-10, 12-13, 18-21, 26-27, 33, 38, 56-57, 91, 98-99, 102-103, 121-123, 136, 138, 142, 144, 161, 163, 165
energeia, 130
epiphany, 109-110
equations, 22, 59, 114, 170
equipping ministry, 145, 148-150, 153
essence, 9-10, 72, 137, 139-141 *See also* temporizing of essence
ethos, 153-155, 166
eugenics, 161
Evangelical, 2, 76, 78-80, 82-83, 85, 91-92, 106, 124, 127, 130-132, 134, 136, 144-145, 150, 154, 163, 166, 171
evil(doers), 19, 25-26, 28-29, 32-33, 40-43, 45-47, 50-52, 59-60, 63, 65, 69, 96, 109-110, 113-114, 141, 162, 166, 170
expectation, 90

experience, 9, 29, 58-59, 92, 100-102, 119, 135, 142, 160
extreme(s), 2, 4, 6, 8, 10-11, 13-14, 17, 24, 29, 31, 37-38, 56, 66, 71, 101, 137, 143 *See also* meaning carried to extreme
fanatic, 2, 47
fatwa(h), 45, 48, 56
final cause/*telos*, 6, 8, 13, 18, 25-26, 33, 43, 50, 52, 55, 58-59, 122-123, 138, 163, 165, 170
Fisher, Jeanne, 24, 27, 33
for the sake of, 48
form, 8, 10, 29, 46, 137-138, 148, 163
free will, 14, 66, 74, 75, 108, 110, 147, 164-165, 171
Freud, Sigmund, 11, 13, 29, 62
fulfilment/fulfillment, 9, 13, 14, 17, 19, 27, 38, 46, 66, 70, 78, 84, 87, 123, 140, 159
generating principle, 128
generation, 8, 19, 98, 103, 107, 122-124, 144, 152, 159
German/y, 76, 79-80, 161, 163
Gog and Magog, 26, 28-29
Hamas, 39
Hart, Roderick, 5, 37
heaven, 9, 21, 26, 40, 62, 95, 98, 109, 121-122, 135, 138, 142, 151-152, 163
Heaven's Gate, 5, 12-13, 30, 70, 103, 161
hierarchy, 144, 156
Hitler, Adolph, 1, 5, 11, 13, 38, 47, 79, 160, 163-165

Holy Spirit, 4, 18, 22, 100-102, 106-107, 114-119, 121, 132-134, 140, 142, 152, 169, 172
hortatory, 3-5, 50, 110
hortatory negative, 108-110
Hussein, Saddam, 37, 45, 47, 61, 63
identification, 11-12, 24, 26, 32, 34, 41, 58, 72, 103, 106, 113, 154-155, 161, 166,
implicit, 7-11, 13, 18, 22-24, 30, 47, 58, 72, 75, 85, 91, 109-111, 113, 123, 128, 131, 156, 165
interpretation, 5-6, 11, 17, 18-19, 25, 29-30, 33, 37-38, 59, 61-63, 77, 90-91, 117-118, 123, 126, 128-129, 135, 145, 149, 151-152, 154, 156-158, 170
intuitive, 108, 155
Iran, 5, 43, 56, 59
Iraq, 1, 37, 43, 45, 48-49, 55-56, 59, 61, 64-65, 170
irony, 12, 26, 32, 85, 108, 134
Jesus, 2-3, 19-21, 23, 40, 69, 85-90, 99-100, 107, 110, 112, 116-118, 120-122, 125, 133-134, 136-137, 145-146, 149, 152-153, 160
Jew/ish, 6-7, 11, 13, 20, 39-41, 43-44, 46, 48, 51-52, 56-57, 59-66, 69-70, 73-74, 76-79, 83, 85-86, 88, 91-92, 95, 97-99, 107, 111, 115, 117-118, 120, 151-153, 155-157, 159-160, 162-166, 170-171
Jihad, 39, 48, 50, 55-56, 64

Jones, Jim, 1, 5-6, 12, 70, 103, 125, 160, 168, 172
Joshua, 51-52, 97, 109
Judas Iscariot, 119, 133, 144
Judaism, 2-3, 7, 40, 61, 70, 80, 98
Kaczynski, Theodore, 6, 70, 162
Khomeini, Ayatollah, 5, 37, 56
kinêsis, 77, 130
Koran (or Qur'an), 3, 37-41, 43, 45-52, 58-64, 70, 91, 99, 106, 161-162, 170
Koresh, David, 1, 5, 12, 17-33, 38, 58, 62-63, 70, 91, 105, 160, 166
labeling, 39, 51-52, 124, 140-141, 145, 149
last apostle, 98, 122-123
last (or latter) days (or times), 2-3, 19-21, 120-121, 132, 152, 169, 172
liver damage, 80-81, 91-92
logos/logology, 9, 14, 33, 66, 108-109
madness, 11, 13
marriage, 18, 20-23, 27-28, 85, 96, 147, 155
martyr, 19, 42, 51-52, 59, 62, 125, 171
Mary, 3, 40-41, 106, 109
Masad, 39
material, Materialism, 30, 72-74, 76, 129, 132-138, 144, 157, 164-167
Mayans, 7, 160
McKeon, Richard, 8
meaning carried to extreme, 11, 13, 29

metamorphosis, 102, 130
metaphor, 8, 18, 30, 32, 107
metaphysics, 132
method/methodology, 5, 13, 25, 27-29, 34, 59, 66, 70-71, 73, 79, 83, 106-107, 110, 113, 115-116, 118-119, 124, 129-130, 133, 164
methodological doubt, 130
metonymy, 32, 107
Miller, John, 44, 48, 50, 58
Milton, John, 24-25, 58-59
minister, 1-2, 4, 38, 62, 69, 134, 141, 148-150, 170
miracles, 2, 85, 97, 107, 109-117, 122, 135, 137-138, 140, 144, 168
modern-day, 4, 7, 30, 63, 102, 106, 113, 119-121, 125, 127, 129-130, 132-134, 137-139, 142-145, 149-150, 169-171
Modernism, 130-131, 136, 145
Mogadishu, 57
Mohammed, 3, 40, 45, 50-52, 60, 62, 64, 69, 96, 99, 106, 170
money, 4, 115, 133-134, 141, 154
Moore, G. F., 107
Mormon/ism, 2-3, 79, 83, 91, 99-101, 121, 163, 171
Moses, 42, 51, 69, 95-97, 109, 111, 136, 148
motive, 6, 8, 10, 24-25, 28, 37, 39, 43, 47-48, 58, 62, 70, 74, 89, 108, 127-131, 133-135, 137-139, 141-142, 144-145, 162, 164
Muhammad, Elijah, 62, 99
naming, 11, 24, 96, 128

narrative, 10, 72, 120, 163
natural, 8, 10, 14, 110, 114, 123, 131, 137-138, 161, 163
Naturalism, 14, 70, 72, 74-76, 78-79, 131, 137, 164-167, 171
nature, 9, 32, 63, 101, 109, 127, 129-130, 137-138, 141, 143, 145, 156, 167
Nazirite, 86-87
necks (smiting), 42, 51
negative, 4, 82, 84, 89, 91-92, 108-110, 143 *See* hortatory negative
nomenclature, 9
Nominalism, 8, 131
not seeing, 1, 11-12
Palestine/-ian, 1-2, 39, 45, 48-49, 56, 61, 159
part . . . whole, 9-10, 107
Pentecost (the day of), 18, 84, 110, 115, 118, 120-121, 132, 152
Pentacostal/ism, 100, 102, 142
pentad, 24-25, 72, 74, 128-129, 144, 164
People's Temple, 1, 5, 12, 30, 70, 103, 160, 168
perfect, 9-11, 13-14, 27, 31, 46, 66, 70, 73, 78, 121-123, 159, 163-164, 167 *See also* rotten with perfection
perhaps, 131
perspective/ism, 29-31, 73-76, 83, 96, 101, 107, 128, 131, 144, 147-157, 164
persuasion, 6, 25, 27, 29, 31, 33-34, 37-38, 59-60, 62-64, 77, 109-110, 125, 130, 151, 153, 155, 157, 167

philosophy, 7-8, 10, 20, 31, 70, 72-75, 129-132, 137, 151, 160-161, 163-167
physical, 9, 22, 28, 105-107, 111, 123-124, 133-134
pious, 32
Plato, 8-9, 130-131
plot, 43, 45
point of view, 30, 38, 46, 127, 151
political, 2, 5, 19, 26, 46-49, 55, 59, 155
political correctness, 70-72, 76, 162-163
positioning, 135
possibly-wrong-yet-possibly-right, 128, 134, 144, 153
Postmodernism, 7, 70, 130-131
Pragmatism, 73, 129, 142, 144-145, 164
prayer, 45, 100, 109-110, 114-115, 135
principle, 7, 10-11, 13, 29-30, 39, 74-75, 83-86, 88, 105, 112, 128-129, 148, 164-166
principles of consistency, 129
process, 5, 8-10, 30, 32-33, 84-85, 91, 106, 110, 123, 130, 147, 151, 153, 163, 165-166, 168
progressive form, 83-84, 142
prohibit (various things), 3, 24, 48, 71, 80
Prohibition, 79-80, 92, 162
Protestant, 3, 6, 60, 76, 78, 99, 101-102, 134, 150, 163
proverbs, 11-12, 91, 97, 163
psychology, 82, 132
psychopath/ic, 29

psychosis, 11, 32, 59, 63, 89, 105
PTL Club, 4, 134
purgation, 163
purgatory, 134
purpose, 9, 11, 44, 74, 77, 96-97, 108-109, 124, 128-129, 131, 136-138, 140, 164
qualifier, 167-170
quickening, 77-78, 171
Qur'an, *See* Koran
racism, 7, 72, 161-162
rational, 29, 62, 65, 167
Reagan, Ronald, 78-79
Realism, 8, 129-132, 144
realm, 8, 108, 130-131, 137
rebuttal, 167-169
recalcitrance, 5-6, 27, 29-31, 33-34, 63, 83, 89, 91, 105-106, 124, 127, 166, 169
reflexive, 12, 90, 135
Relativism, 70, 131
revelation, 70, 98, 99, 119
Revelation, The book of, 17-21, 25-29, 32-33, 38, 106-107, 111, 119, 123, 133, 136, 151, 160
Robertson, Pat, 170
Roosevelt, Theodore, 58
roots, 8, 29, 74, 86, 123, 155
rotten with perfection, 10-11
Saddat, Anwar, 57, 65
salvation, 20, 134, 145
Samson, 24-25, 58-59, 61, 97
Samuel, 97
science, 73-74
Scientology, 160

scripture, 5-7, 19, 37-38, 40, 46, 59, 70, 75-76, 83, 89, 99, 101, 103, 108, 113, 132, 142, 145, 150, 153 See also Bible, biblical, Koran, and *sola scriptura*
secular, 69-71, 73, 77, 82, 89, 92, 165
selective interpretation, 11
selective organization, 11
selective perception, 11
seven seals (of Revelation), 17, 19-23, 26, 32-33
Sicarii, 64
Simon the Sorcerer, 115-116, 133, 144, 169, 172
situation, 5, 128, 131
Smith, Joseph, 3, 91, 99-100, 163
sola scriptura, 99, 150
Solar Tradition (Order of the), 12, 30, 103, 160
Somalia, 57
Spiech, David, 46
stress, 89-90, 147, 154-155
suicide, 5-6, 12, 24-25, 33, 58-59, 61-62, 65, 80, 103, 160-161-162, 168-169, 171-172
supernatural, 2-3, 110
symbol, 8-10, 19, 25, 31, 57, 59, 64, 106, 113-114, 116, 135
synecdoche, 25, 32, 107
system (-builder), 6, 10, 19, 22, 25-26, 31-33, 75, 106, 113-114, 116, 129, 131, 135, 149, 151, 156
Tabor, James D., 17, 19, 23, 25, 27-31, 33-34, 62, 105, 166
Talmud, 74, 80

technology/technologism, 6, 70, 76-77, 83-84, 162
teleion/-os, 122-124
teleology, 136, 138
telos, See final cause/*telos*
temporizing of essence, 9-10, 72
tendency, 13-14, 25, 27, 29, 31, 66, 70, 78, 155, 159
terminology, 8-9, 11, 13-14, 23-24, 27, 31, 45, 64, 66, 70, 72, 78, 95, 102, 106, 113-116, 118, 124, 129, 150, 159
Theists, 78-79
theory, 7-8, 14, 32, 66, 75, 107, 127, 132, 139, 141, 161
Tomlinson, H. M., 11
Toulmin, Stephen, 167
tragedy, 34, 43, 65, 167
trained incapacity, 11
transcendence, 39, 133
tropes, 27, 32, 34, 107
ultimate, 51, 58, 75, 137, 139
unbelievers, 41-42, 46, 50-52, 59, 60-61, 63, 170
uncertainty, 156-157
values, 3, 7, 32, 40, 70-72, 78, 135
Veblen, Thorstein, 11
vicious circle, 102
victimage, 43, 60
villain, 11
vinegar, 87-88, 91, 163
voices, 113, 161, 171 See also Bat Qol
Waco, 12, 17-34, 38, 103, 105, 125, 160-161
Wagner, Peter, 142
warrant, 167-170

weapons of mass destruction, 43, 60
whole, *See* part . . . whole
wine, 79-89, 91, 109-110, 162-163
word, 1, 33, 84, 86-88, 91, 95, 97, 106-113, 122-123, 128, 131, 135-136, 141, 147-151, 154, 163, 167
WWJD, 141
Zealot, 64

www.ingramcontent.com/pod-product-compliance
Lightning Source LLC
Chambersburg PA
CBHW021405290426
44108CB00010B/397